To Alexandra!

Antwn
Kokua

FOR ALEXANDRA!

-TODD HERMAN

20
17

PLANET ITH WAS ONCE RULED BY A RACE OF THINKERS
KNOWN AS THE AH'KEE,
BUT DURING A TIME OF PLAGUE,
THE AH'KEE VANISHED.

THE SURVIVORS OF THE PLAGUE,
A TRIBAL RACE KNOWN AS THE KA'II,
WAGED WAR OVER

THE GLEAM OF DISTANCE.

THE DIVINE AMULET OF
THE GODDESS TION.

FOR IT WAS SAID, "WHOEVER WIELDS
THE GLEAM WILL RISE AS
THE CHAMPION OF ITH."

BUT THE AGE OF BLOOD ENDED
WHEN THE WARLORDS PUT DOWN THEIR
BLADES TO LIVE IN PEACE.

CENTURIES LATER...A NEW THREAT WOULD COME
FROM THE STARS.
NOW - THE GODDESS TION MUST FIND
HER CHAMPION!

ANDREW KAFOURY'S

NO'MADD
CITY OF EMPTY TOWERS

STORY
ANDREW KAFOURY

ART
TODD HERMAN

DESIGN
TODD HERMAN

LETTERS
ANDREW KAFOURY

MAP
TODD HERMAN

COVER
CHRIS FACCONE &
TODD HERMAN

DIGITALS
ANDREW KAFOURY

ISBN: 978-0-615-92455-7
Copyright (c) 2013 Andrew Kafoury
All rights reserved. The stories,
characters, and incidents, featured in
this publication are entirely fictional.
No'madd, and all related characters
featured in this publication, the
distinctive likeness thereof, and all
related incidia are trademarks of
Andrew Kafoury.

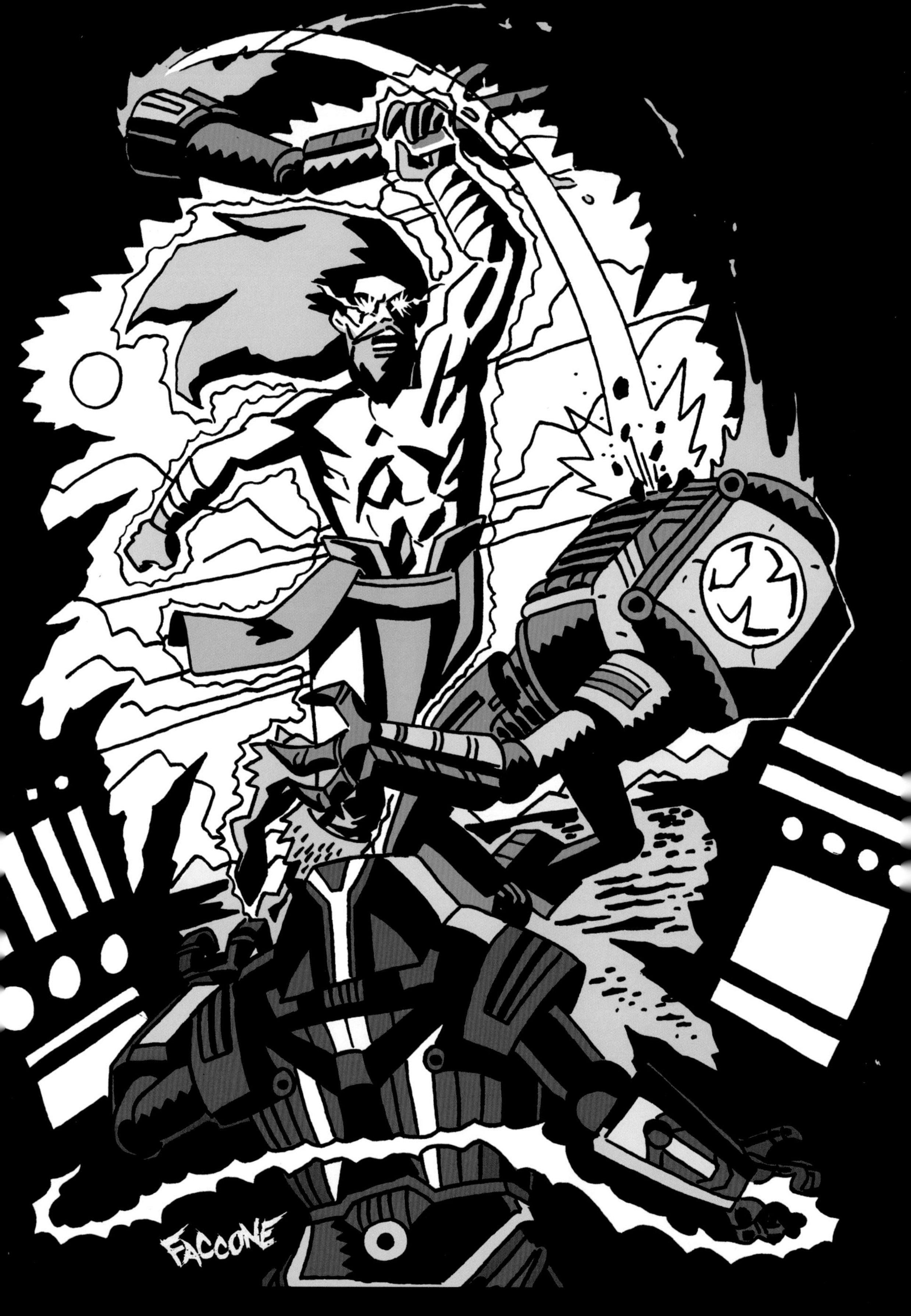
FACCONE

~ PLATU'S PATH ~

A MAP
OF PLANET ITH

PLANET ITH IS A SMALL
WORLD WITH TWO
LANDS:

BARROX AND
PLATU.

THESE LANDS ARE
SEPARATED AT SEA BY
THE UNCONQUERABLE
WALL OF STORMS
KNOWN AS

THE CHAIN OF WRATH!

NO'MADD'S PEOPLE - THE KA'II -
LIVE ON BARROX.

YET - NO KA'II HAS CROSSED
THE CHAIN - OR SEEN
PLATU.

THEREFORE
PLATU IS KNOWN AS

"THE UNSEEN LAND"

OR

"PLATU: THE UNSEEN."

PLATU

LEGEND

⌂	No'madd's HUT
⇧	B'LINN
⌘	The STEEP
⊞	ITO'DELL

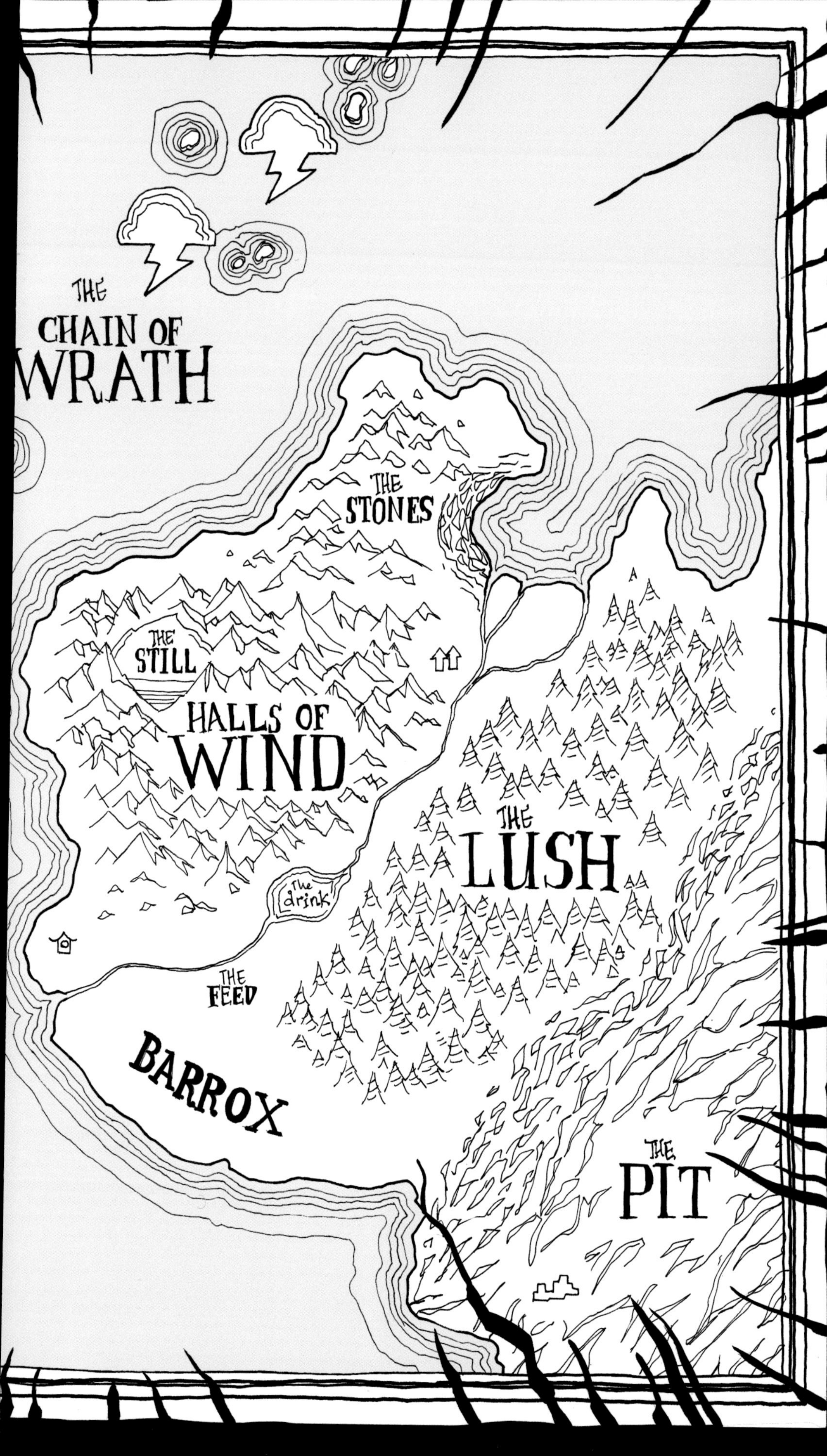
THE CHAIN OF WRATH
THE STONES
THE STILL
HALLS OF WIND
THE LUSH
The drink
THE FEED
BARROX
THE PIT

FOR JOEY, WHO DANCED ACROSS THE CHAIN.
- DREW

CHAPTER ONE

NO'MADD

"HOME.

WHAT A BEAUTIFUL WORD..."

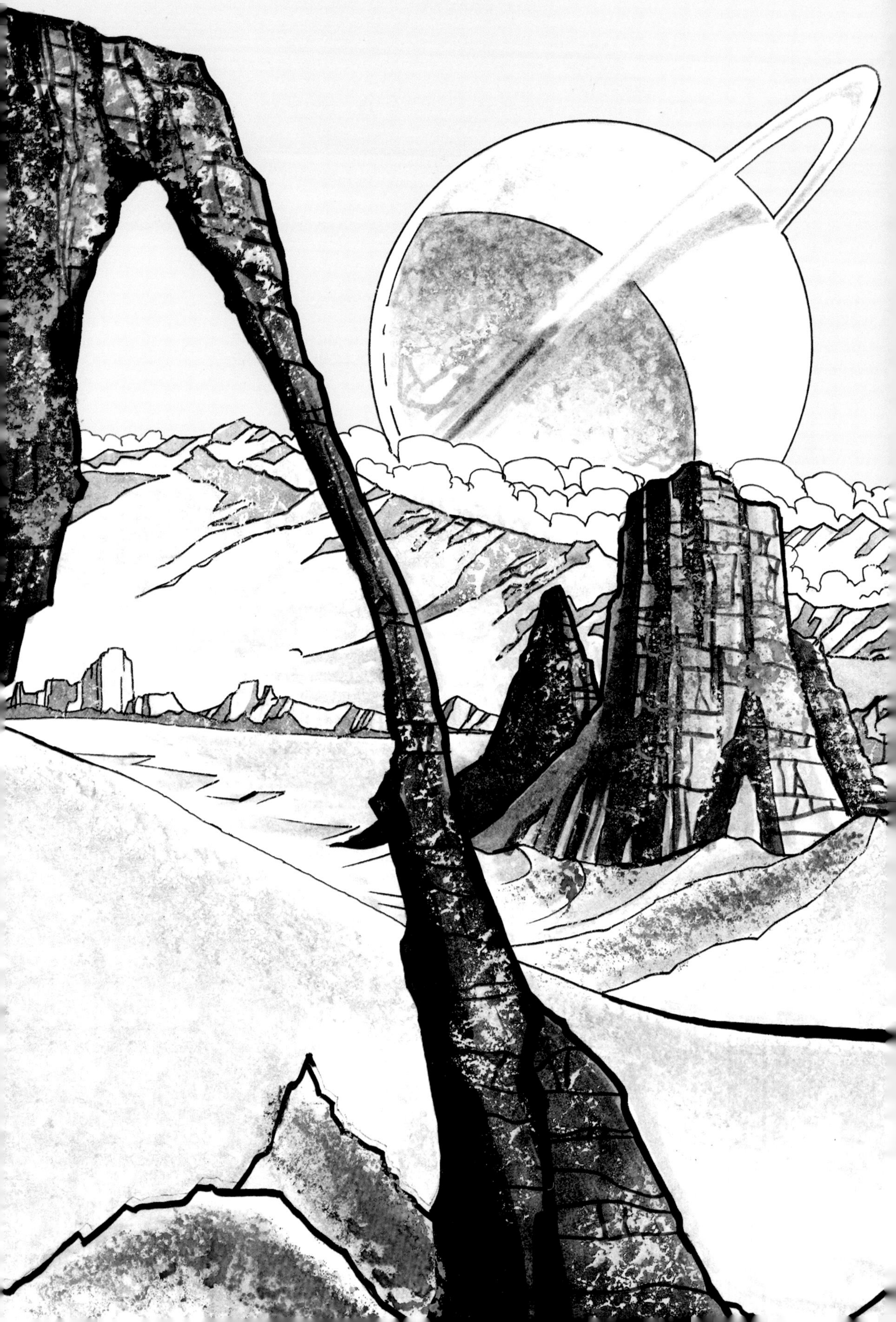

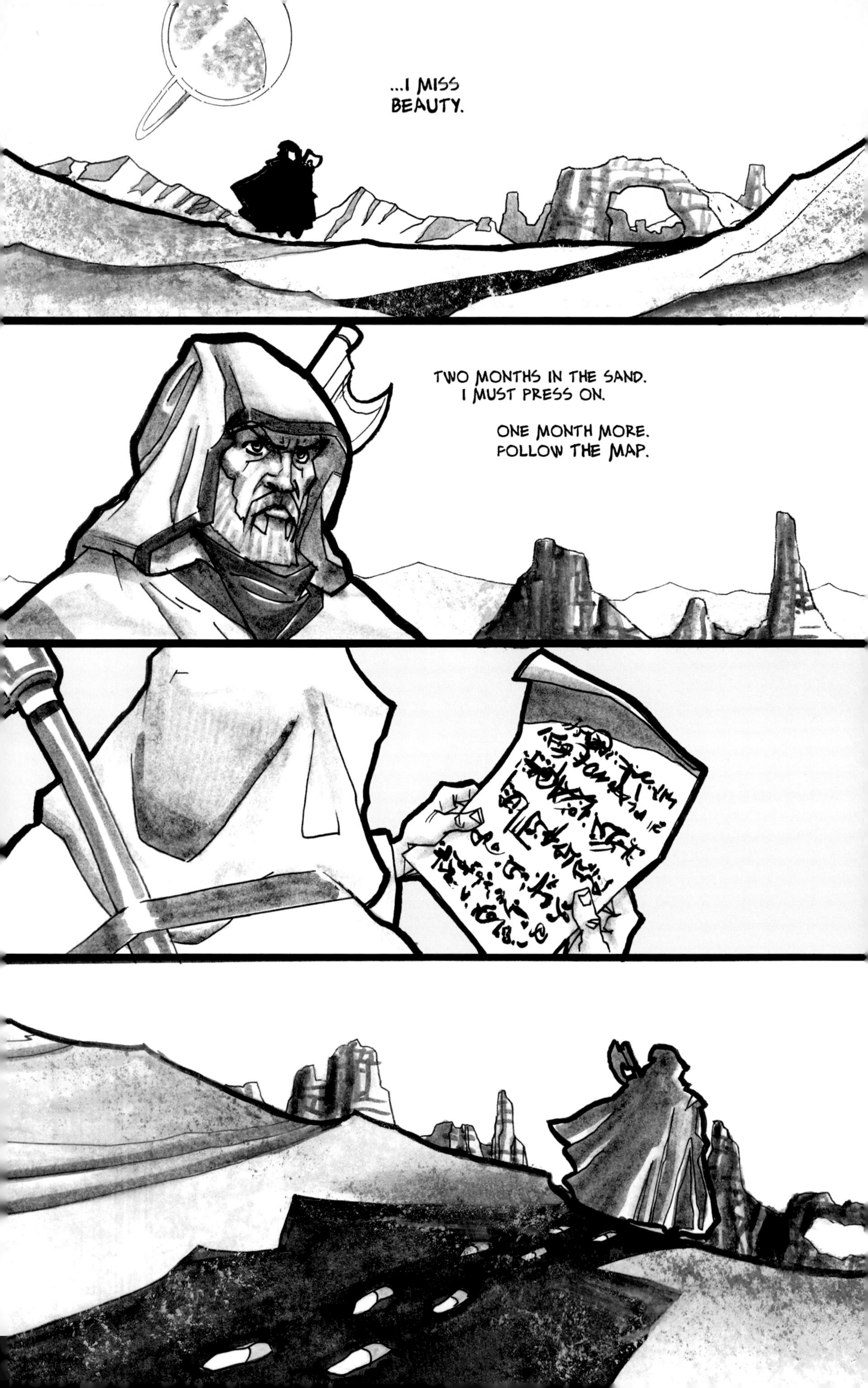
...I MISS BEAUTY.
TWO MONTHS IN THE SAND. I MUST PRESS ON.
ONE MONTH MORE. FOLLOW THE MAP.

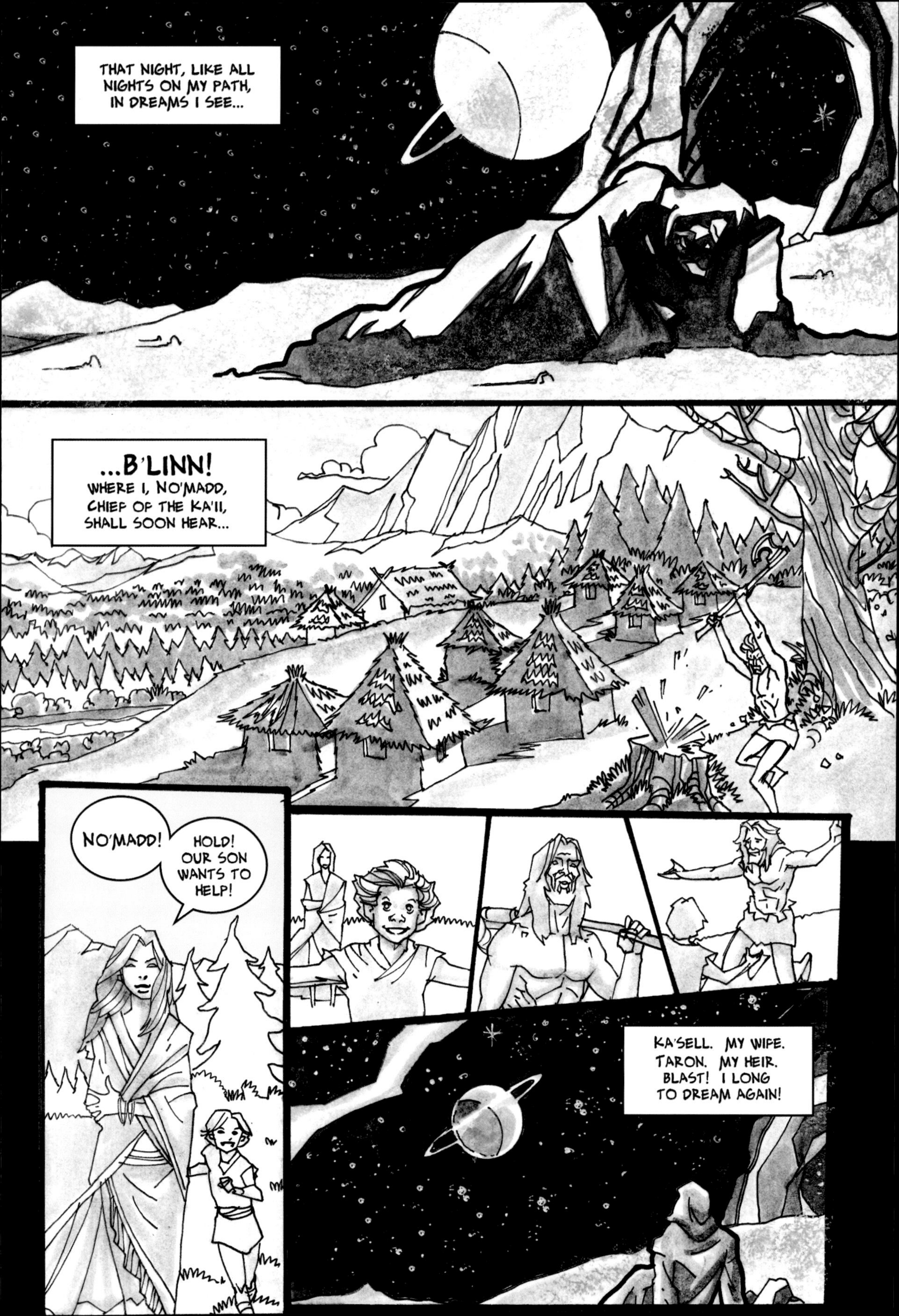

THAT NIGHT, LIKE ALL NIGHTS ON MY PATH, IN DREAMS I SEE...
...B'LINN! WHERE I, NO'MADD, CHIEF OF THE KA'II, SHALL SOON HEAR...
NO'MADD!
HOLD! OUR SON WANTS TO HELP!
KA'SELL. MY WIFE. TARON. MY HEIR. BLAST! I LONG TO DREAM AGAIN!

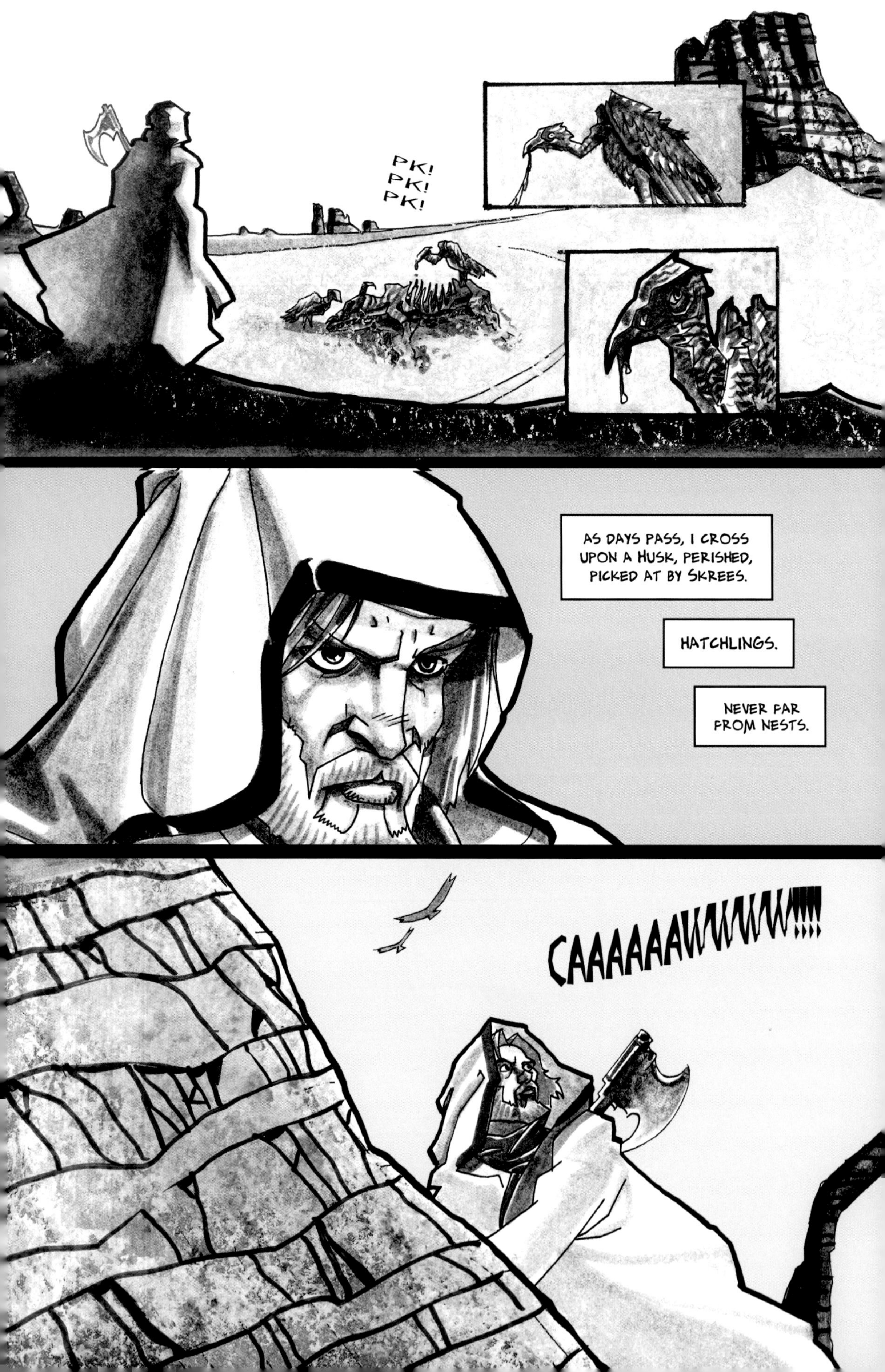
PK!
PK!
PK!
AS DAYS PASS, I CROSS UPON A HUSK, PERISHED, PICKED AT BY SKREES.
HATCHLINGS.
NEVER FAR FROM NESTS.
CAAAAAAWWWW!!!!

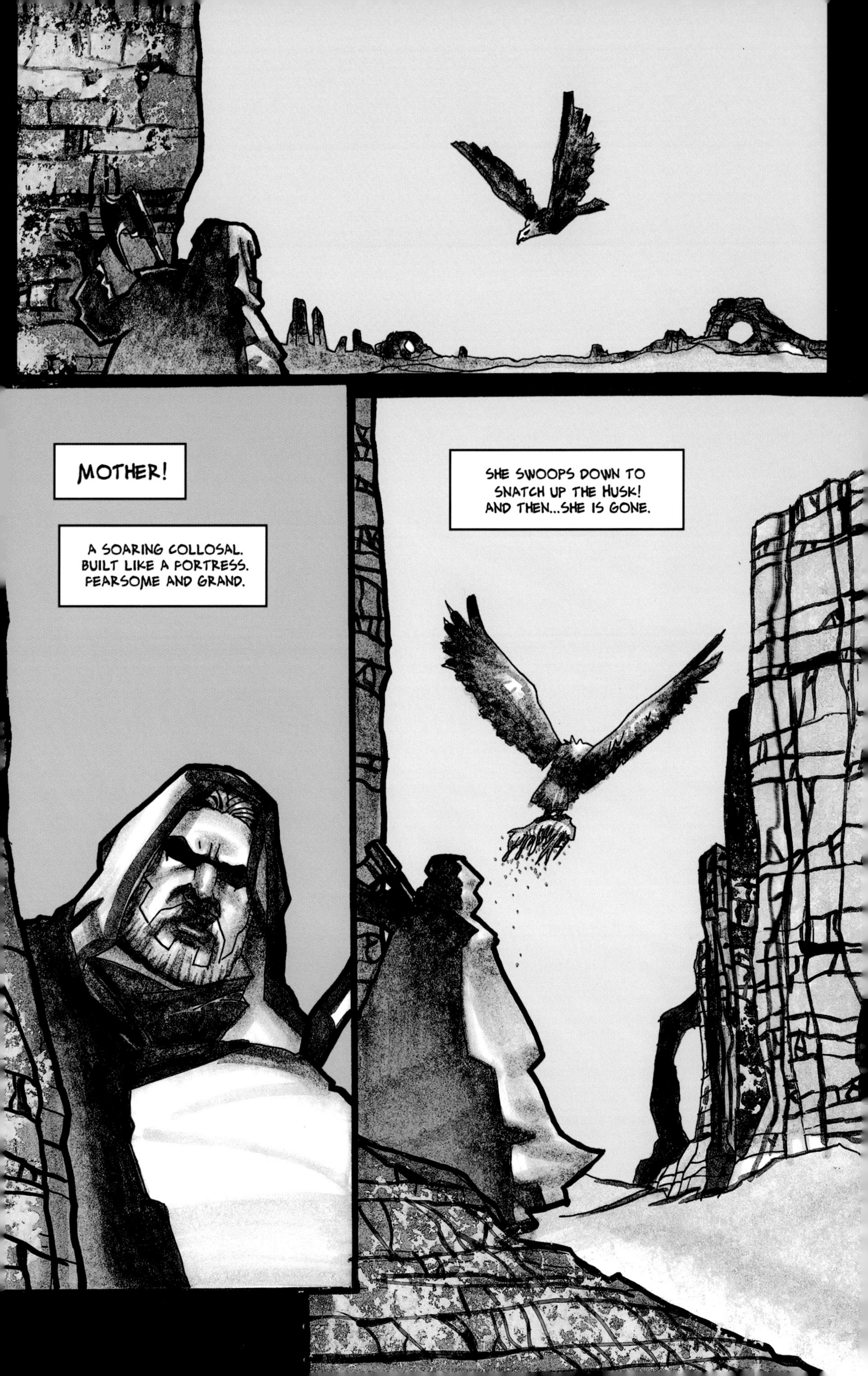
MOTHER!
A SOARING COLLOSAL. BUILT LIKE A FORTRESS. FEARSOME AND GRAND.
SHE SWOOPS DOWN TO SNATCH UP THE HUSK! AND THEN...SHE IS GONE.

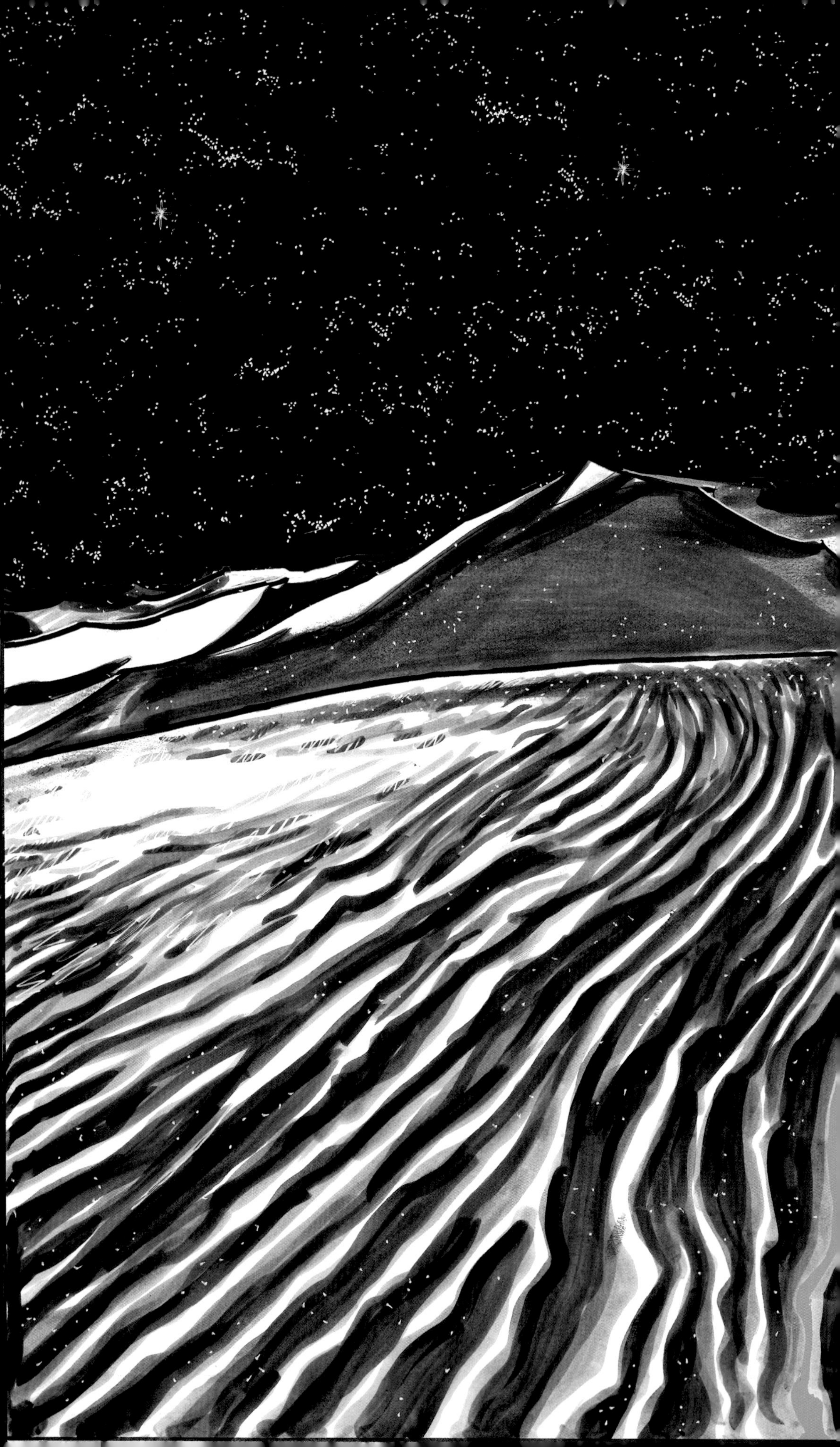

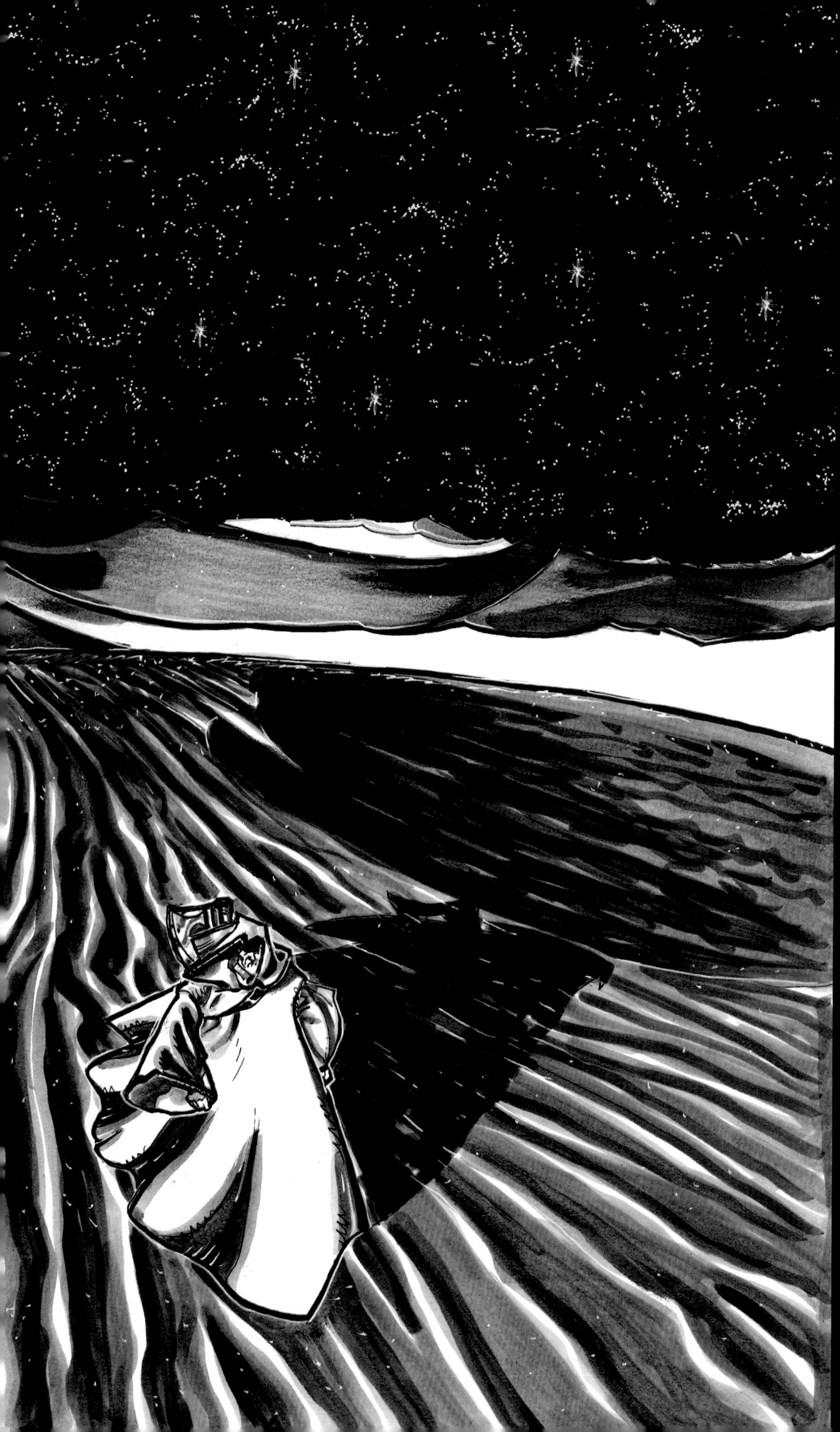

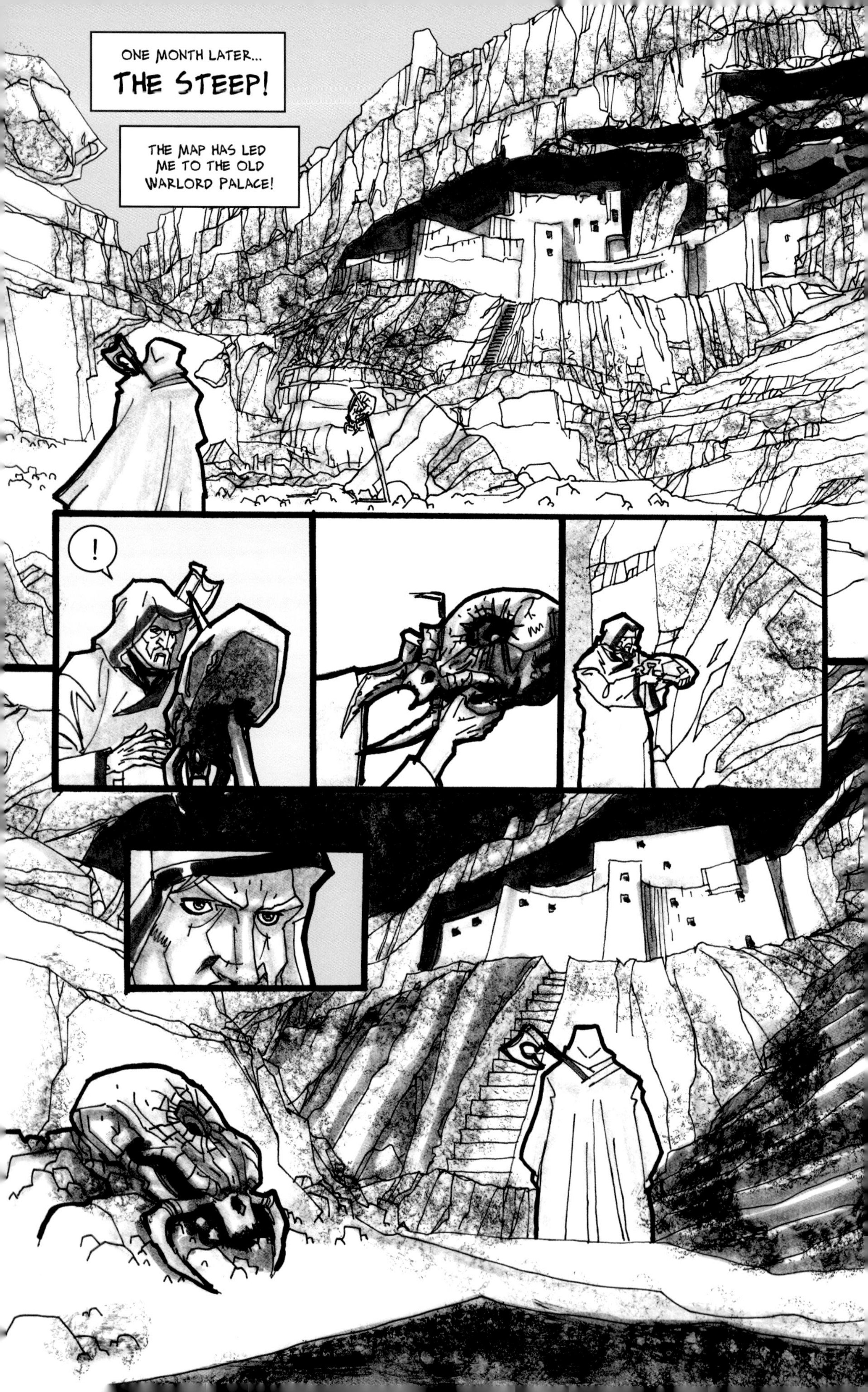
ONE MONTH LATER...
THE STEEP!
THE MAP HAS LED ME TO THE OLD WARLORD PALACE!
!

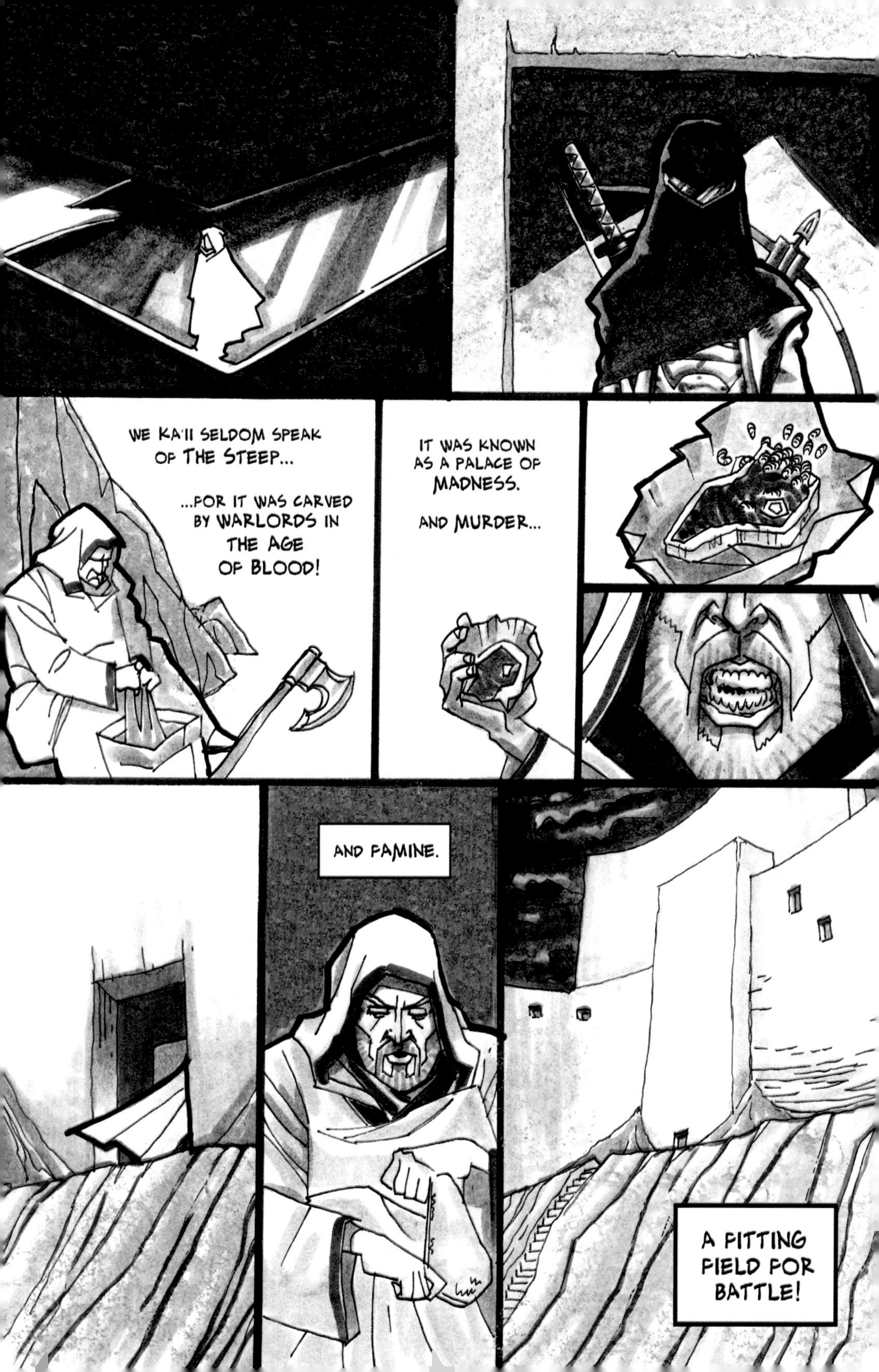
WE KA'II SELDOM SPEAK OF THE STEEP...
...FOR IT WAS CARVED BY WARLORDS IN THE AGE OF BLOOD!
IT WAS KNOWN AS A PALACE OF MADNESS.
AND MURDER...
AND FAMINE.
A FITTING FIELD FOR BATTLE!

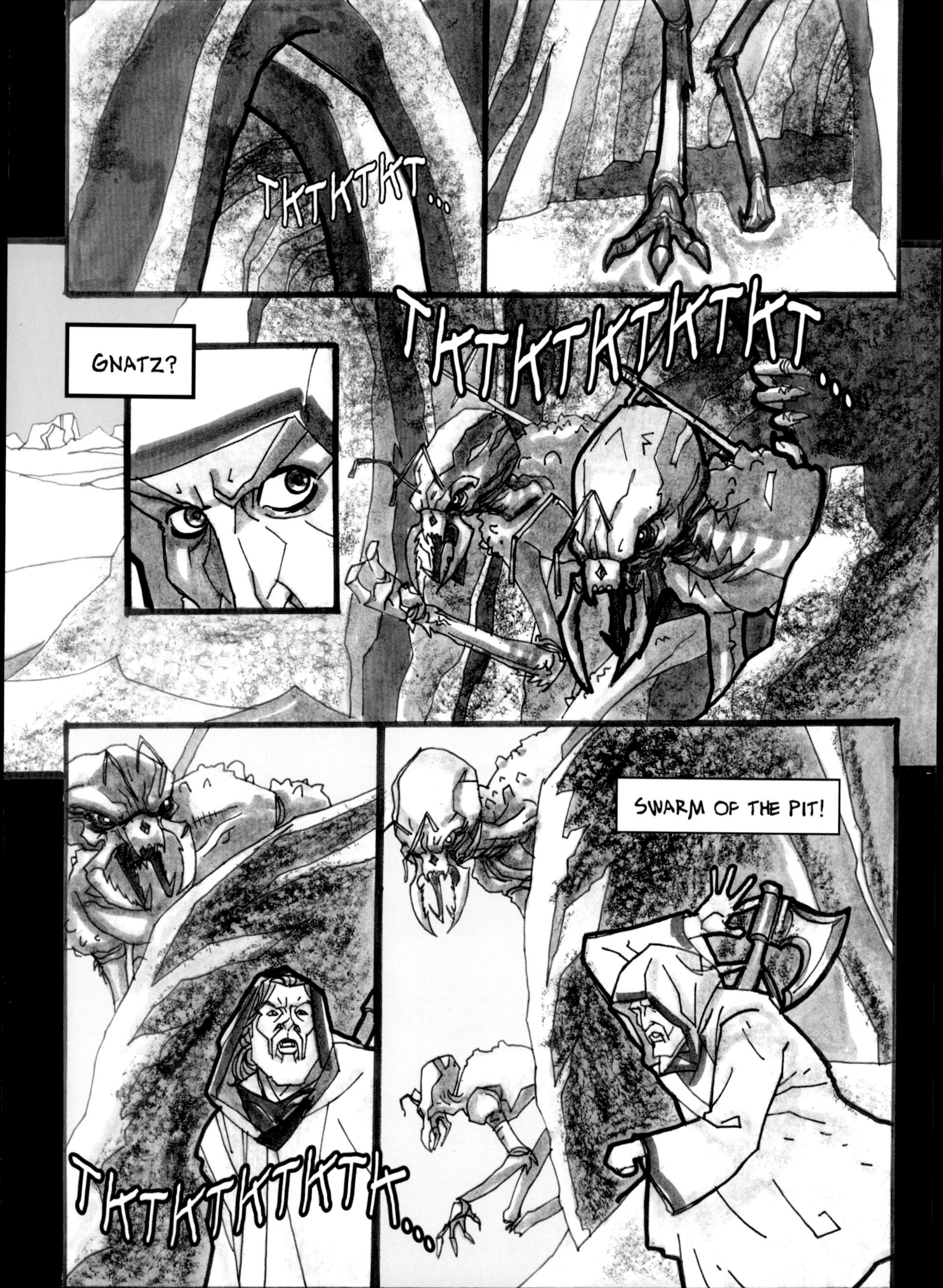
TKTKTKT...
TKTKTKTKTKT...
GNATZ?
SWARM OF THE PIT!
TKTKTKTKTK...

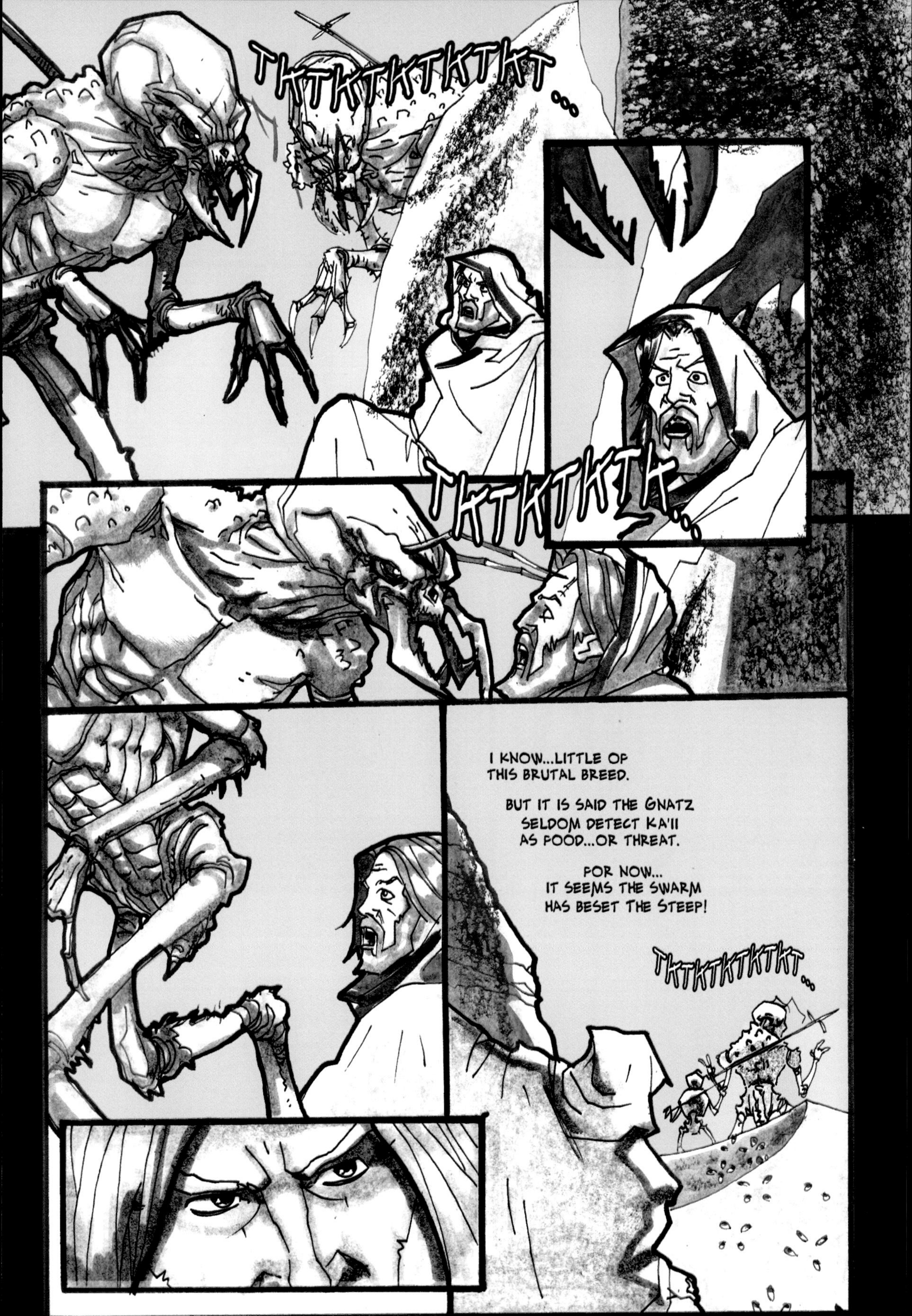
TKTKTKTKTKT...
TKTKTKTK...
I KNOW...LITTLE OF THIS BRUTAL BREED.
BUT IT IS SAID THE GNATZ SELDOM DETECT KA'II AS FOOD...OR THREAT.
FOR NOW... IT SEEMS THE SWARM HAS BESET THE STEEP!
TKTKTKTKTKT...

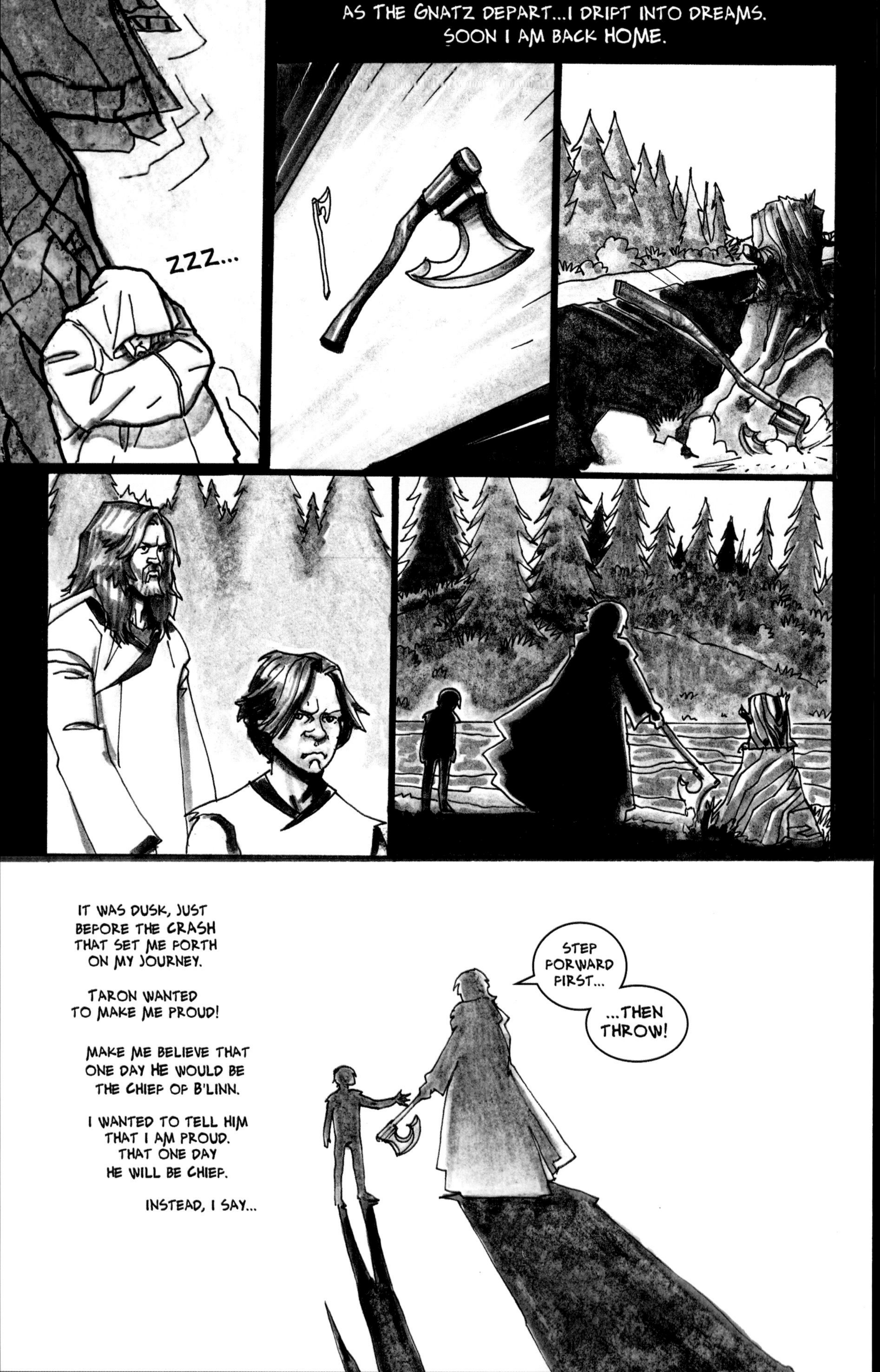
AS THE GNATZ DEPART...I DRIFT INTO DREAMS. SOON I AM BACK HOME.
ZZZ...
IT WAS DUSK, JUST BEFORE THE CRASH THAT SET ME FORTH ON MY JOURNEY.
TARON WANTED TO MAKE ME PROUD!
MAKE ME BELIEVE THAT ONE DAY HE WOULD BE THE CHIEF OF B'LINN.
I WANTED TO TELL HIM THAT I AM PROUD. THAT ONE DAY HE WILL BE CHIEF.
INSTEAD, I SAY...
STEP FORWARD FIRST...
...THEN THROW!

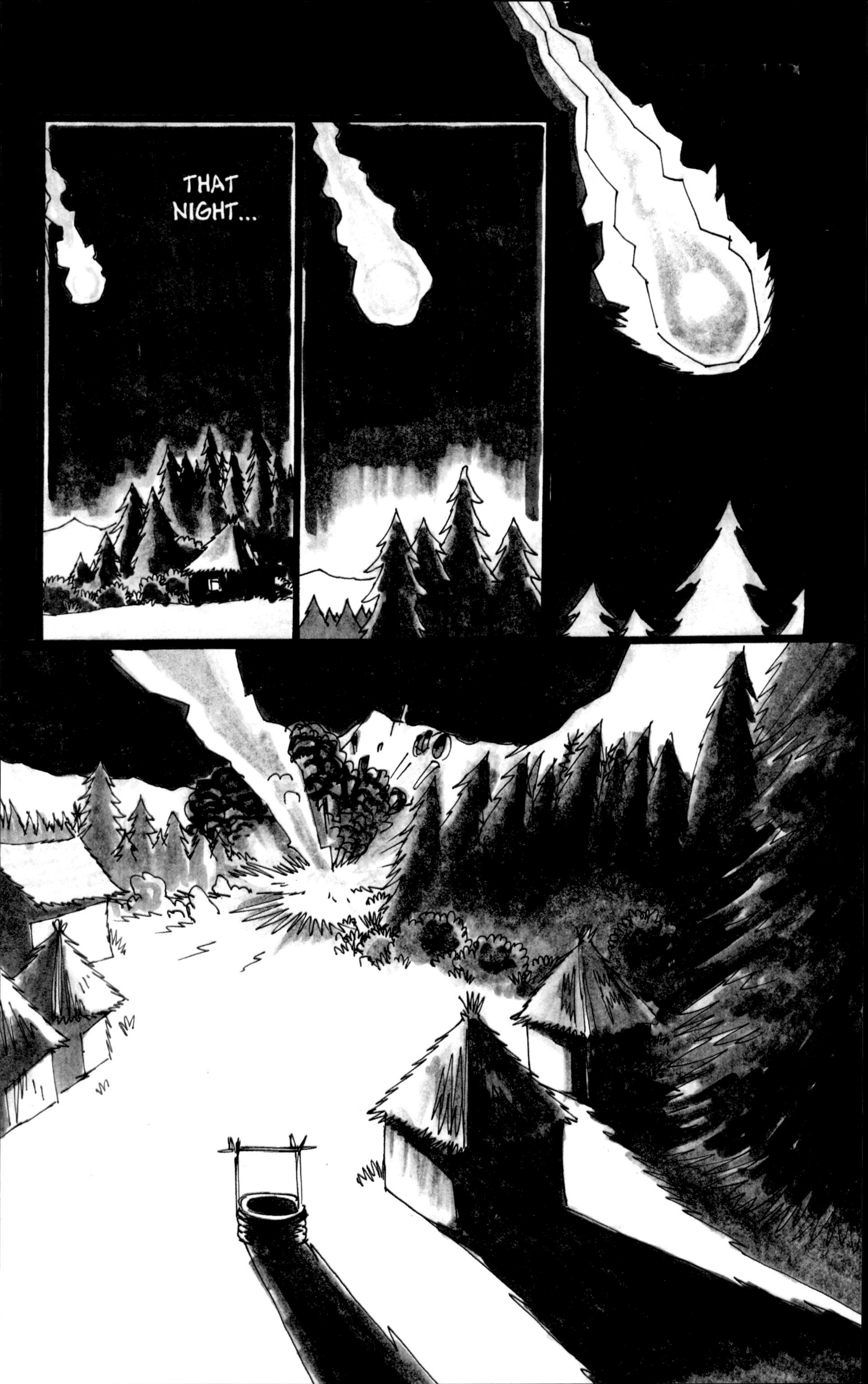
THAT NIGHT...

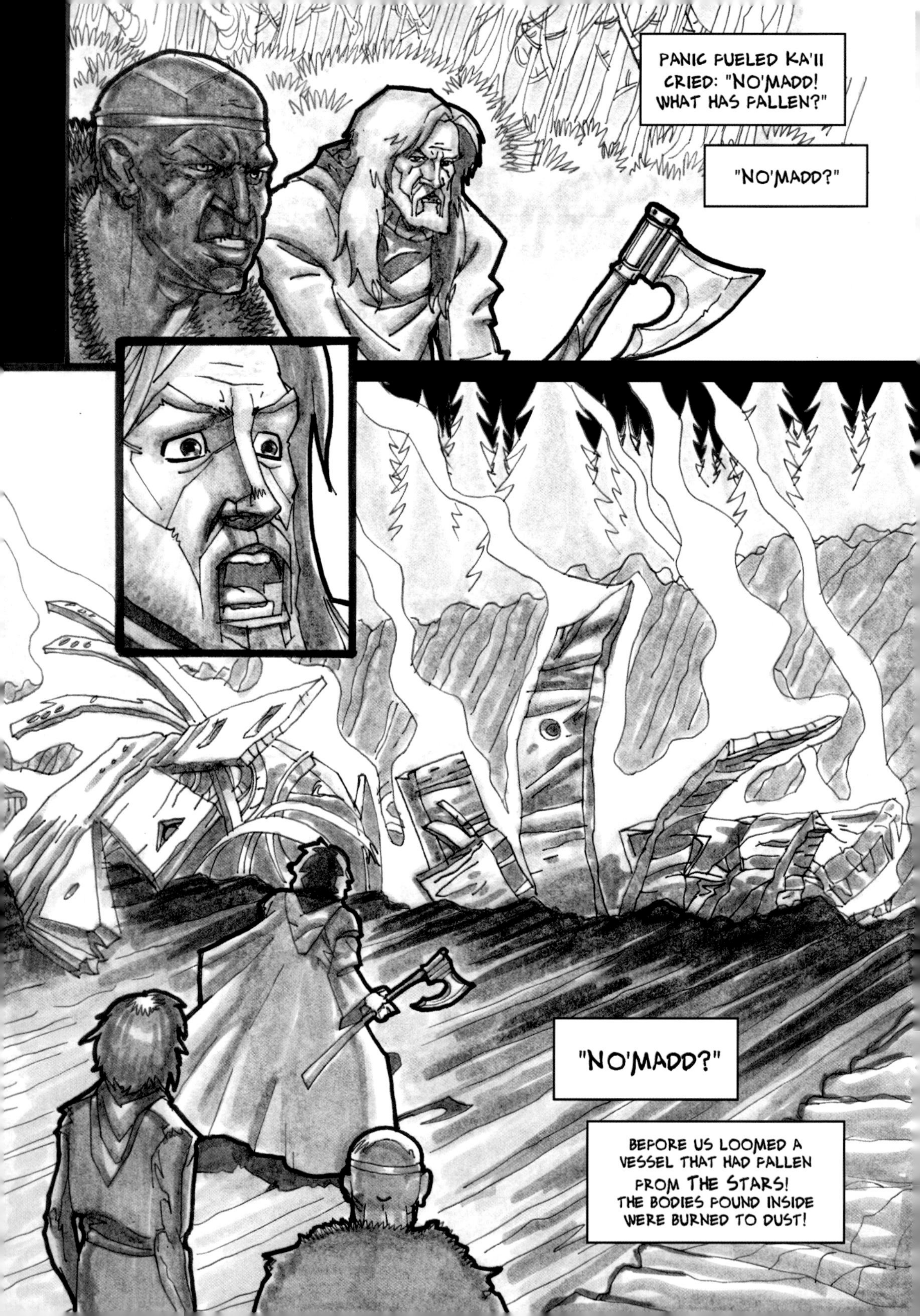
PANIC FUELED KA'II CRIED: "NO'MADD! WHAT HAS FALLEN?"
"NO'MADD?"
"NO'MADD?"
BEFORE US LOOMED A VESSEL THAT HAD FALLEN FROM THE STARS! THE BODIES FOUND INSIDE WERE BURNED TO DUST!

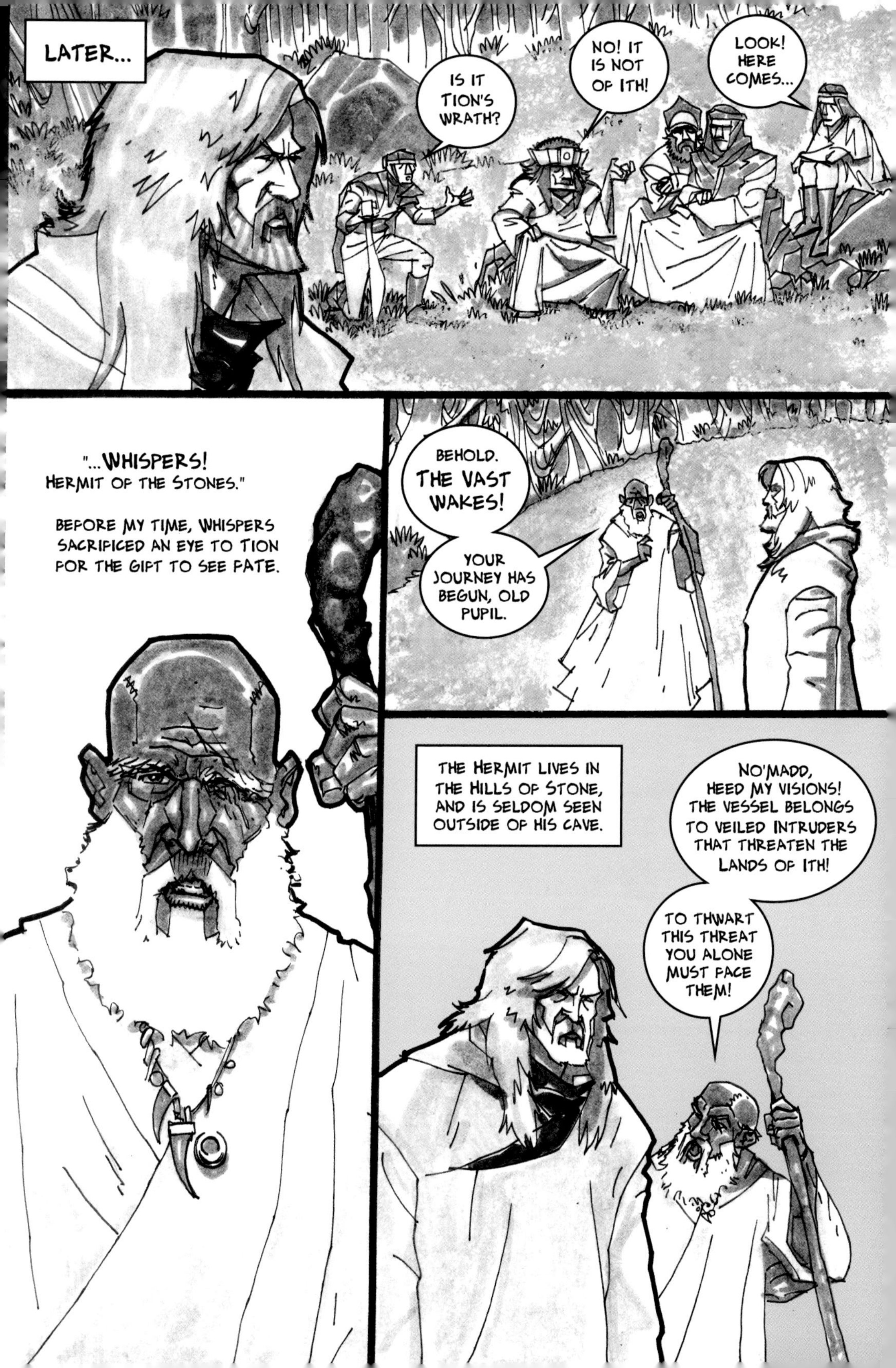
LATER...
IS IT TION'S WRATH?
NO! IT IS NOT OF ITH!
LOOK! HERE COMES...
"...WHISPERS! HERMIT OF THE STONES."
BEFORE MY TIME, WHISPERS SACRIFICED AN EYE TO TION FOR THE GIFT TO SEE FATE.
BEHOLD. THE VAST WAKES!
YOUR JOURNEY HAS BEGUN, OLD PUPIL.
THE HERMIT LIVES IN THE HILLS OF STONE, AND IS SELDOM SEEN OUTSIDE OF HIS CAVE.
NO'MADD, HEED MY VISIONS! THE VESSEL BELONGS TO VEILED INTRUDERS THAT THREATEN THE LANDS OF ITH!
TO THWART THIS THREAT YOU ALONE MUST FACE THEM!

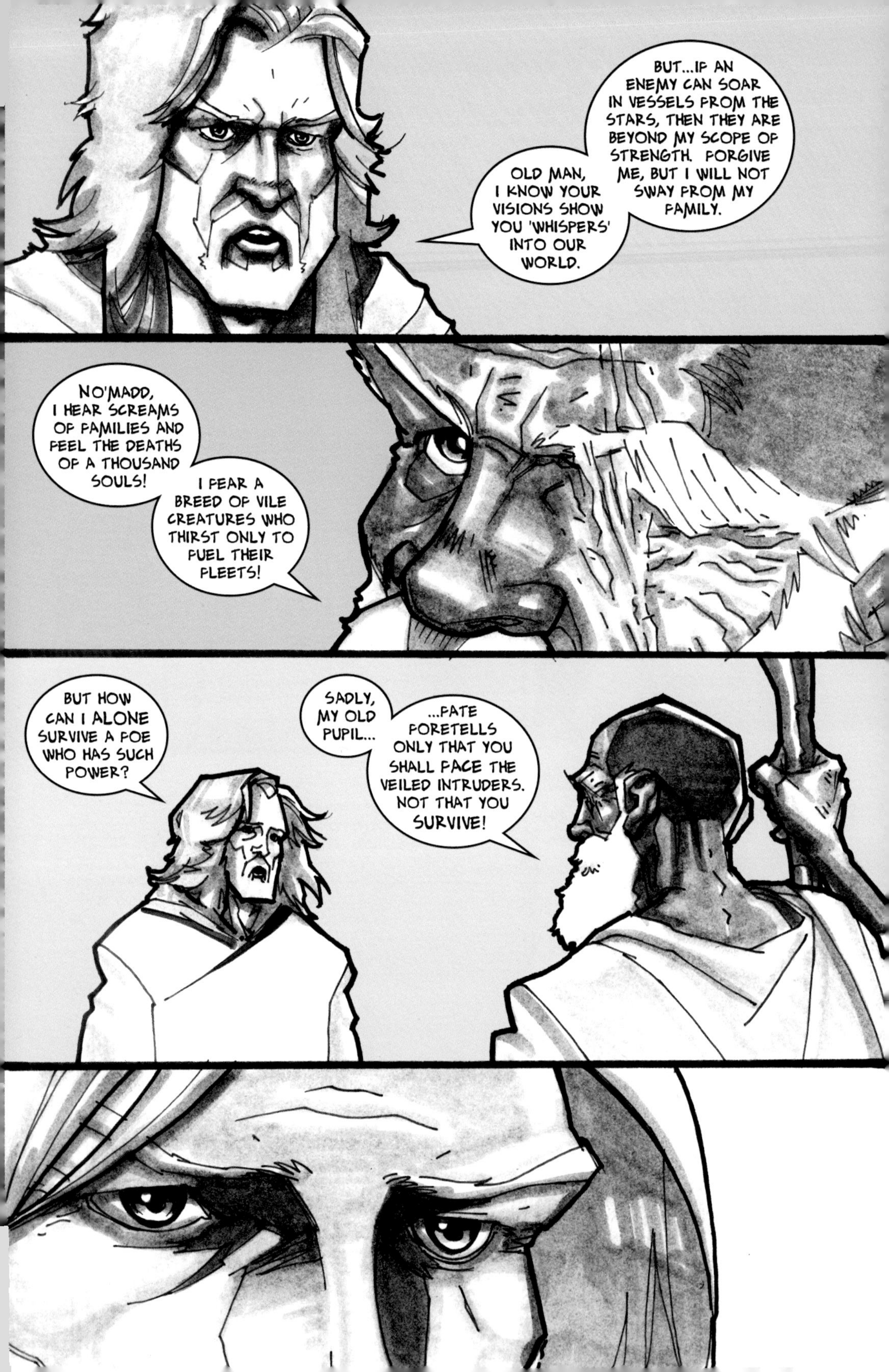
OLD MAN, I KNOW YOUR VISIONS SHOW YOU 'WHISPERS' INTO OUR WORLD.
BUT...IF AN ENEMY CAN SOAR IN VESSELS FROM THE STARS, THEN THEY ARE BEYOND MY SCOPE OF STRENGTH. FORGIVE ME, BUT I WILL NOT SWAY FROM MY FAMILY.
NO'MADD, I HEAR SCREAMS OF FAMILIES AND FEEL THE DEATHS OF A THOUSAND SOULS!
I FEAR A BREED OF VILE CREATURES WHO THIRST ONLY TO FUEL THEIR FLEETS!
BUT HOW CAN I ALONE SURVIVE A FOE WHO HAS SUCH POWER?
SADLY, MY OLD PUPIL...
...FATE FORETELLS ONLY THAT YOU SHALL FACE THE VEILED INTRUDERS. NOT THAT YOU SURVIVE!

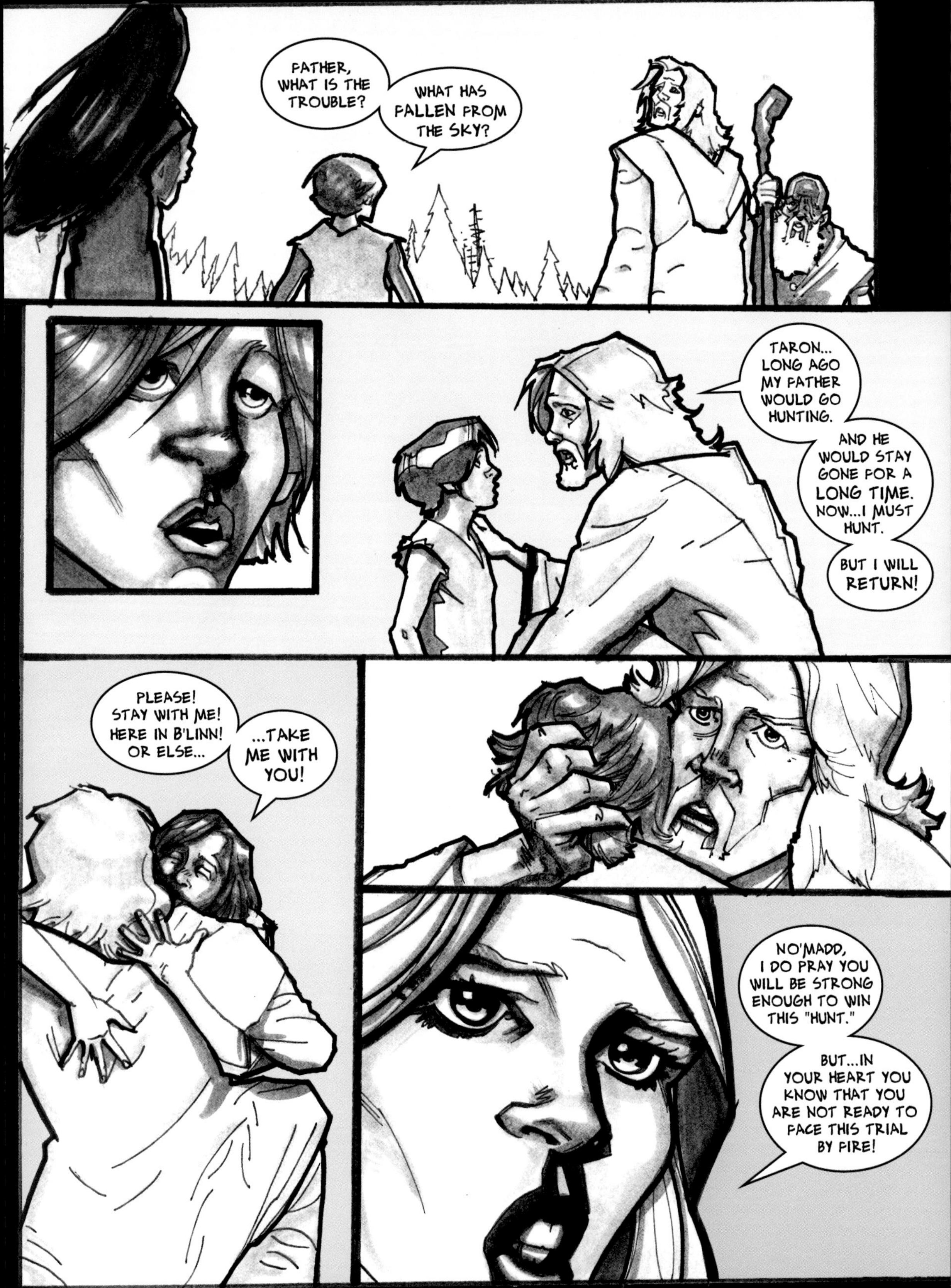
FATHER, WHAT IS THE TROUBLE?
WHAT HAS FALLEN FROM THE SKY?
TARON... LONG AGO MY FATHER WOULD GO HUNTING.
AND HE WOULD STAY GONE FOR A LONG TIME. NOW...I MUST HUNT.
BUT I WILL RETURN!
PLEASE! STAY WITH ME! HERE IN B'LINN! OR ELSE...
...TAKE ME WITH YOU!
NO'MADD, I DO PRAY YOU WILL BE STRONG ENOUGH TO WIN THIS "HUNT."
BUT...IN YOUR HEART YOU KNOW THAT YOU ARE NOT READY TO FACE THIS TRIAL BY FIRE!

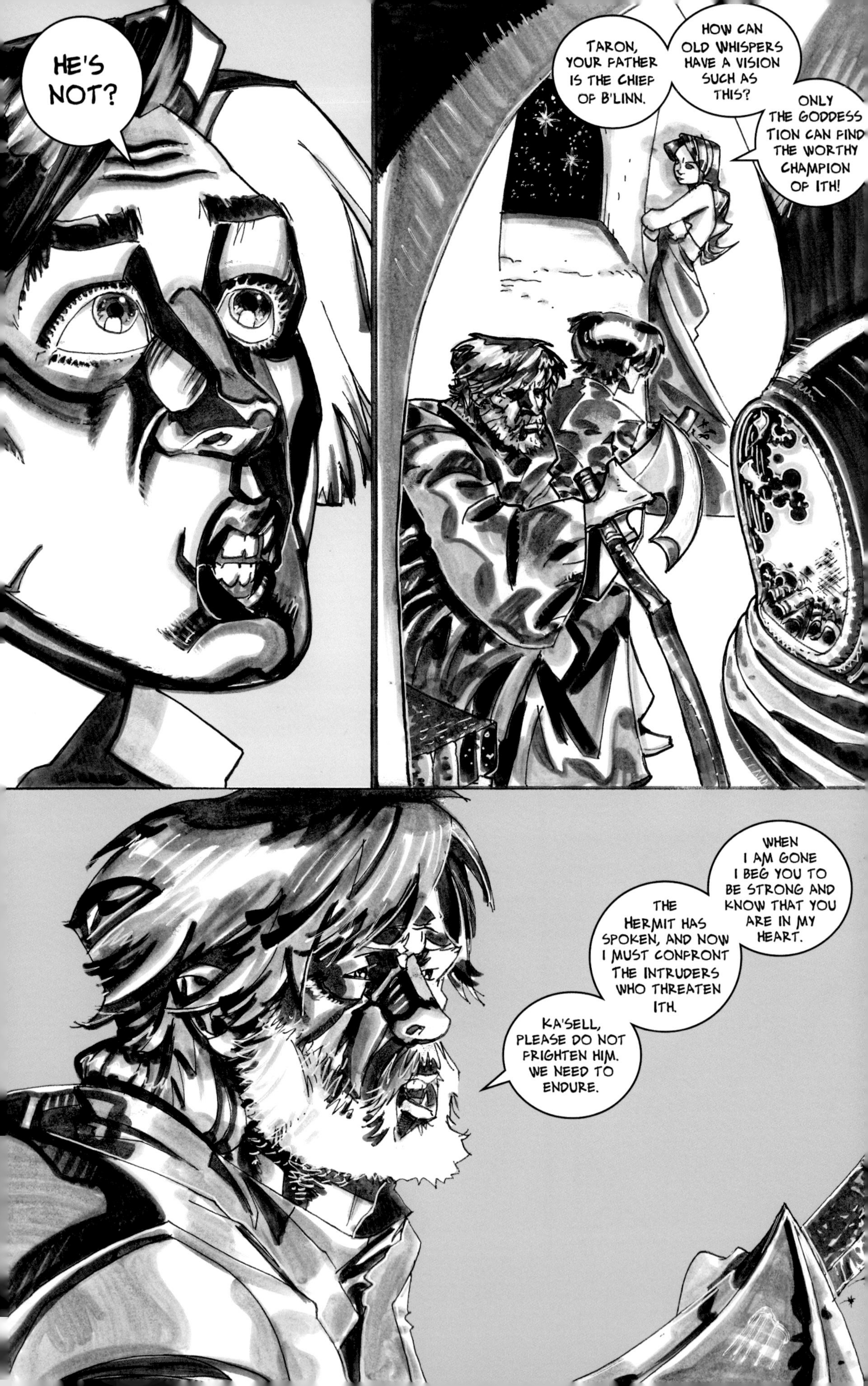
HE'S NOT?
TARON, YOUR FATHER IS THE CHIEF OF B'LINN.
HOW CAN OLD WHISPERS HAVE A VISION SUCH AS THIS?
ONLY THE GODDESS TION CAN FIND THE WORTHY CHAMPION OF ITH!
KA'SELL, PLEASE DO NOT FRIGHTEN HIM. WE NEED TO ENDURE.
THE HERMIT HAS SPOKEN, AND NOW I MUST CONFRONT THE INTRUDERS WHO THREATEN ITH.
WHEN I AM GONE I BEG YOU TO BE STRONG AND KNOW THAT YOU ARE IN MY HEART.

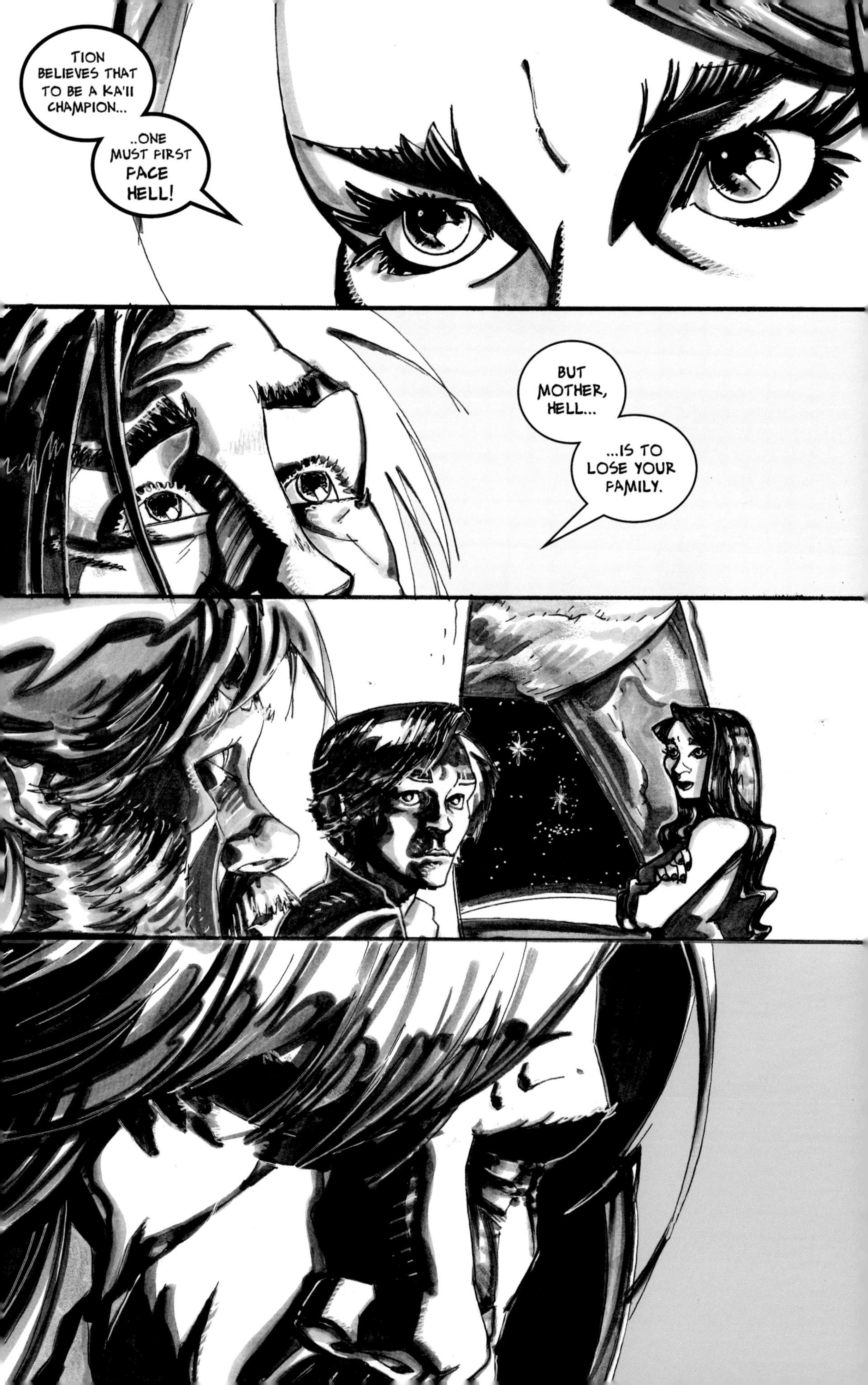
TION BELIEVES THAT TO BE A KA'II CHAMPION...
..ONE MUST FIRST FACE HELL!
BUT MOTHER, HELL...
...IS TO LOSE YOUR FAMILY.

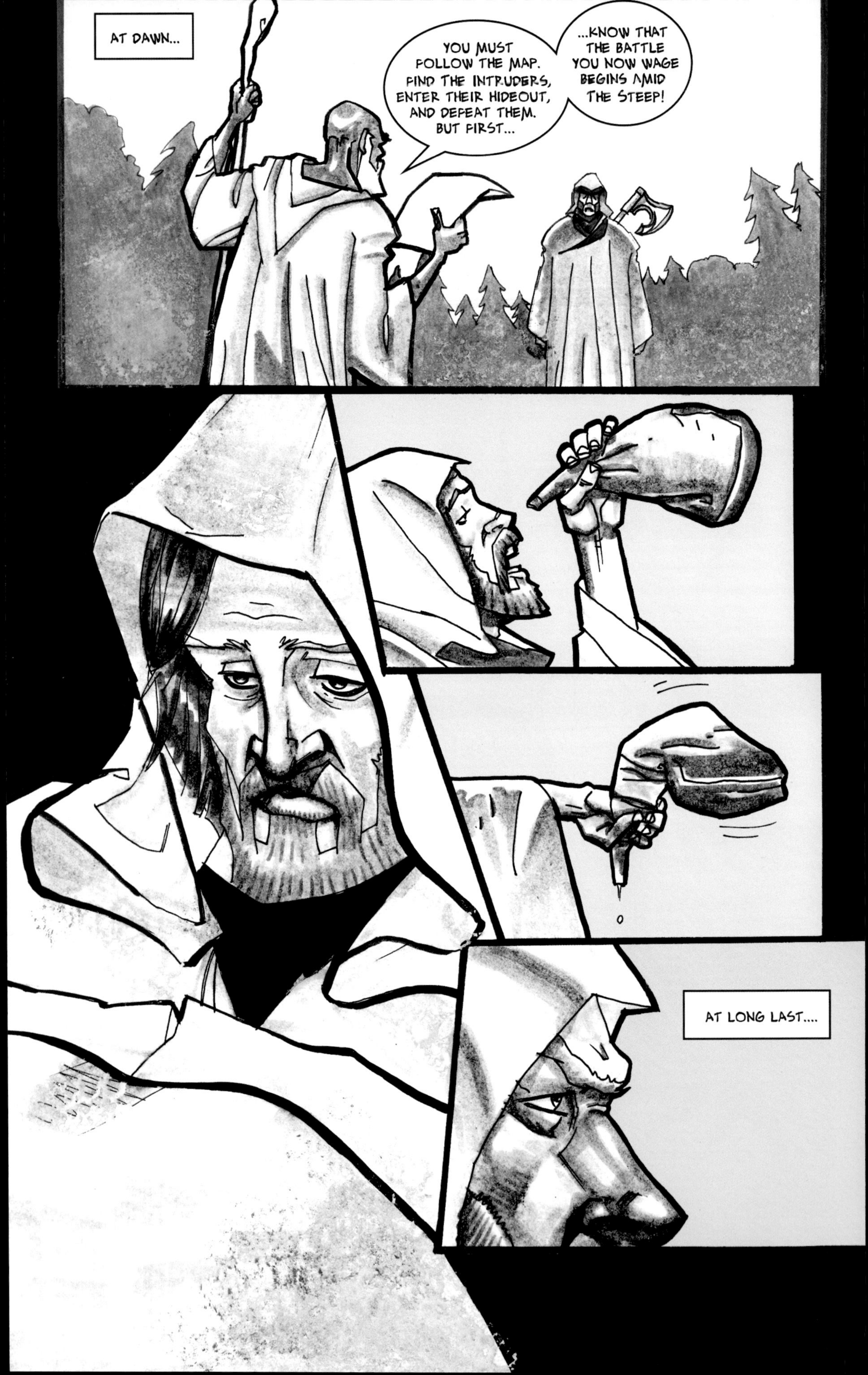
AT DAWN...
YOU MUST FOLLOW THE MAP. FIND THE INTRUDERS, ENTER THEIR HIDEOUT, AND DEFEAT THEM. BUT FIRST...
...KNOW THAT THE BATTLE YOU NOW WAGE BEGINS AMID THE STEEP!
AT LONG LAST....

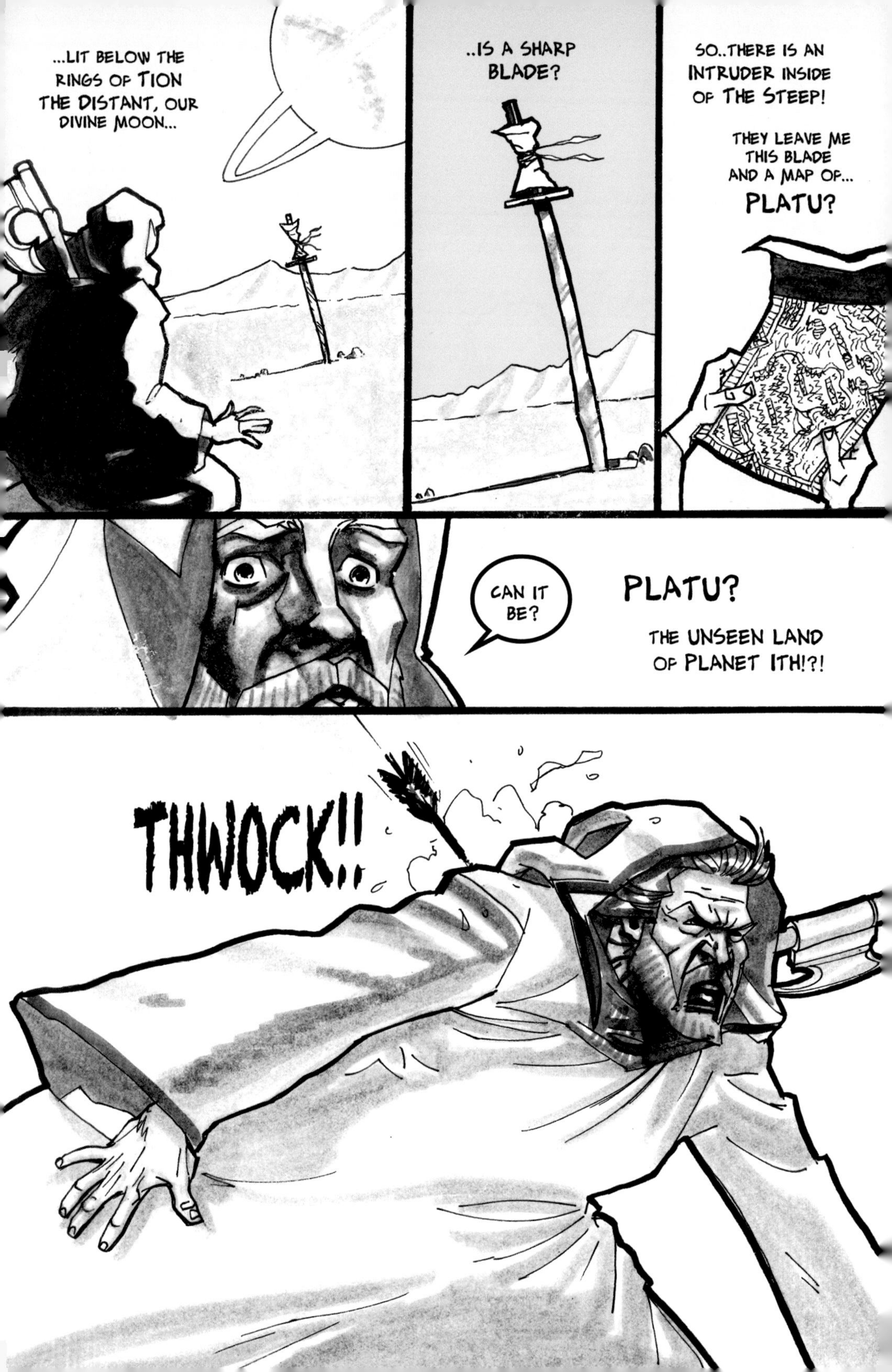
...LIT BELOW THE RINGS OF TION THE DISTANT, OUR DIVINE MOON...
..IS A SHARP BLADE?
SO..THERE IS AN INTRUDER INSIDE OF THE STEEP!
THEY LEAVE ME THIS BLADE AND A MAP OF...
PLATU?
CAN IT BE?
PLATU?
THE UNSEEN LAND OF PLANET ITH!?!
THWOCK!!

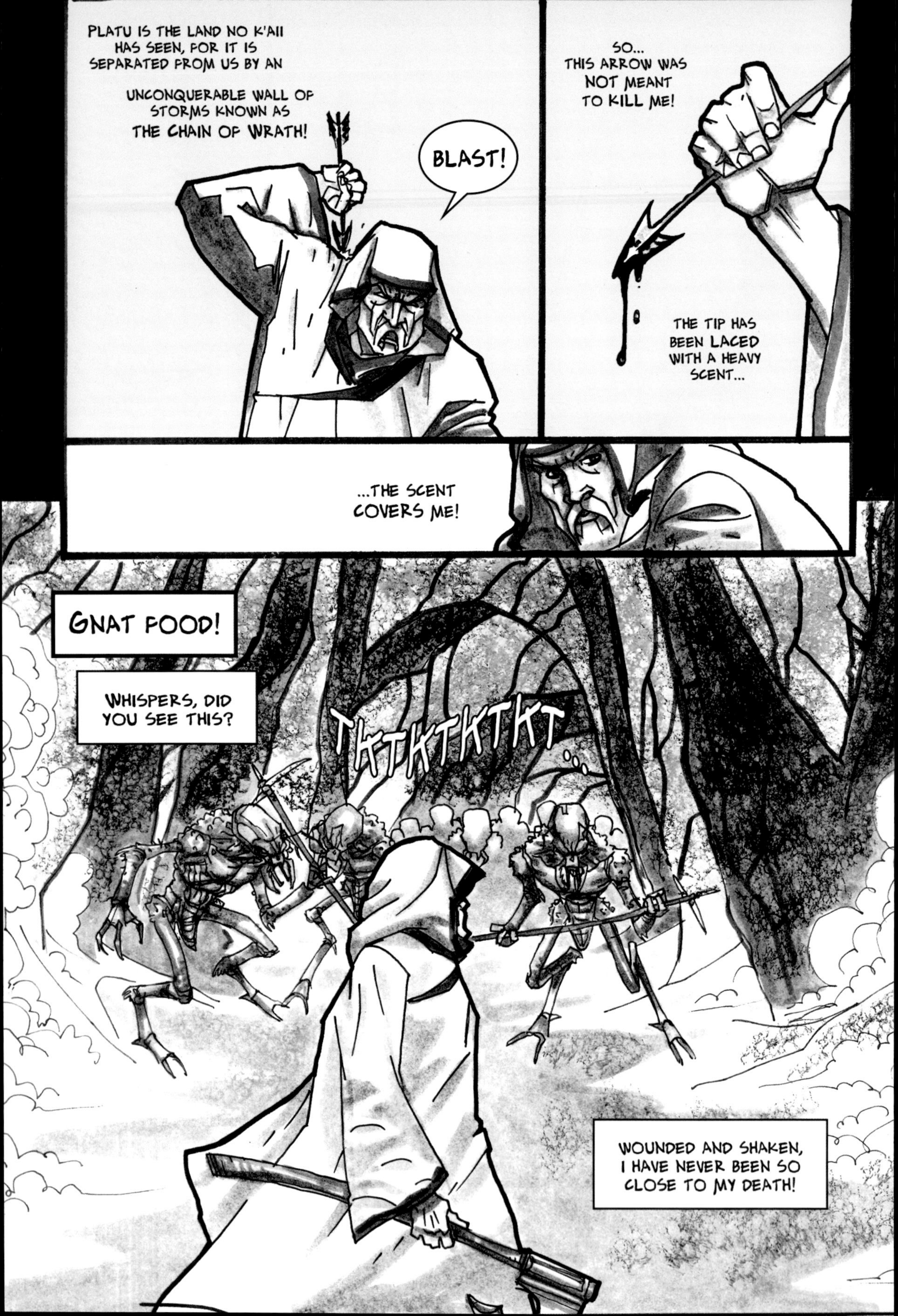

PLATU IS THE LAND NO K'AII HAS SEEN, FOR IT IS SEPARATED FROM US BY AN
UNCONQUERABLE WALL OF STORMS KNOWN AS THE CHAIN OF WRATH!
BLAST!
SO... THIS ARROW WAS NOT MEANT TO KILL ME!
THE TIP HAS BEEN LACED WITH A HEAVY SCENT...
...THE SCENT COVERS ME!
GNAT FOOD!
WHISPERS, DID YOU SEE THIS?
THTHTHTHT
WOUNDED AND SHAKEN, I HAVE NEVER BEEN SO CLOSE TO MY DEATH!

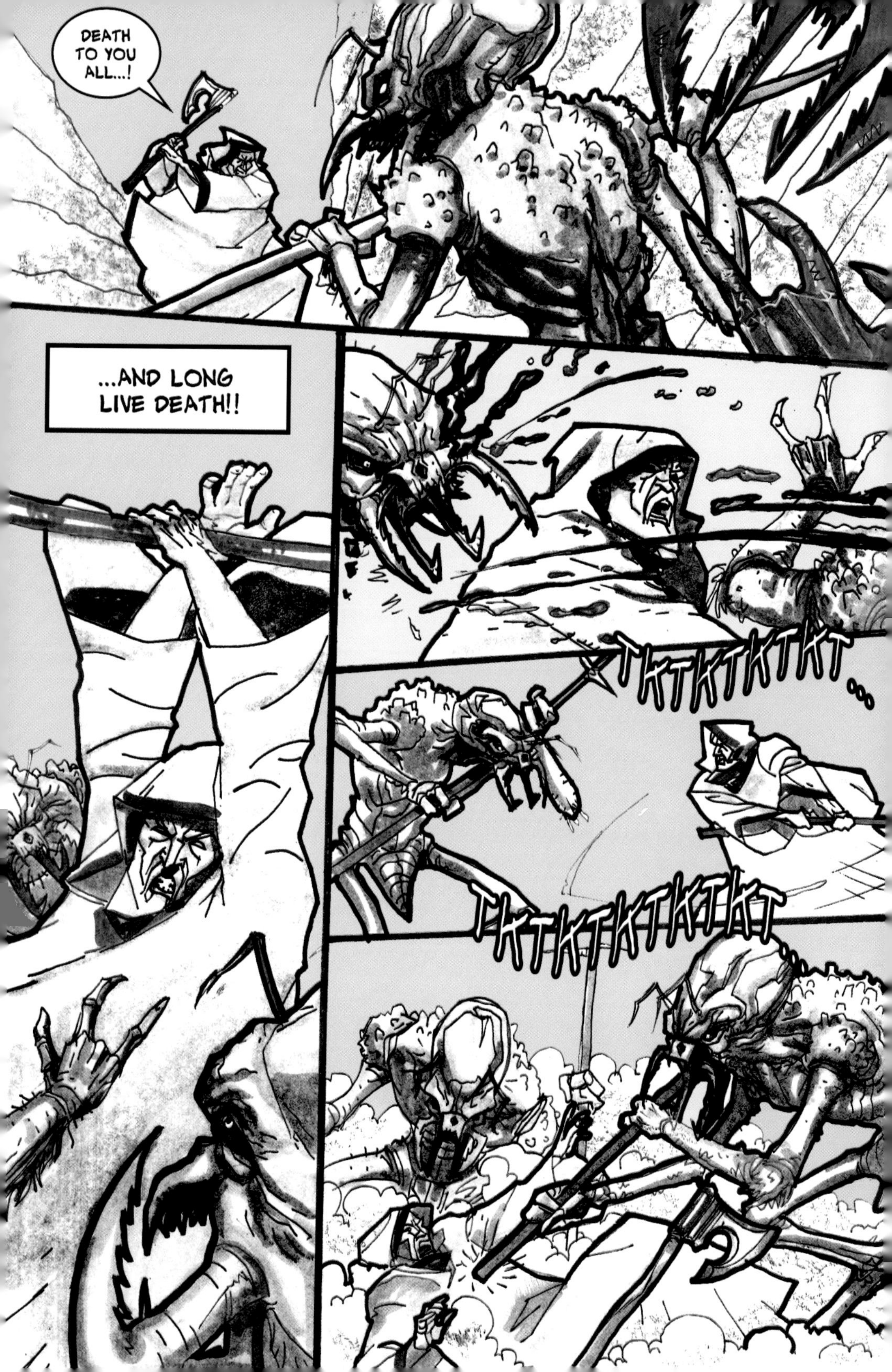
DEATH TO YOU ALL...!
...AND LONG LIVE DEATH!!
TKTKTKTKTKT...
TKTKTKTKTKTKT

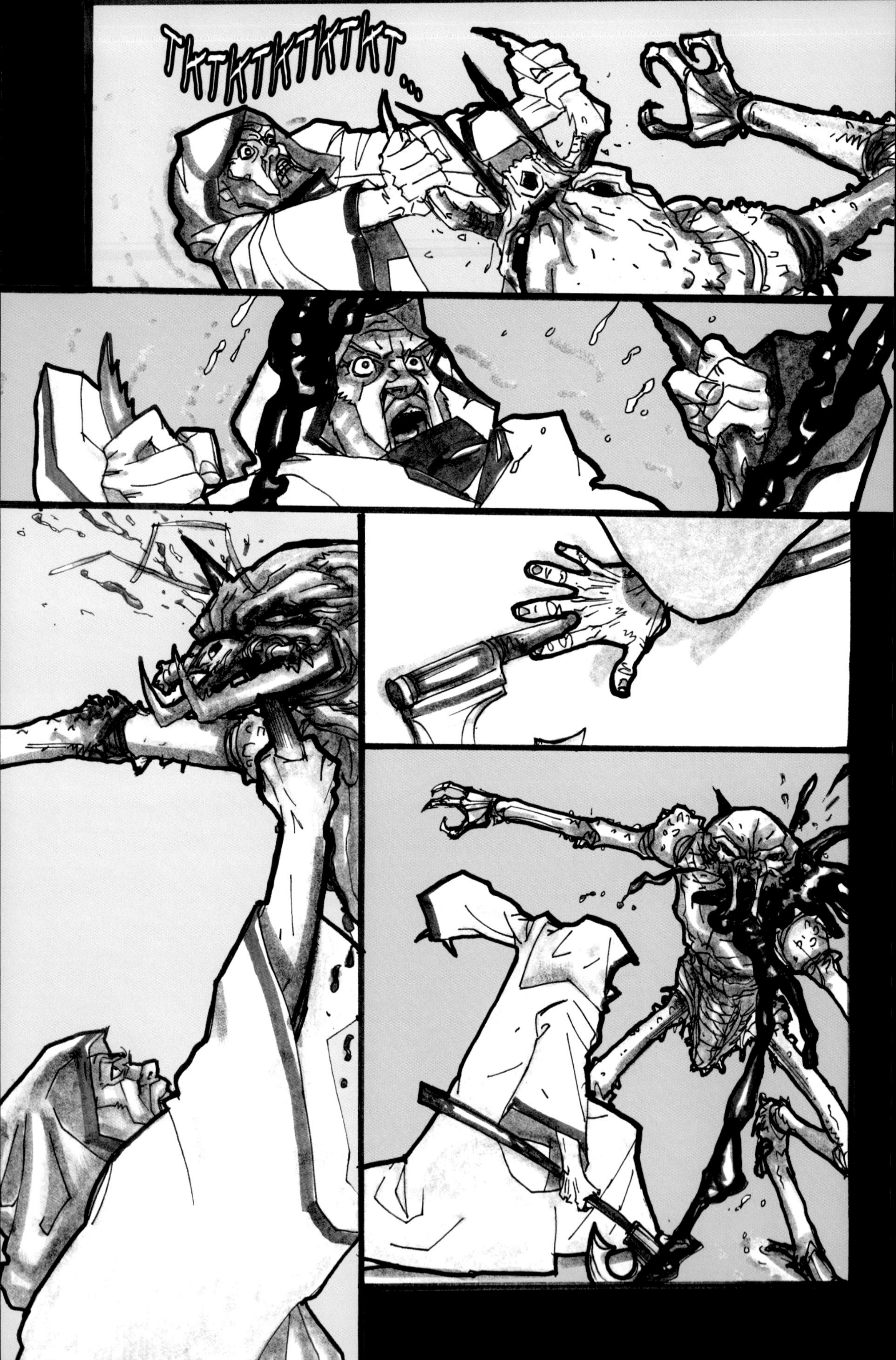
TKTKTKTKTKT...

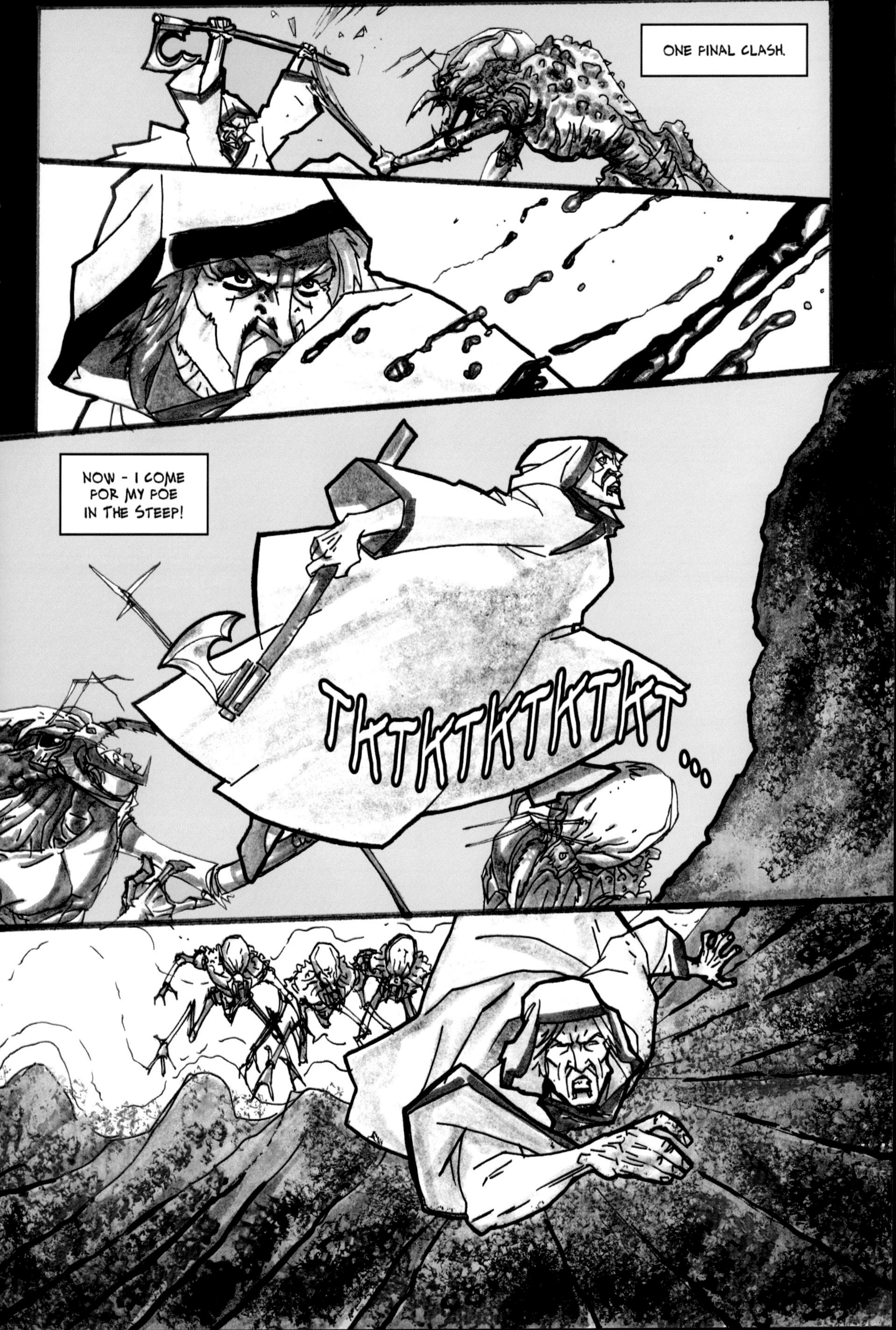
ONE FINAL CLASH.
NOW - I COME FOR MY FOE IN THE STEEP!
TKTKTKTKTKT...

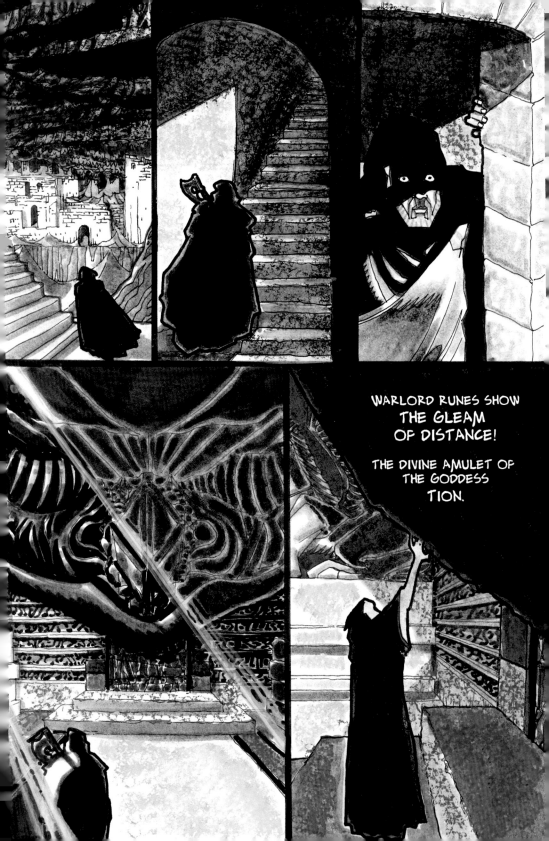

WARLORD RUNES SHOW
THE GLEAM
OF DISTANCE!

THE DIVINE AMULET OF
THE GODDESS
TION.

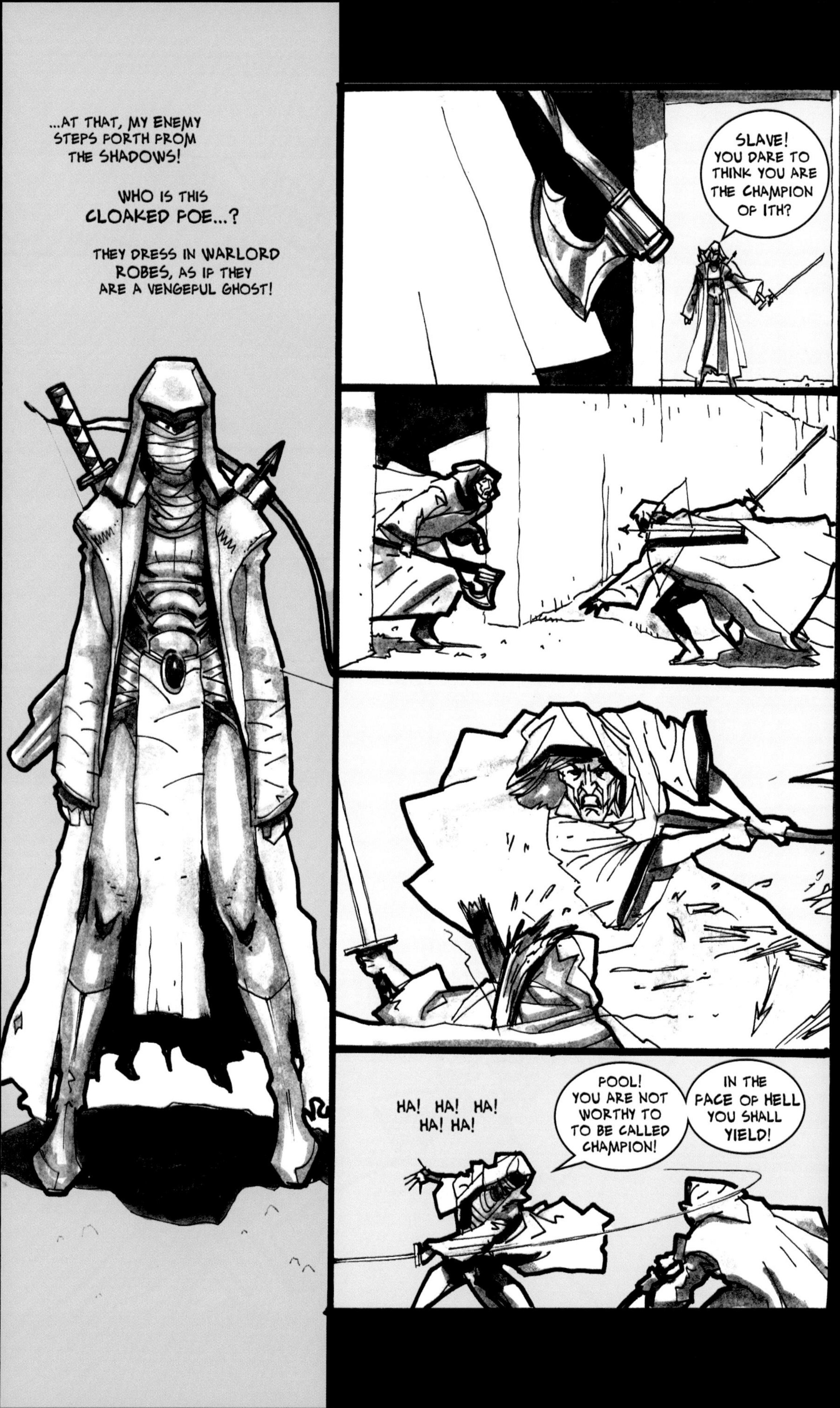
...AT THAT, MY ENEMY STEPS FORTH FROM THE SHADOWS!
WHO IS THIS CLOAKED FOE...?
THEY DRESS IN WARLORD ROBES, AS IF THEY ARE A VENGEFUL GHOST!
SLAVE! YOU DARE TO THINK YOU ARE THE CHAMPION OF ITH?
HA! HA! HA! HA! HA!
FOOL! YOU ARE NOT WORTHY TO TO BE CALLED CHAMPION!
IN THE FACE OF HELL YOU SHALL YIELD!

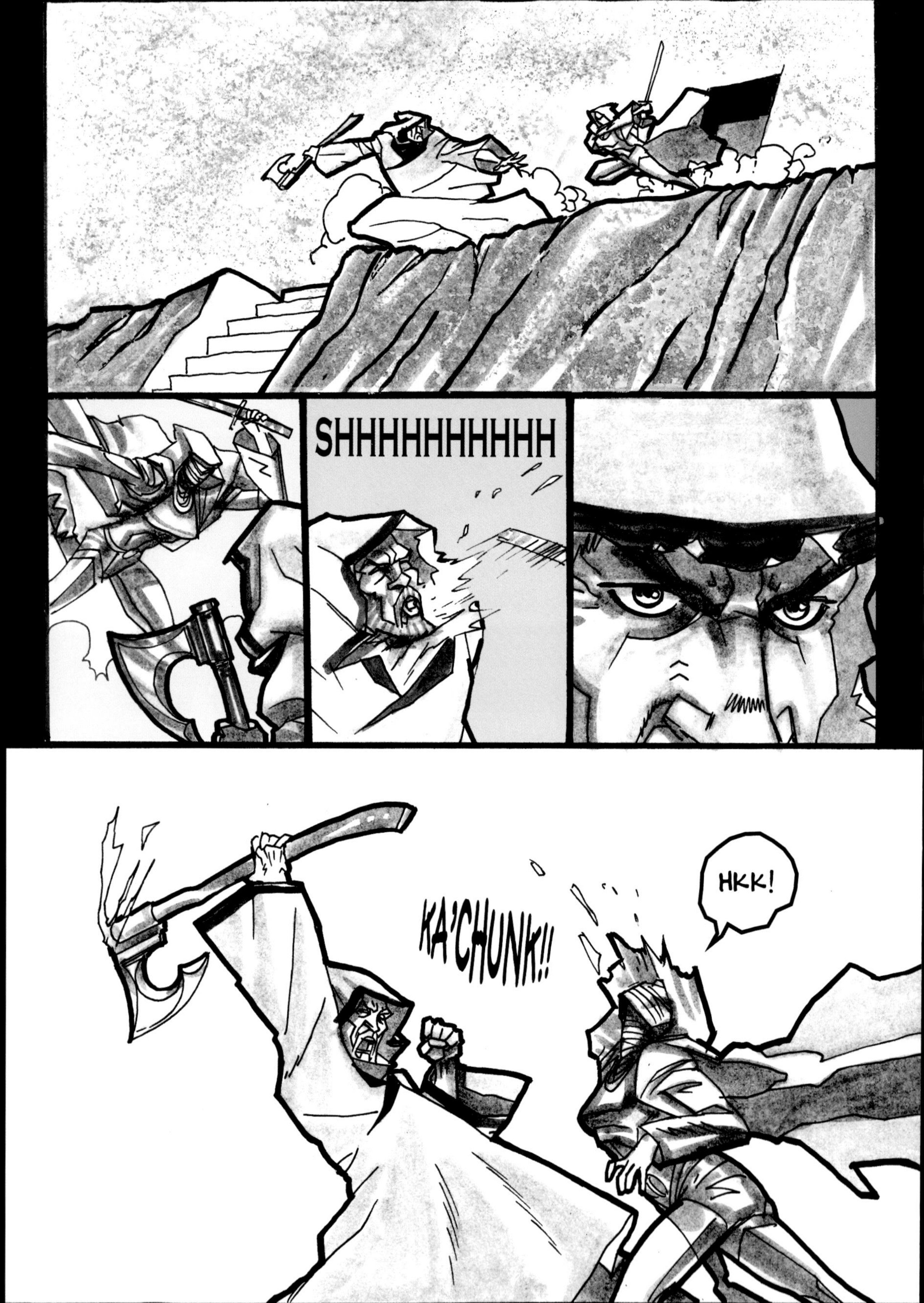
SHHHHHHHHHH
KA'CHUNK!!
HKK!

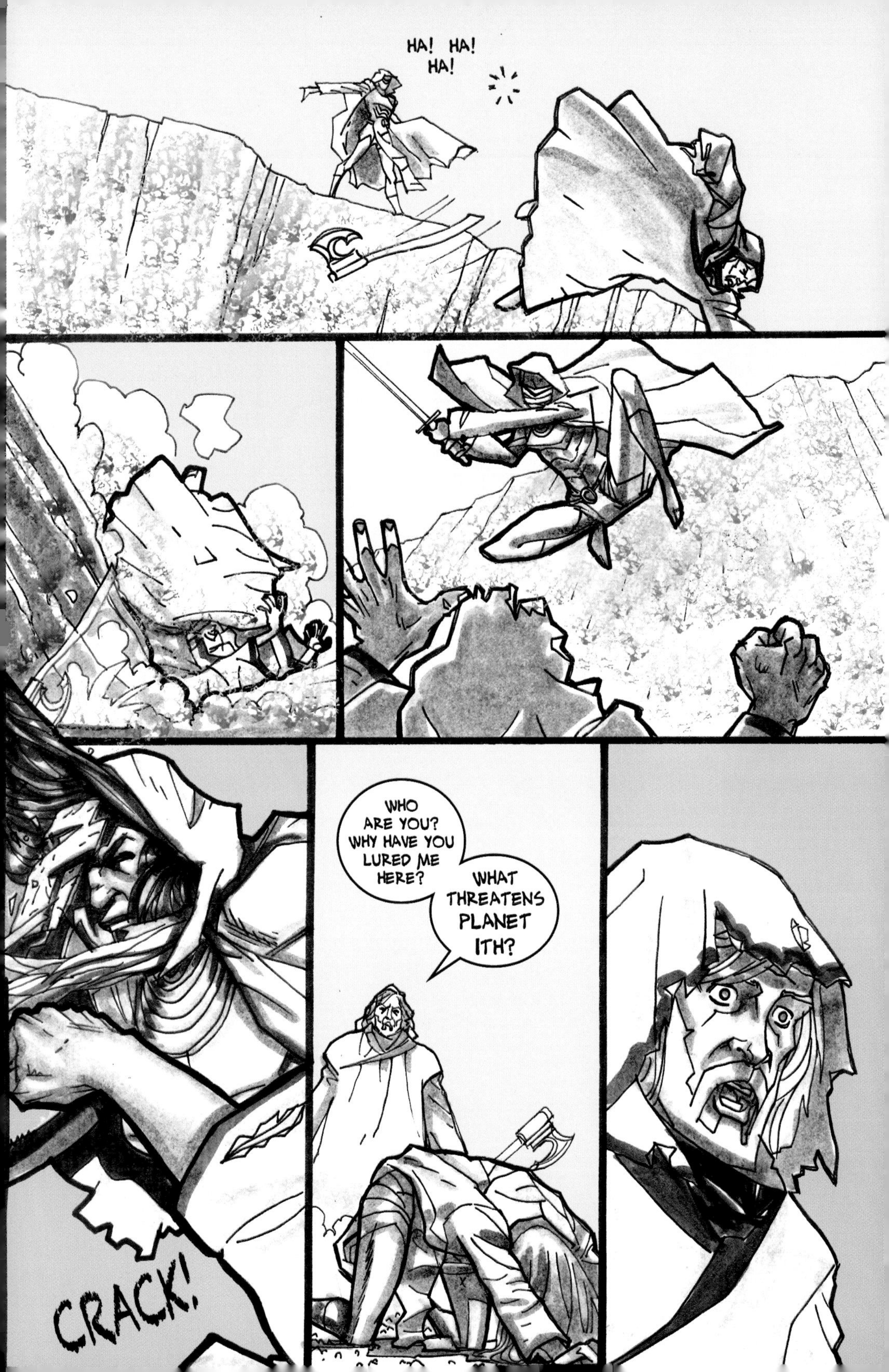
HA! HA!
HA!
WHO ARE YOU? WHY HAVE YOU LURED ME HERE?
WHAT THREATENS PLANET ITH?
CRACK!

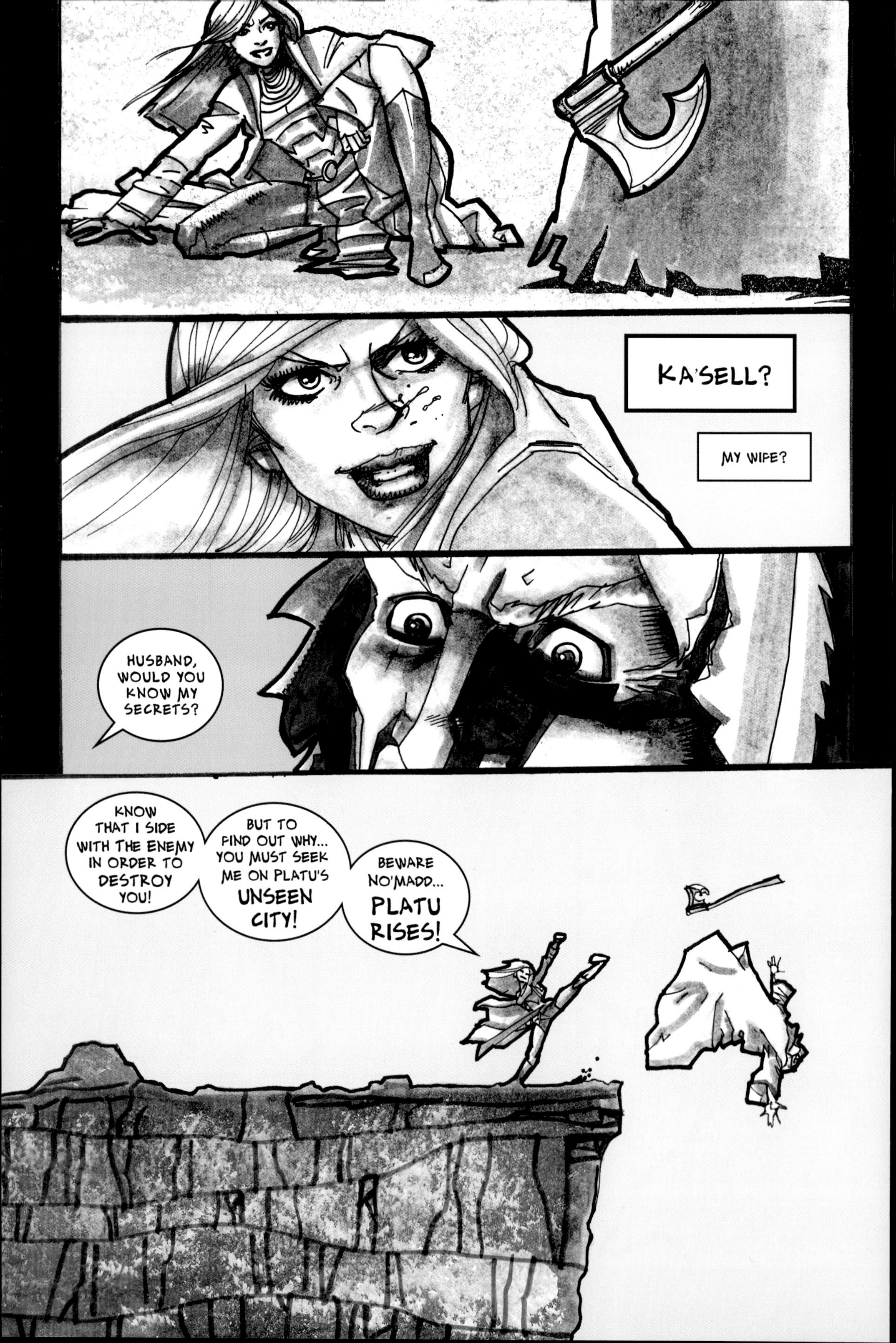
KA'SELL?
MY WIFE?
HUSBAND, WOULD YOU KNOW MY SECRETS?
KNOW THAT I SIDE WITH THE ENEMY IN ORDER TO DESTROY YOU!
BUT TO FIND OUT WHY... YOU MUST SEEK ME ON PLATU'S UNSEEN CITY!
BEWARE NO'MADD... PLATU RISES!

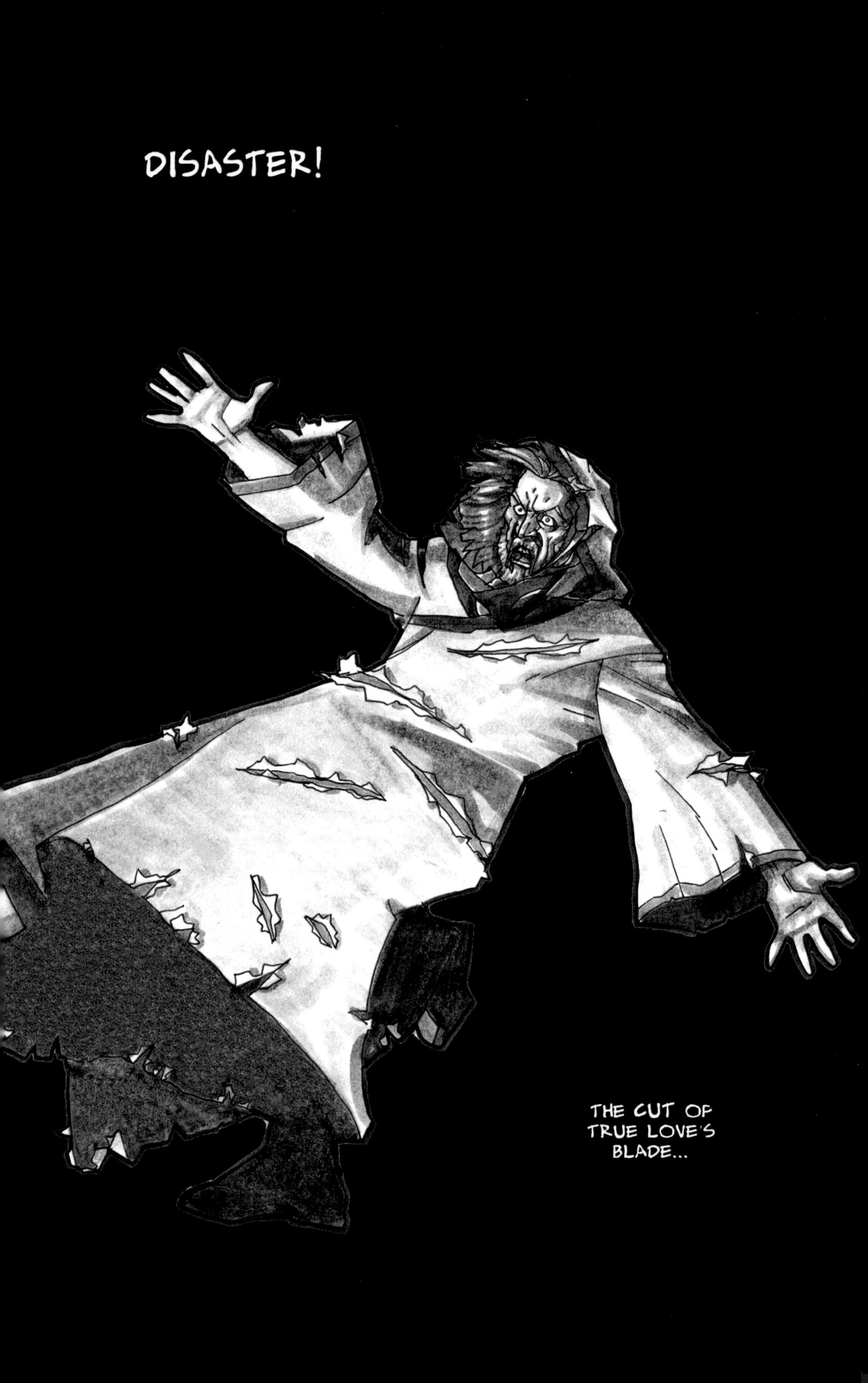
DISASTER!
THE CUT OF TRUE LOVE'S BLADE...

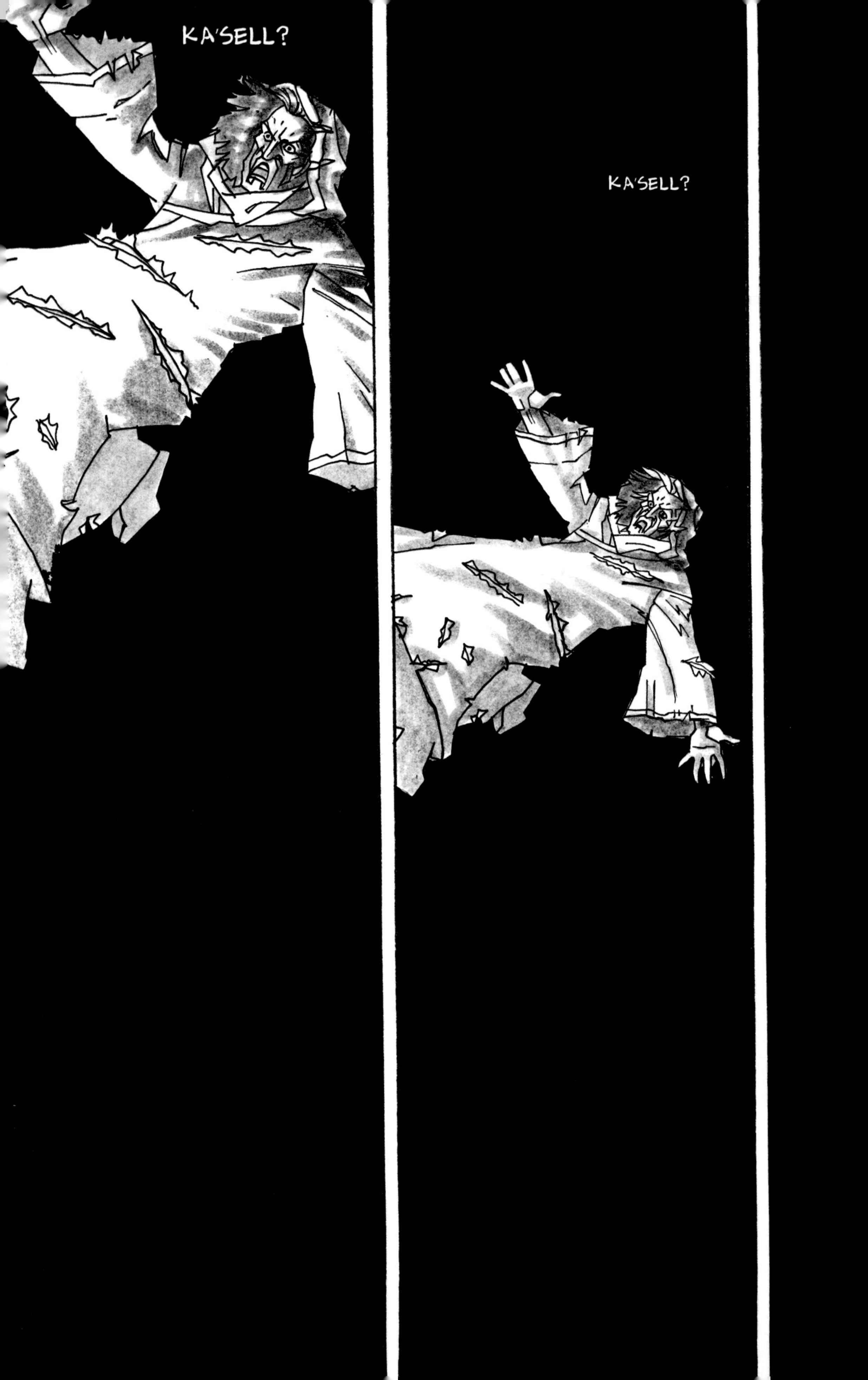
KA'SELL?
KA'SELL?

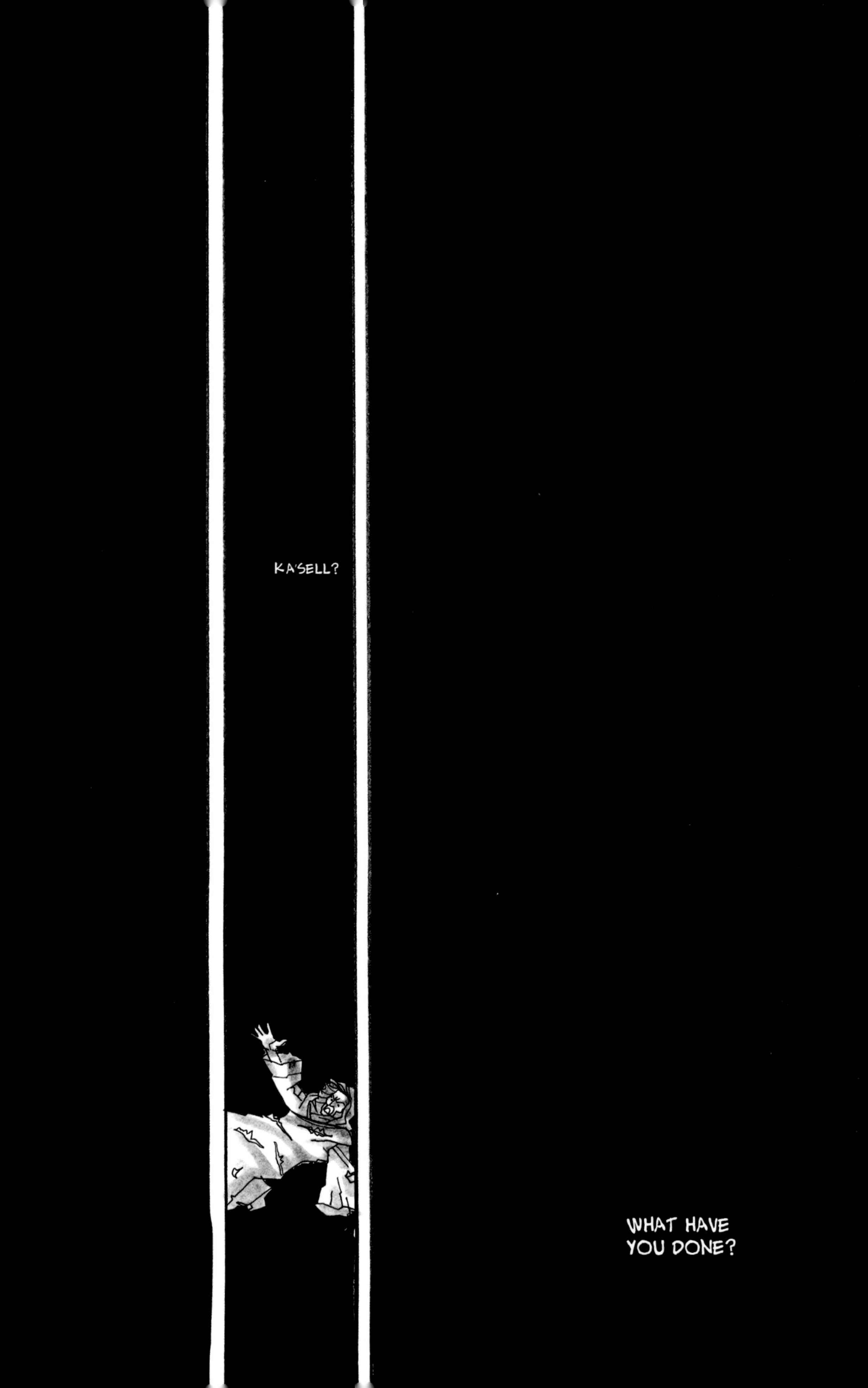
KA'SELL?
WHAT HAVE YOU DONE?

TKTKTKTKTKT...

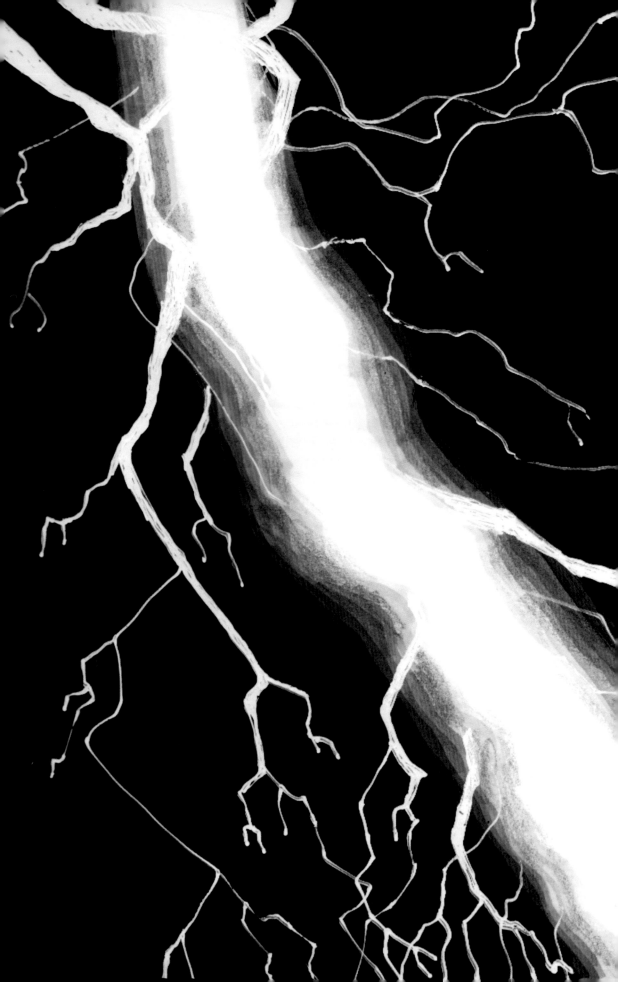

CHAPTER TWO

KA'SELL

"BETRAYED...

...I ROAM TO
THE ROAR OF WAVES."

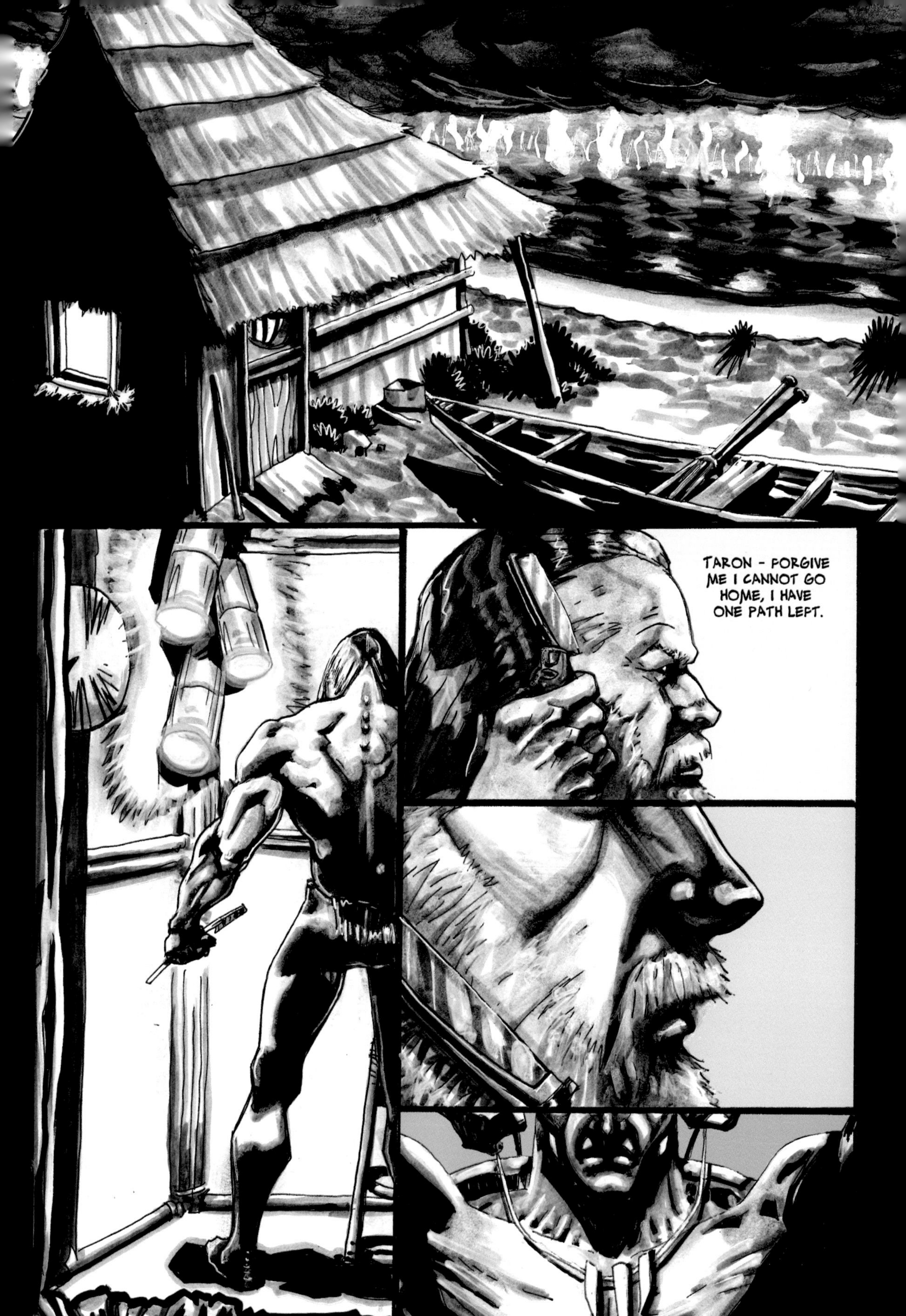
TARON - FORGIVE ME I CANNOT GO HOME, I HAVE ONE PATH LEFT.

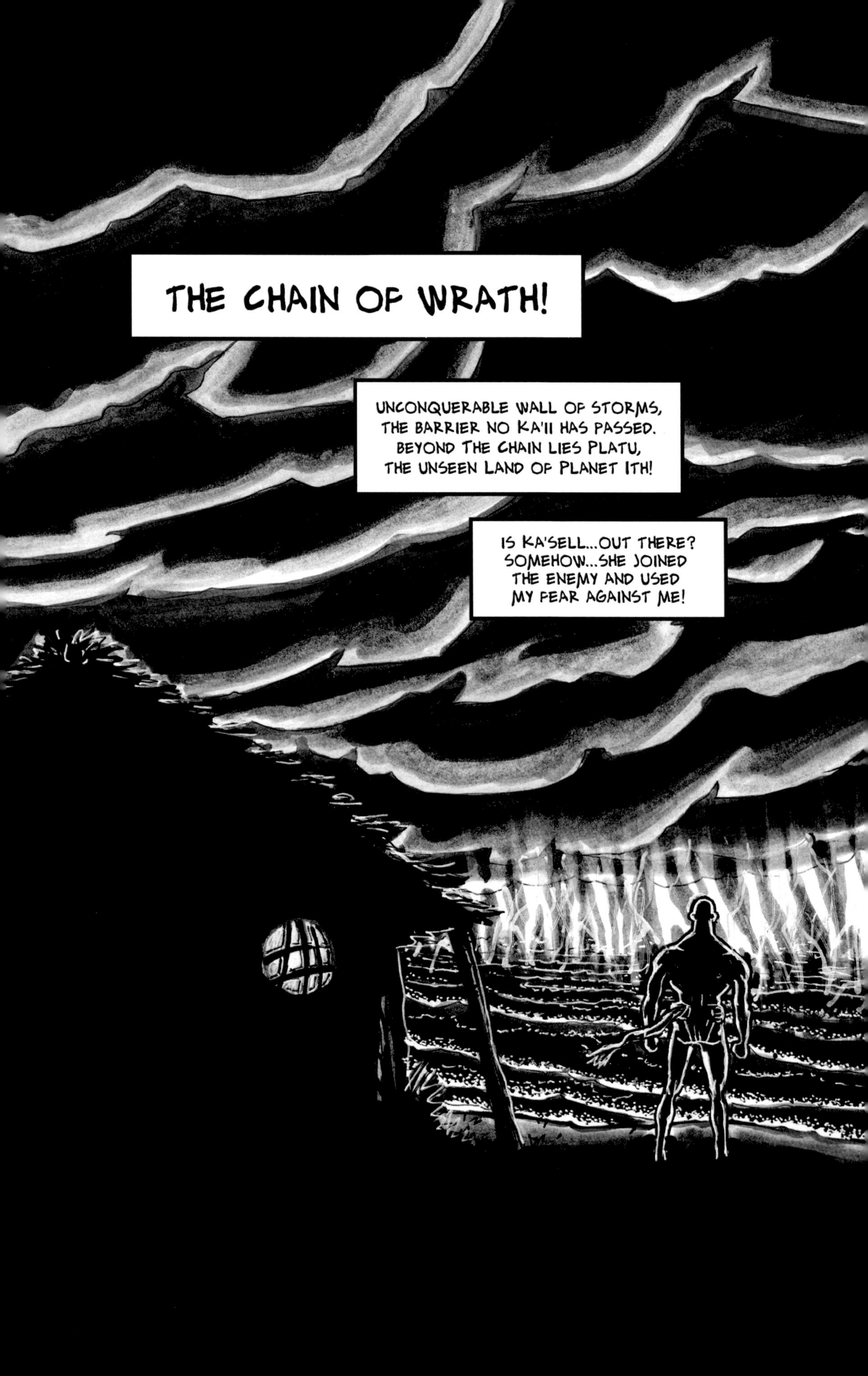
THE CHAIN OF WRATH!
UNCONQUERABLE WALL OF STORMS, THE BARRIER NO KA'II HAS PASSED. BEYOND THE CHAIN LIES PLATU, THE UNSEEN LAND OF PLANET ITH!
IS KA'SELL...OUT THERE? SOMEHOW...SHE JOINED THE ENEMY AND USED MY FEAR AGAINST ME!

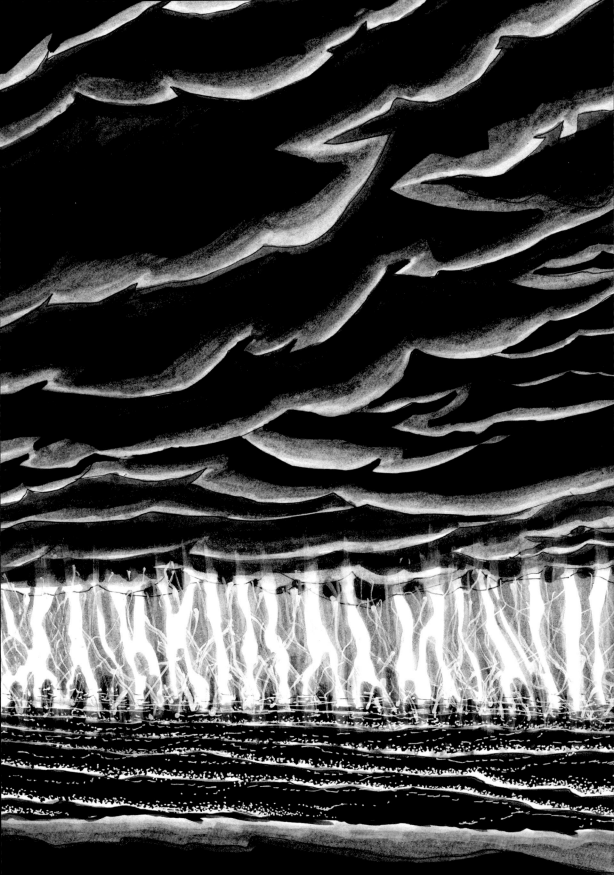

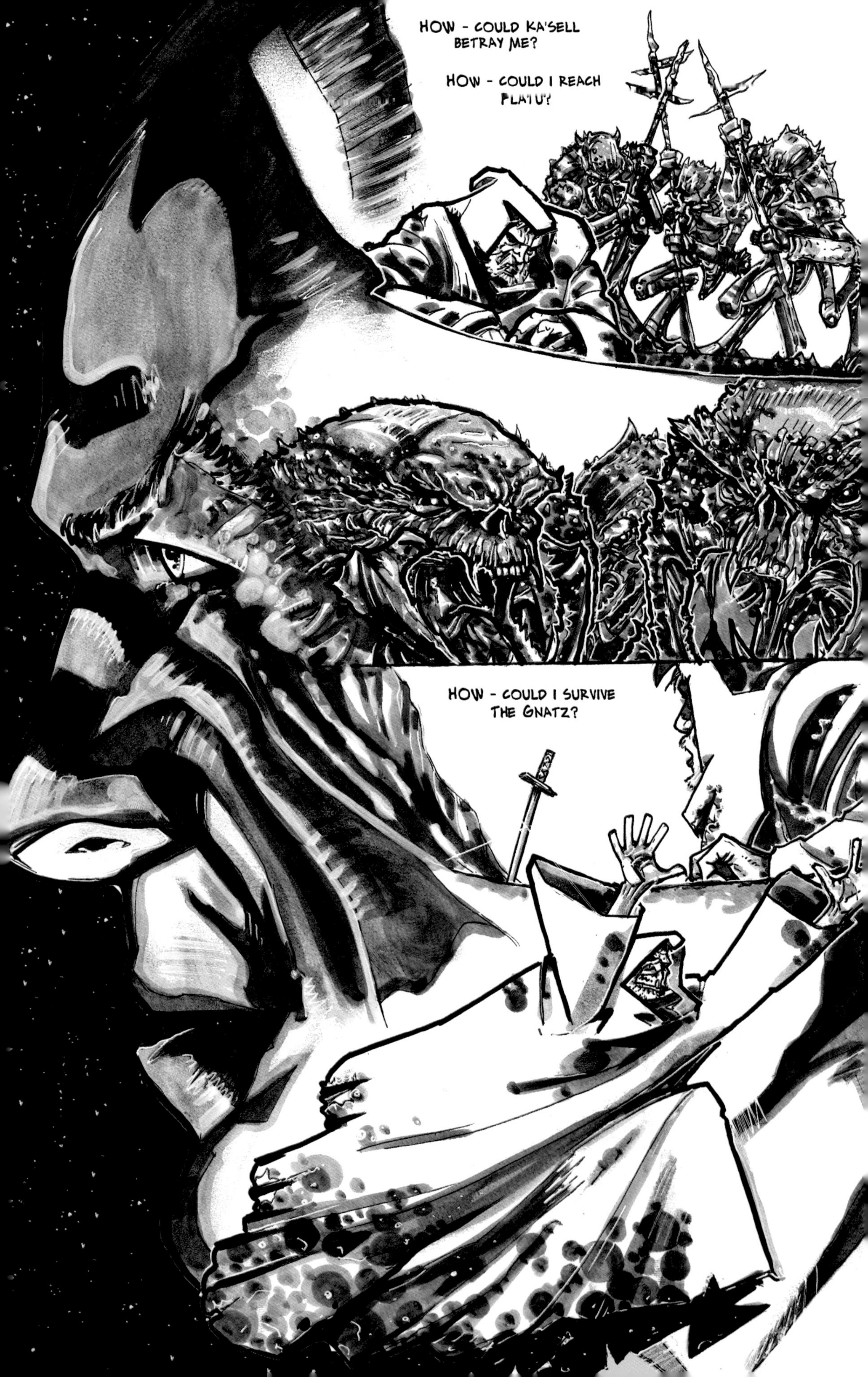
HOW - COULD KA'SELL BETRAY ME?
HOW - COULD I REACH PLATU?
HOW - COULD I SURVIVE THE GNATZ?

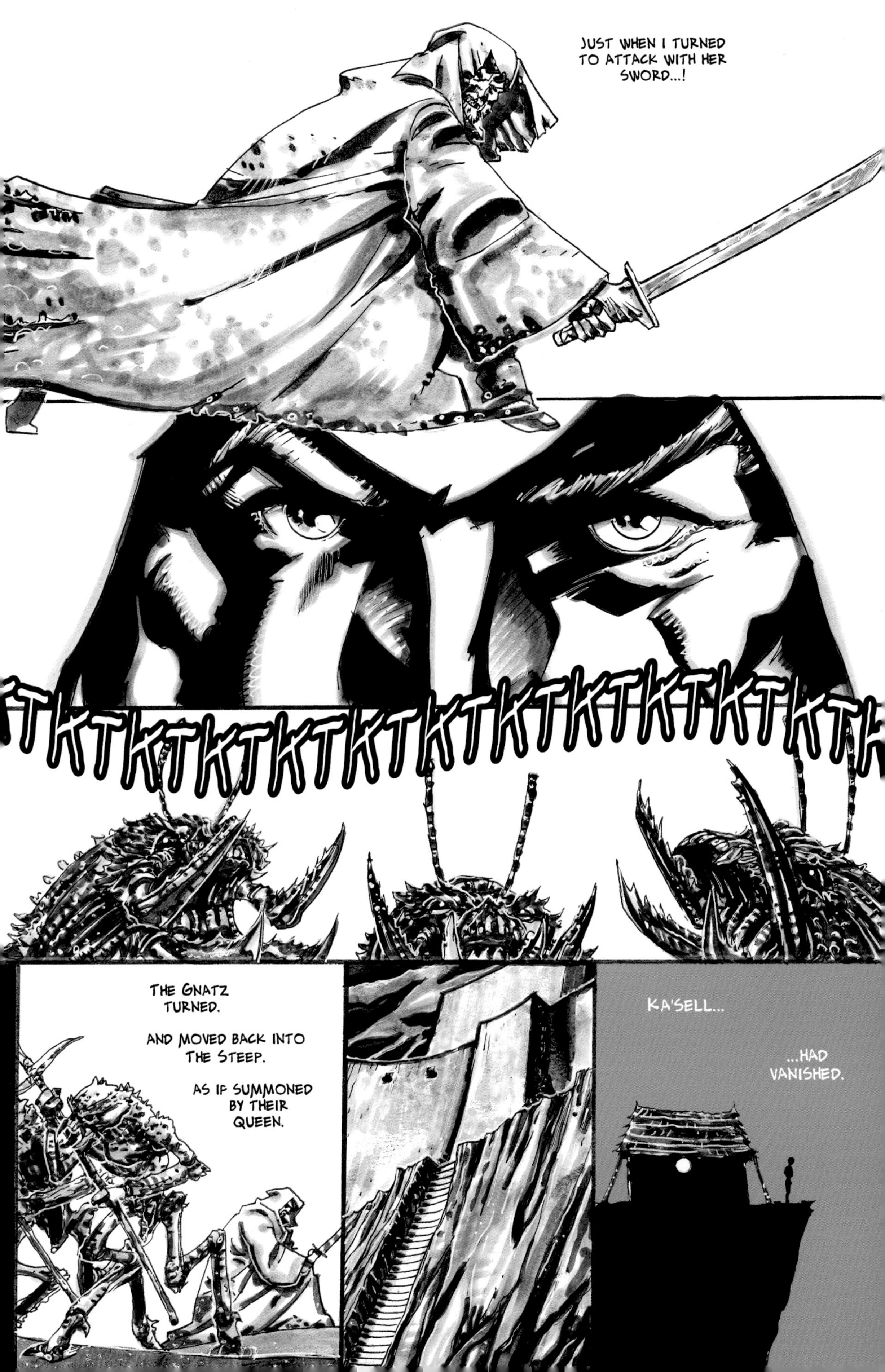
JUST WHEN I TURNED TO ATTACK WITH HER SWORD...!
TKTKTKTKTKTKTKTKTKTKTKTKTKTKTK
THE GNATZ TURNED.
AND MOVED BACK INTO THE STEEP.
AS IF SUMMONED BY THEIR QUEEN.
KA'SELL...
...HAD VANISHED.

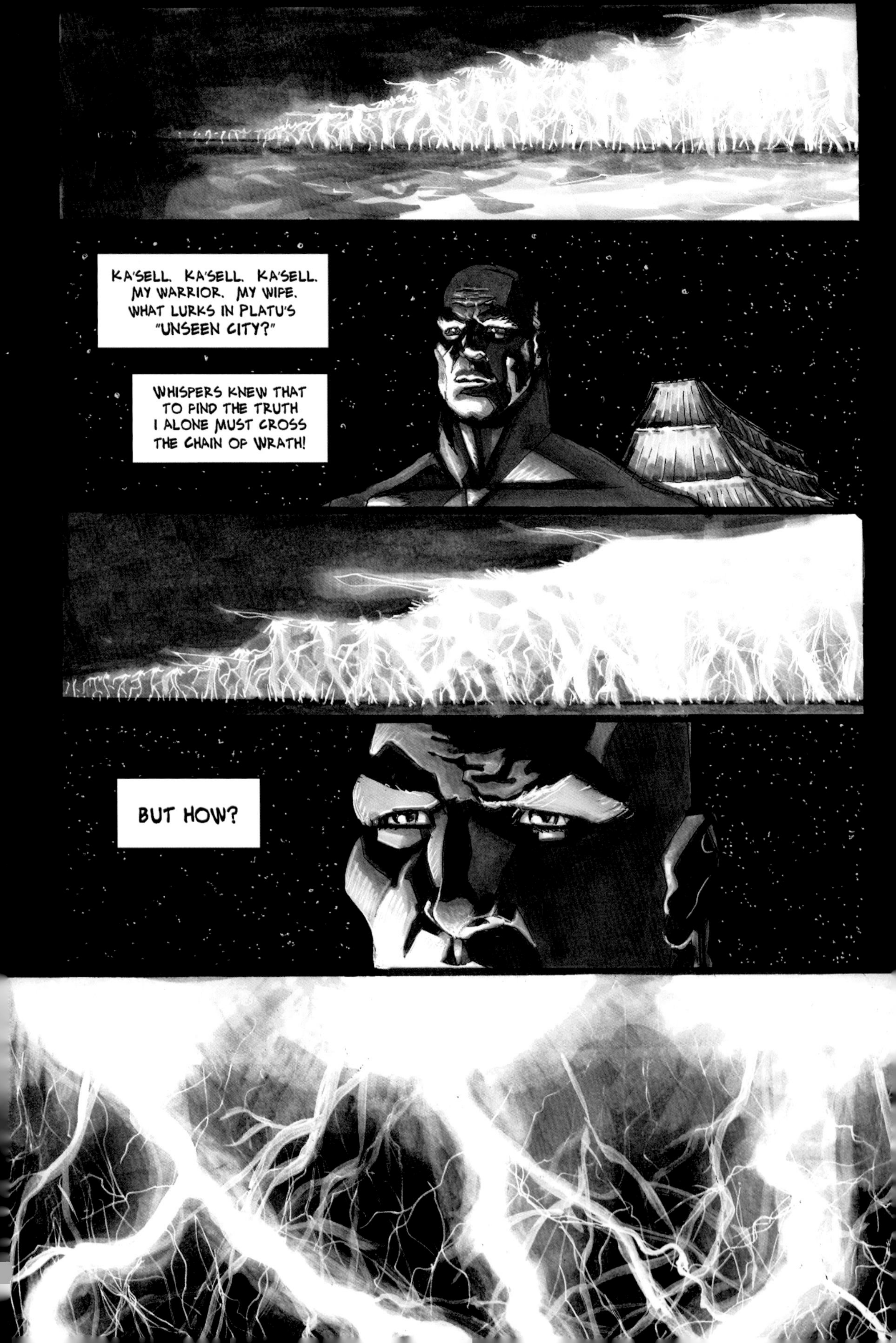
KA'SELL. KA'SELL. KA'SELL. MY WARRIOR. MY WIFE. WHAT LURKS IN PLATU'S "UNSEEN CITY?"
WHISPERS KNEW THAT TO FIND THE TRUTH I ALONE MUST CROSS THE CHAIN OF WRATH!
BUT HOW?

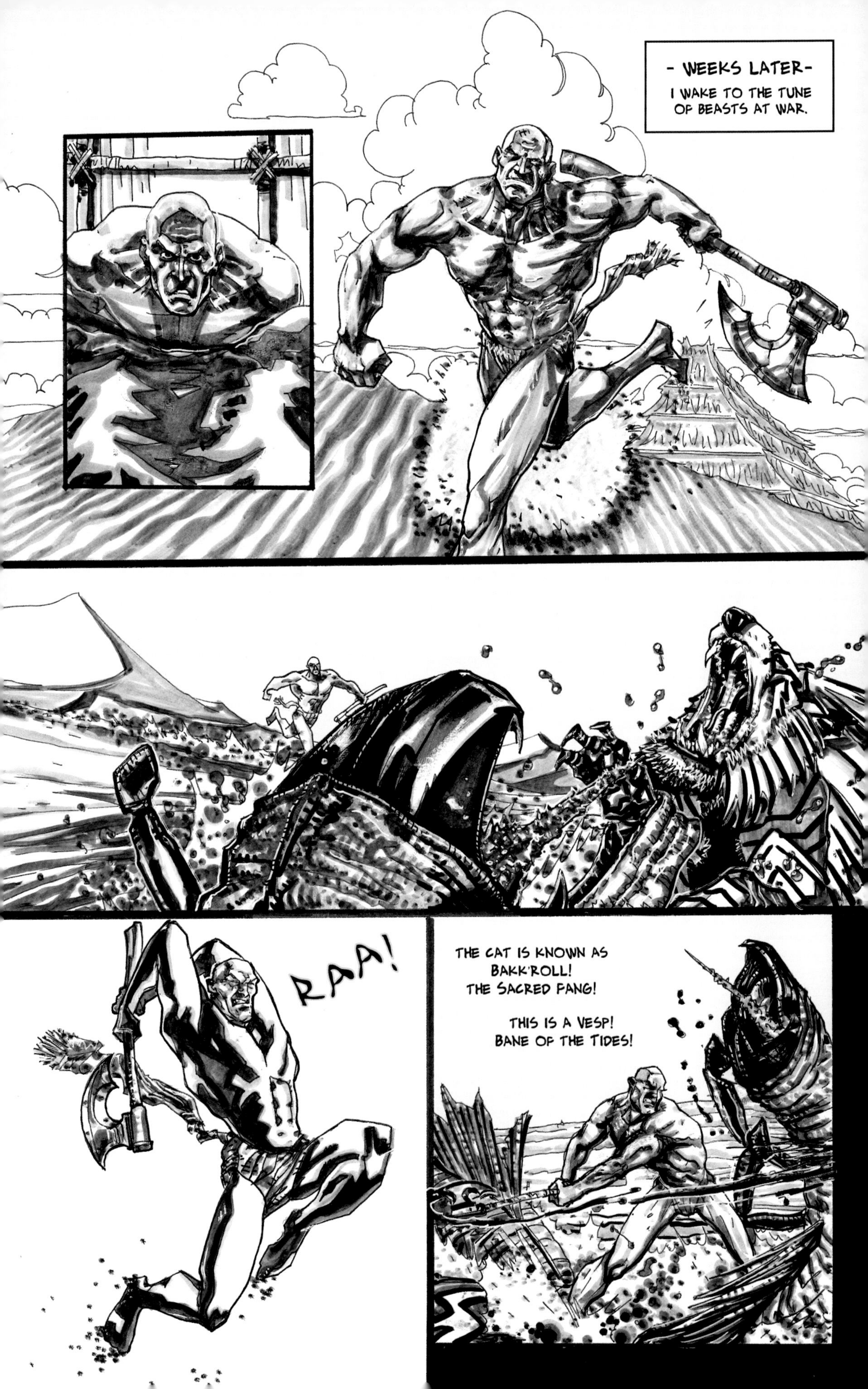
- WEEKS LATER-
I WAKE TO THE TUNE OF BEASTS AT WAR.
RAA!
THE CAT IS KNOWN AS BAKK'ROLL! THE SACRED FANG!
THIS IS A VESP! BANE OF THE TIDES!

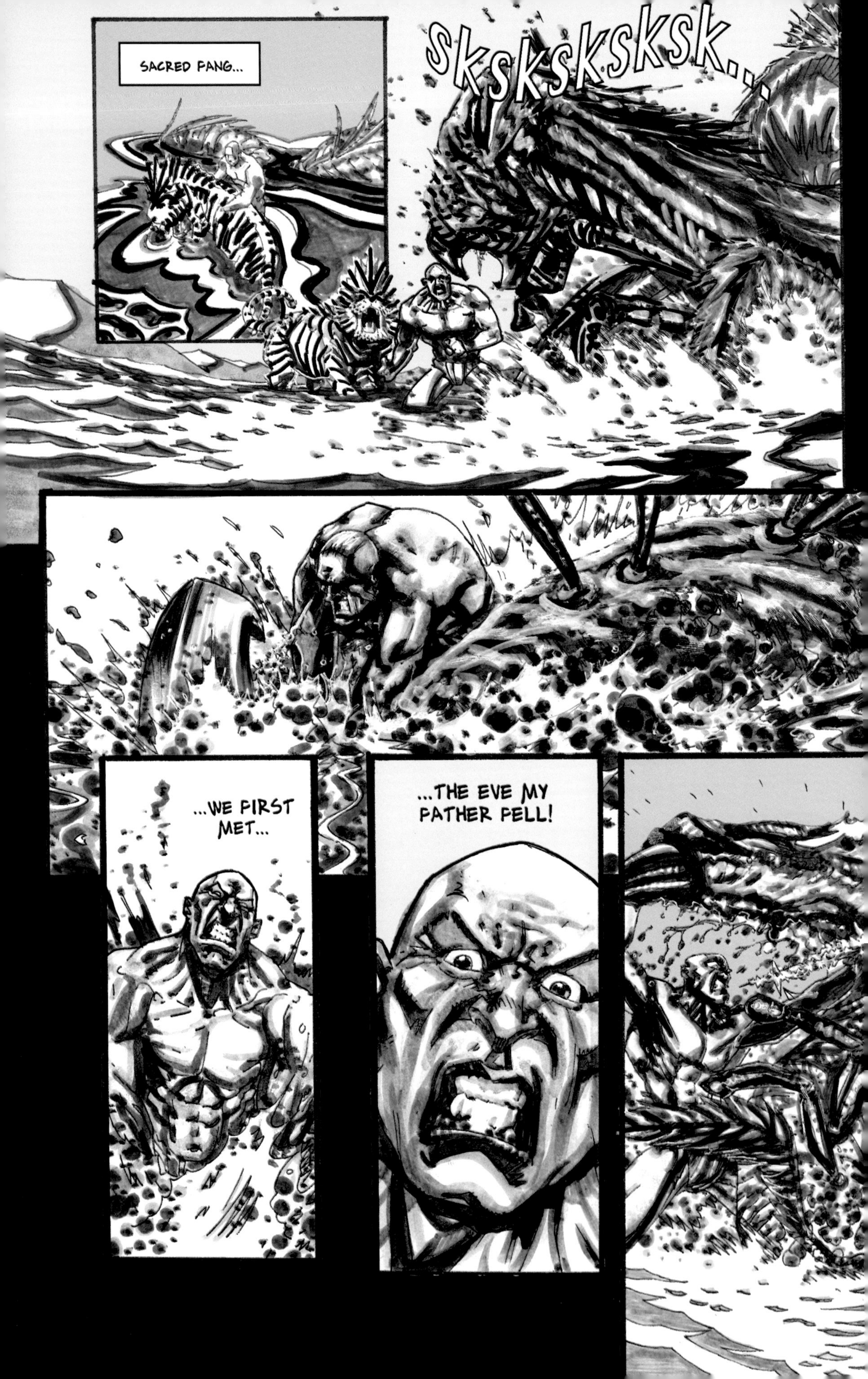
SACRED FANG...
SKSKSKSKSK...
...WE FIRST MET...
...THE EVE MY FATHER FELL!

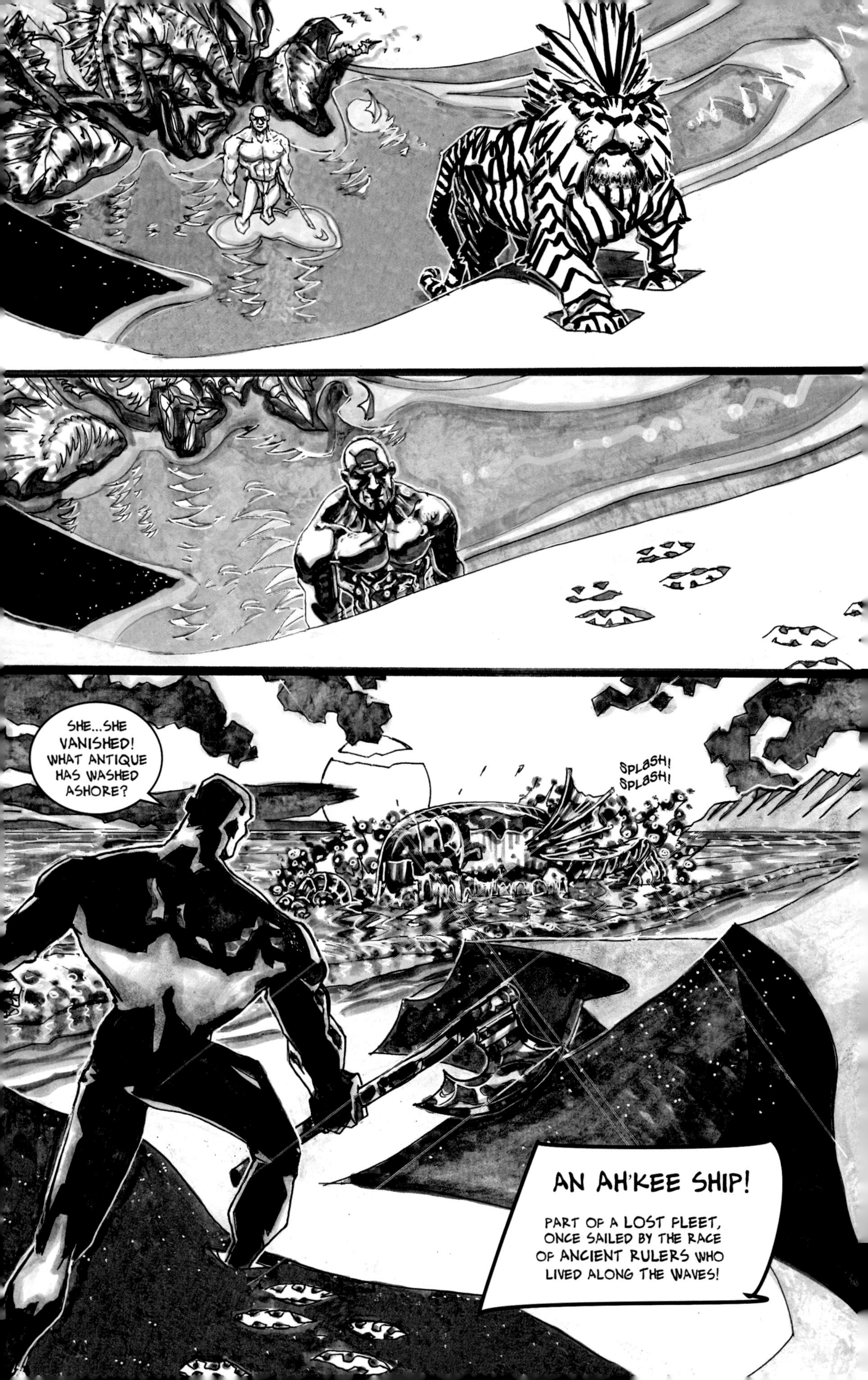
SHE...SHE VANISHED! WHAT ANTIQUE HAS WASHED ASHORE?
SPLASH! SPLASH!
AN AH'KEE SHIP!
PART OF A LOST FLEET, ONCE SAILED BY THE RACE OF ANCIENT RULERS WHO LIVED ALONG THE WAVES!

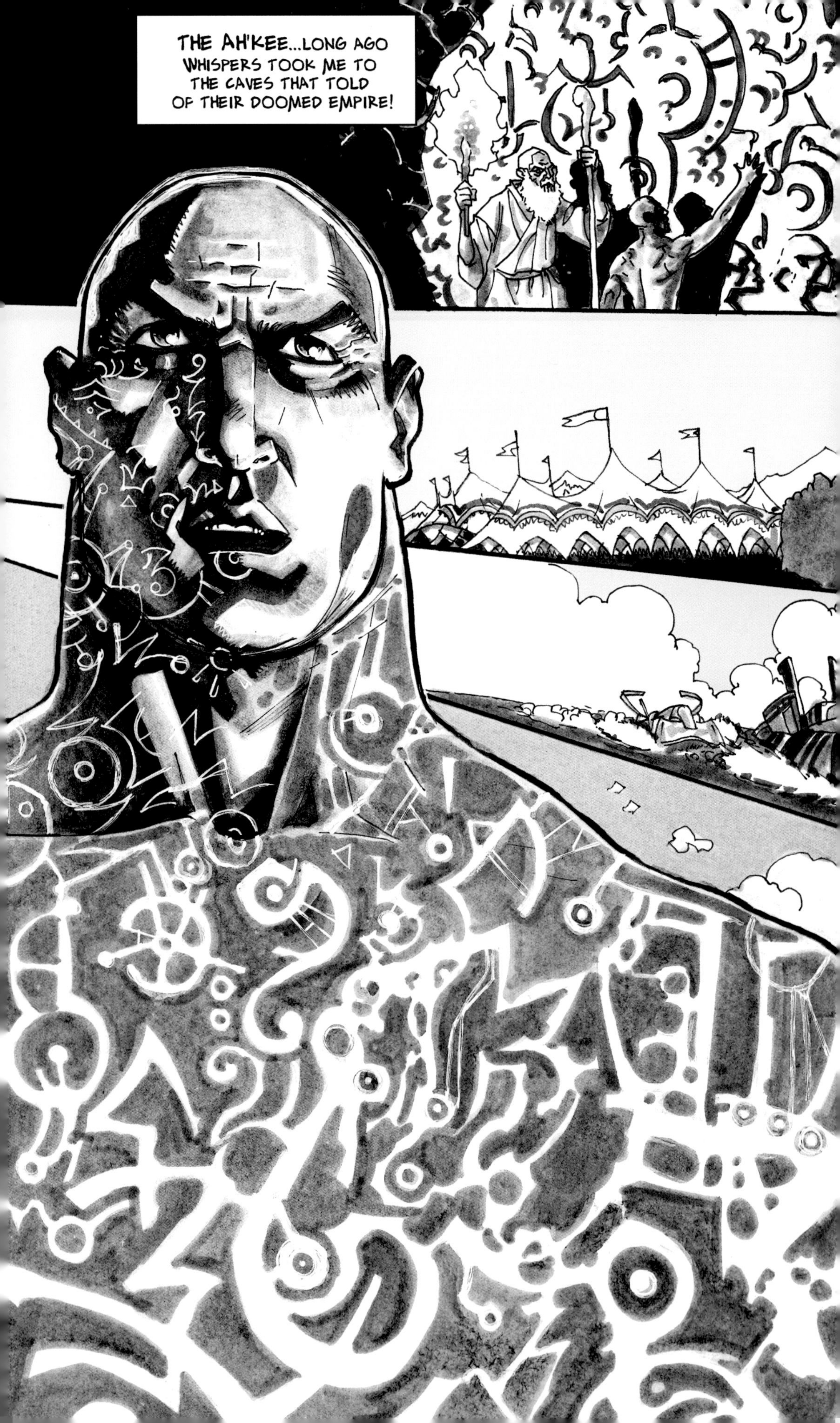
THE AH'KEE...LONG AGO WHISPERS TOOK ME TO THE CAVES THAT TOLD OF THEIR DOOMED EMPIRE!

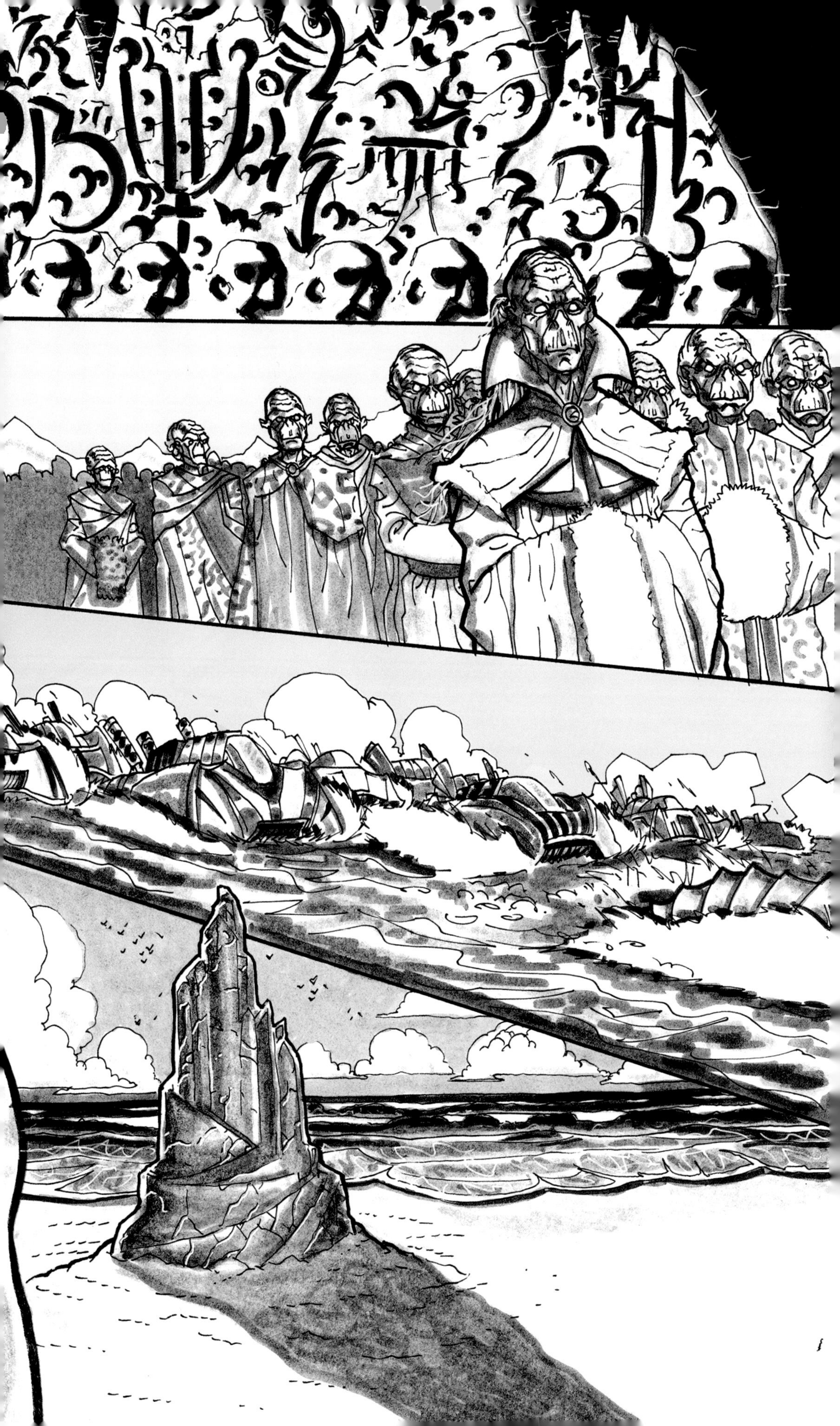

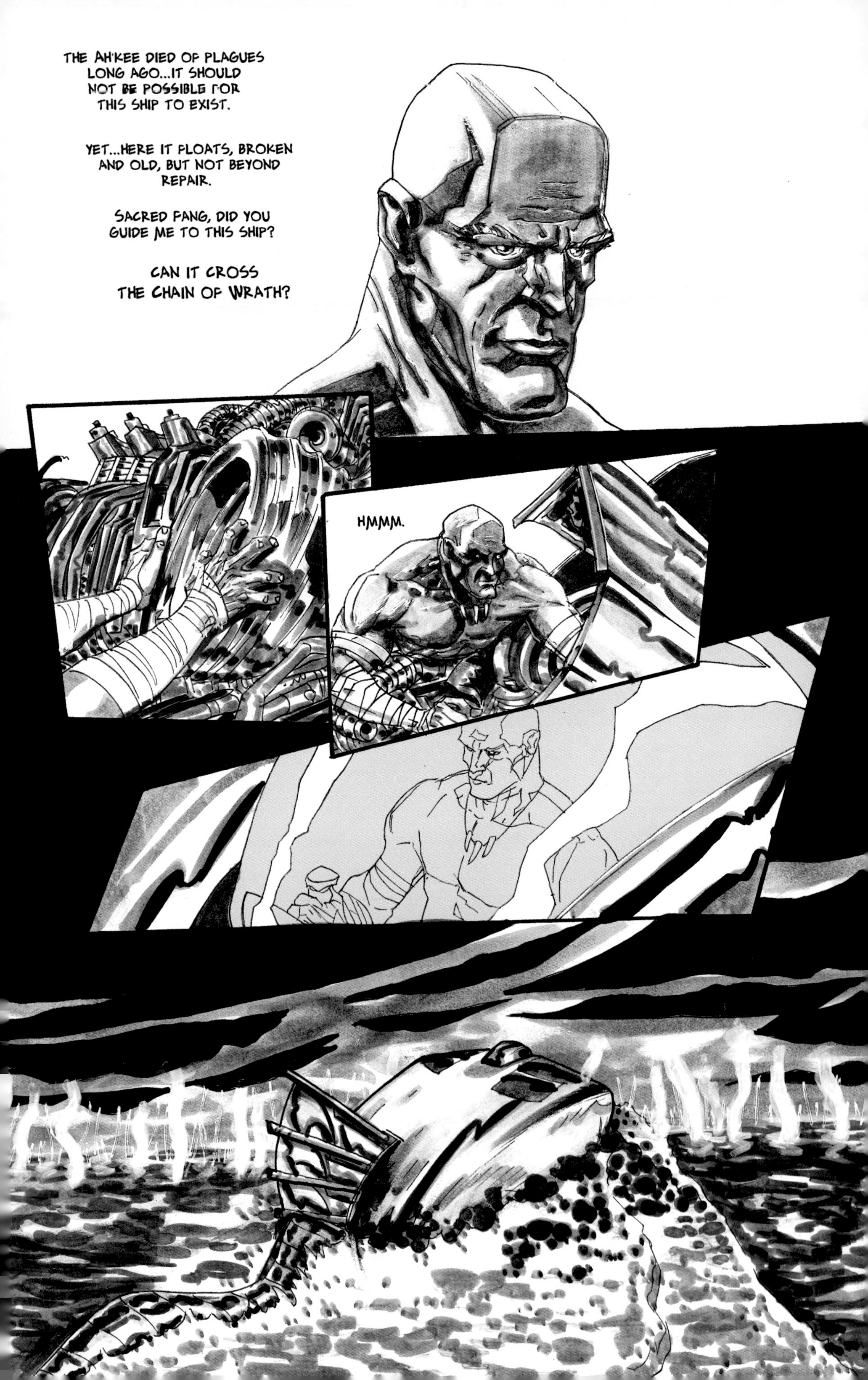
THE AH'KEE DIED OF PLAGUES LONG AGO...IT SHOULD NOT BE POSSIBLE FOR THIS SHIP TO EXIST.
YET...HERE IT FLOATS, BROKEN AND OLD, BUT NOT BEYOND REPAIR.
SACRED FANG, DID YOU GUIDE ME TO THIS SHIP?
CAN IT CROSS THE CHAIN OF WRATH?
HMMM.

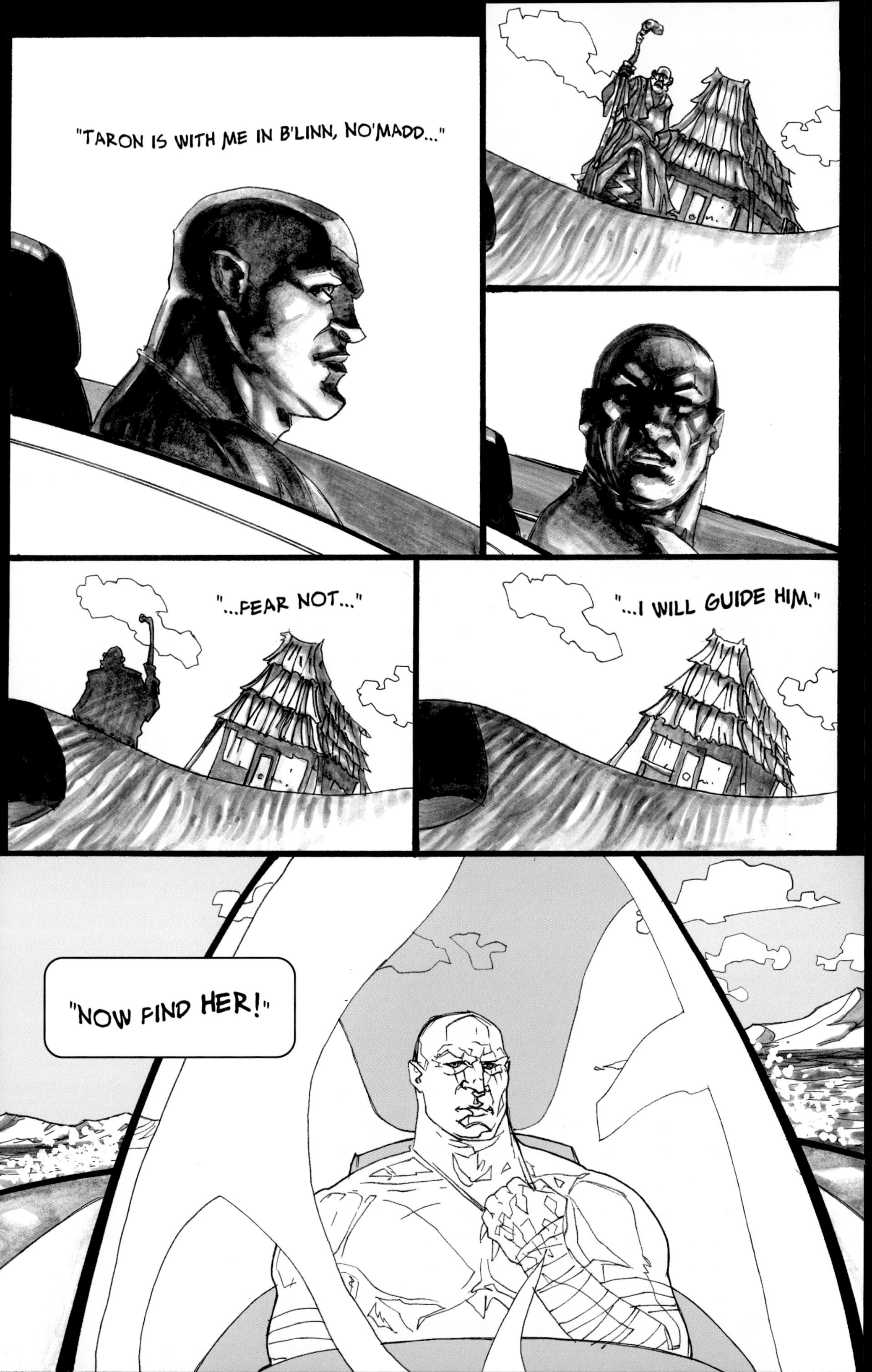
"TARON IS WITH ME IN B'LINN, NO'MADD..."
"...FEAR NOT..."
"...I WILL GUIDE HIM."
"NOW FIND HER!"

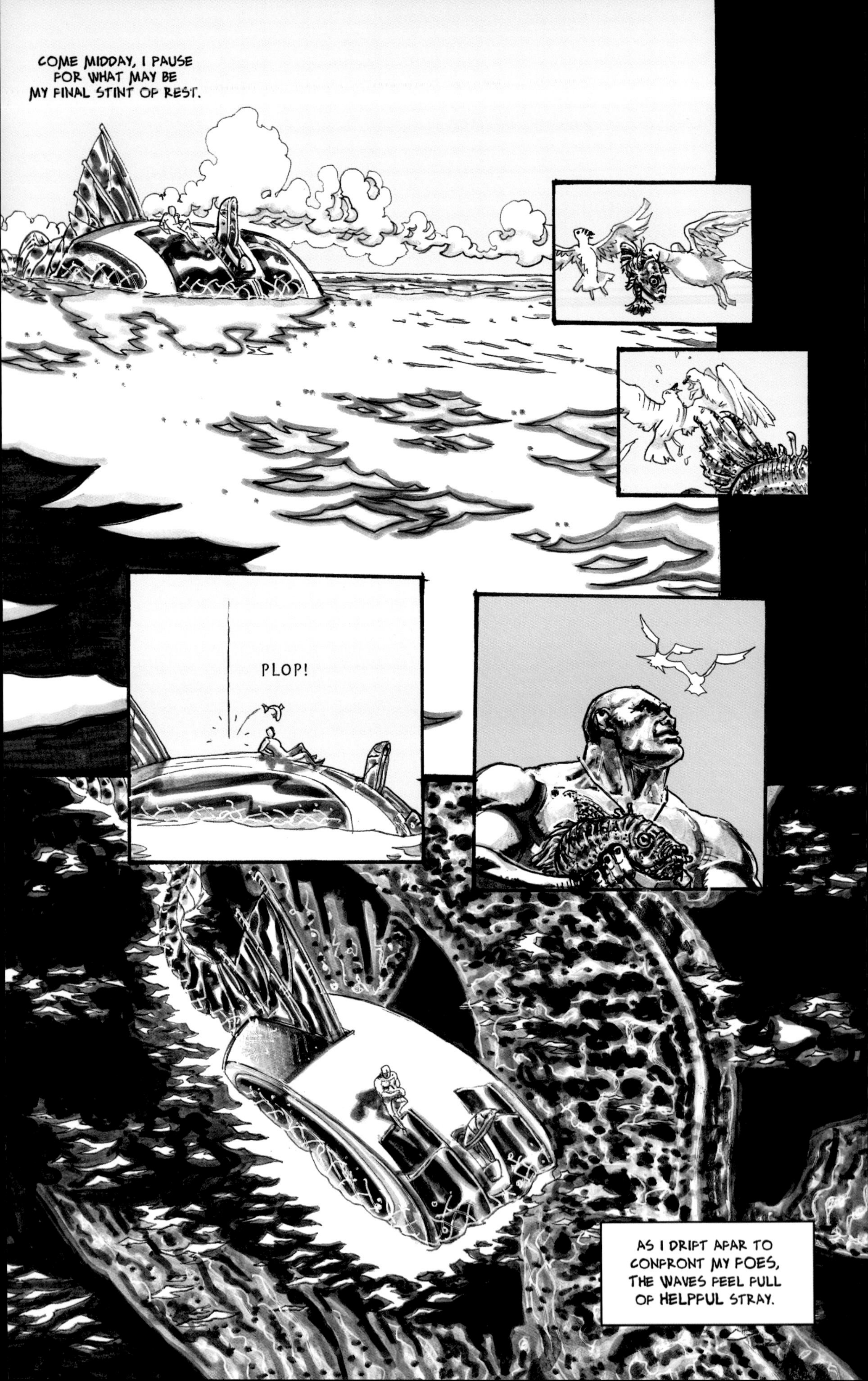
COME MIDDAY, I PAUSE FOR WHAT MAY BE MY FINAL STINT OF REST.
PLOP!
AS I DRIFT AFAR TO CONFRONT MY FOES, THE WAVES FEEL FULL OF HELPFUL STRAY.

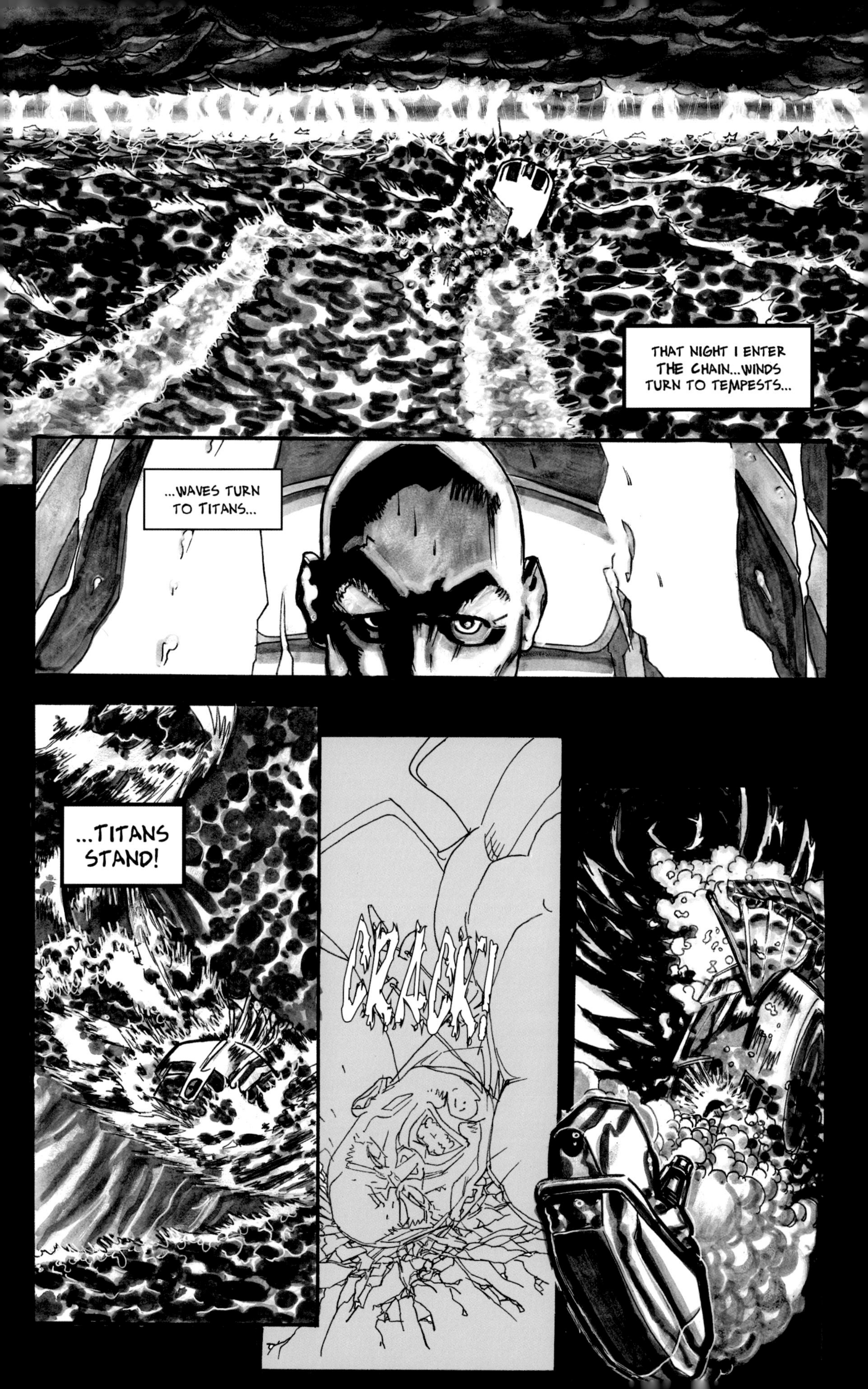
THAT NIGHT I ENTER THE CHAIN...WINDS TURN TO TEMPESTS...
...WAVES TURN TO TITANS...
...TITANS STAND!
CRACK!

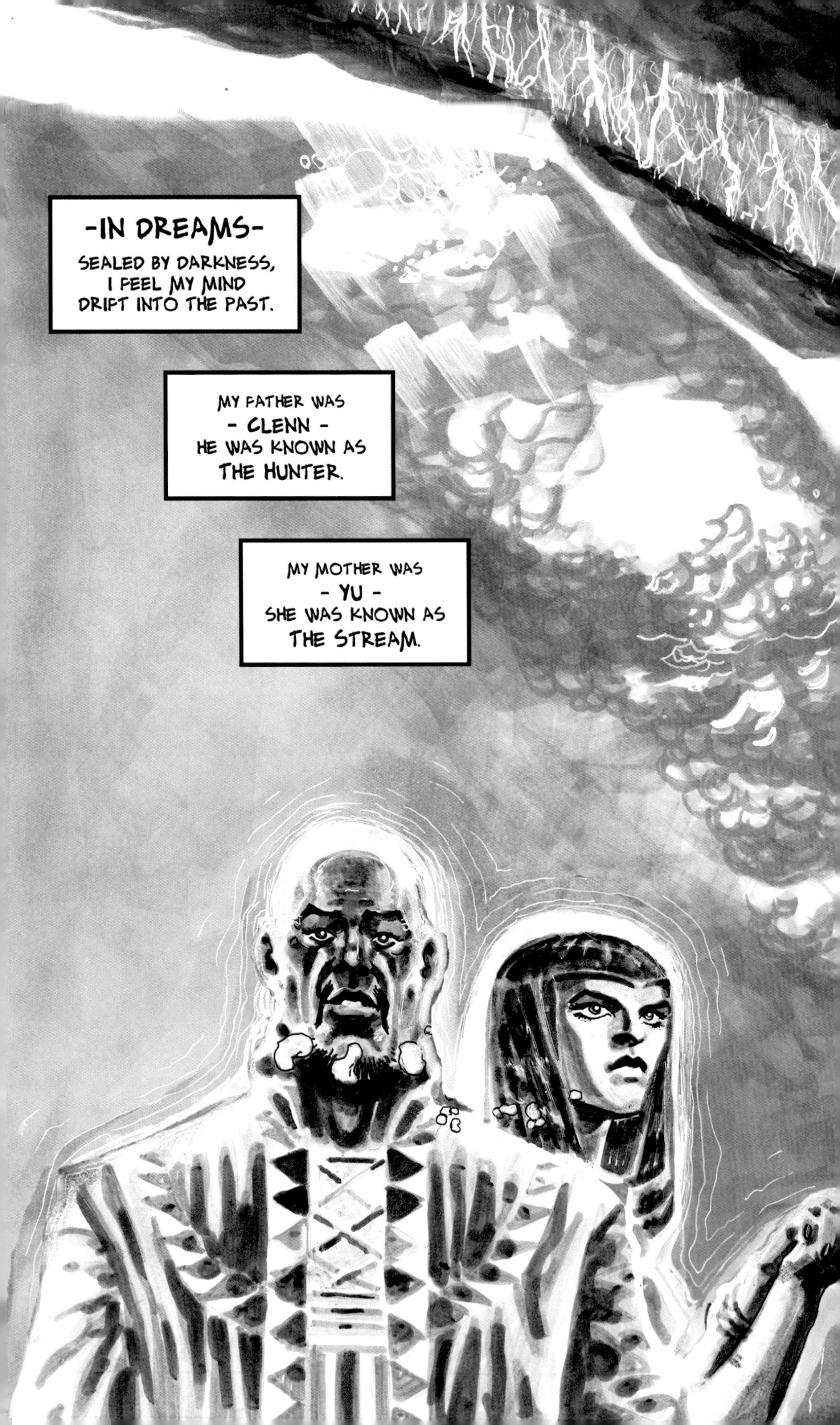
-IN DREAMS-
SEALED BY DARKNESS, I FEEL MY MIND DRIFT INTO THE PAST.
MY FATHER WAS - CLENN - HE WAS KNOWN AS THE HUNTER.
MY MOTHER WAS - YU - SHE WAS KNOWN AS THE STREAM.

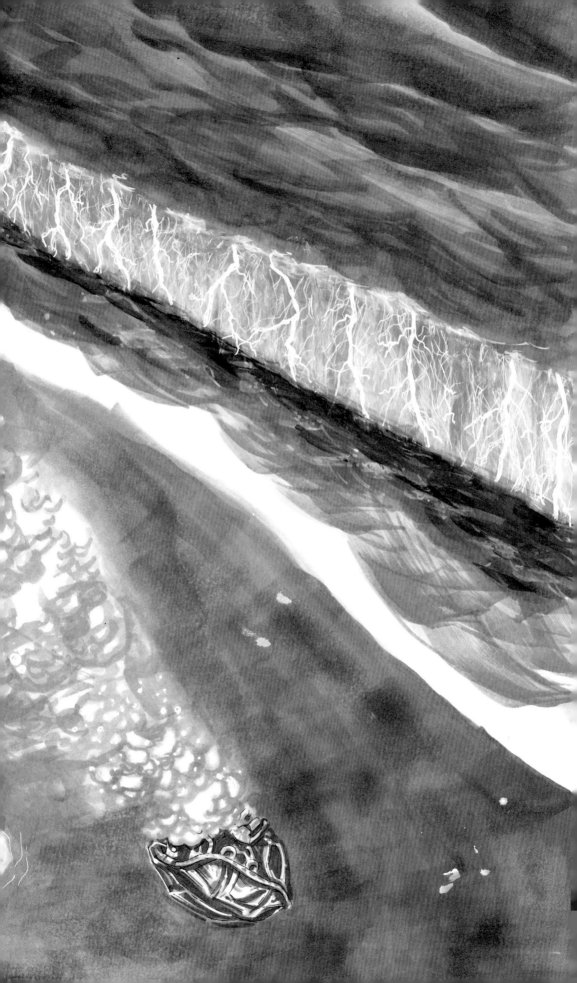

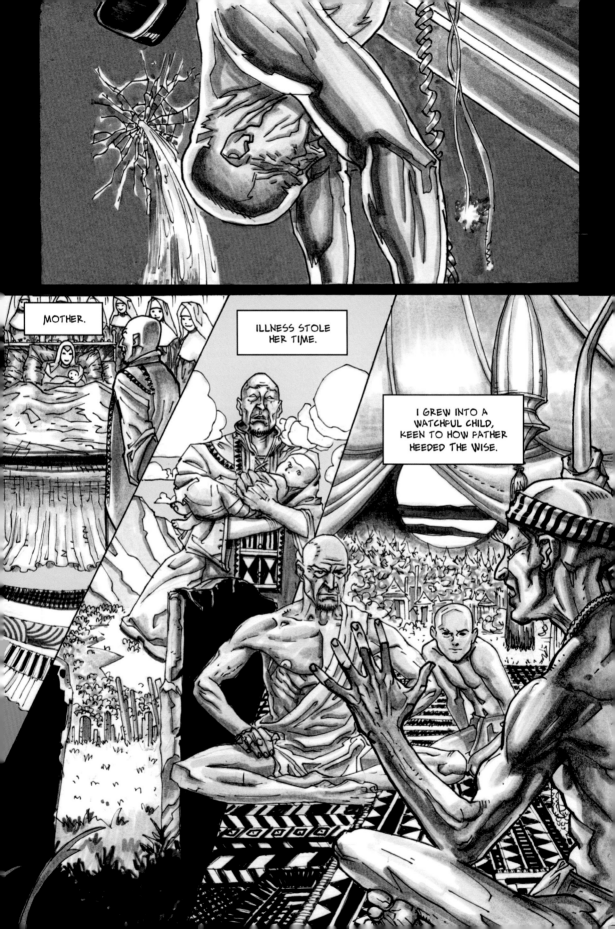

MOTHER.

ILLNESS STOLE HER TIME.

I GREW INTO A WATCHFUL CHILD, KEEN TO HOW FATHER HEEDED THE WISE.

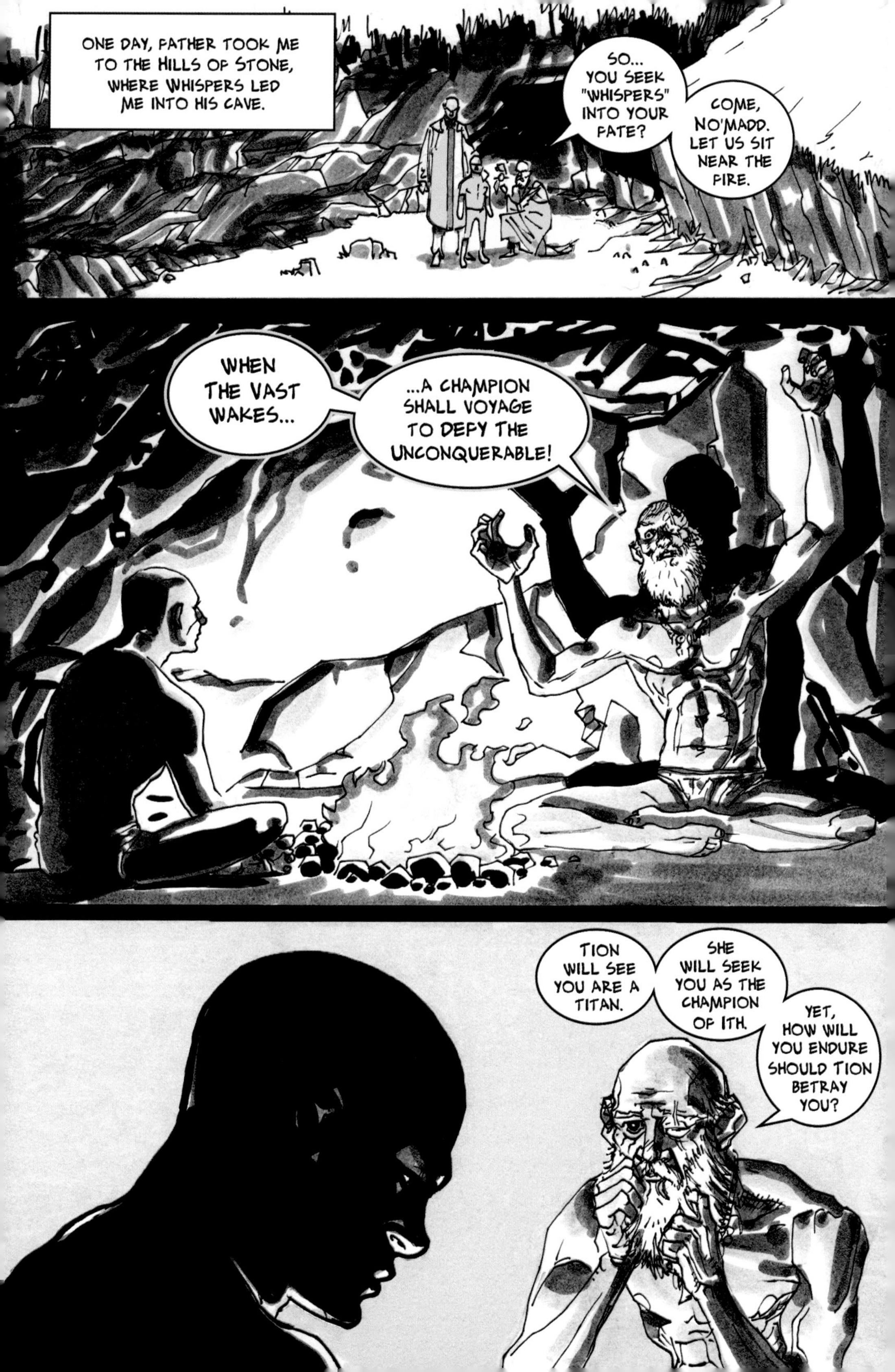

ONE DAY, FATHER TOOK ME TO THE HILLS OF STONE, WHERE WHISPERS LED ME INTO HIS CAVE.
SO... YOU SEEK "WHISPERS" INTO YOUR FATE?
COME, NO'MADD. LET US SIT NEAR THE FIRE.
WHEN THE VAST WAKES...
...A CHAMPION SHALL VOYAGE TO DEFY THE UNCONQUERABLE!
TION WILL SEE YOU ARE A TITAN.
SHE WILL SEEK YOU AS THE CHAMPION OF ITH.
YET, HOW WILL YOU ENDURE SHOULD TION BETRAY YOU?

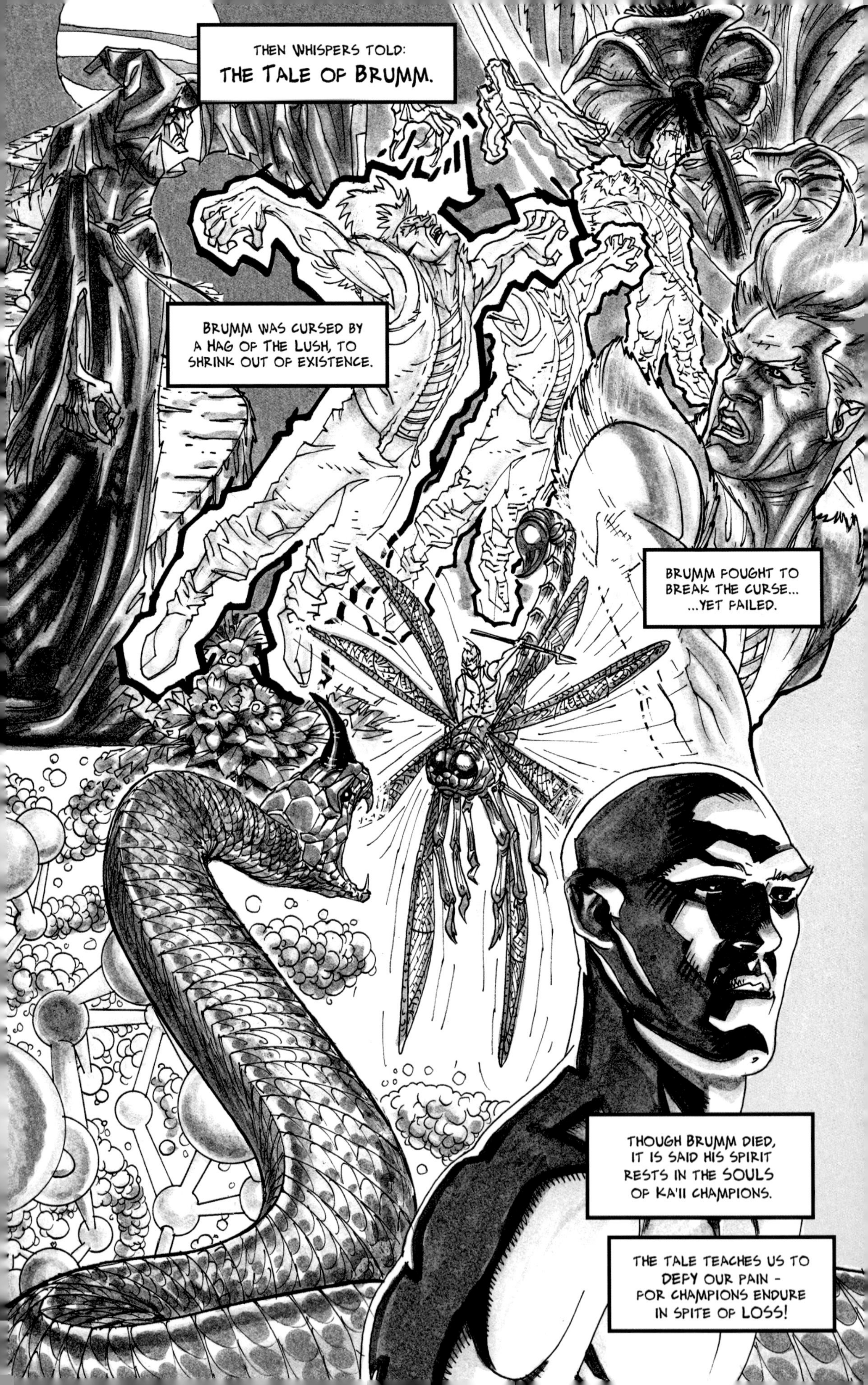
THEN WHISPERS TOLD:
THE TALE OF BRUMM.
BRUMM WAS CURSED BY A HAG OF THE LUSH, TO SHRINK OUT OF EXISTENCE.
BRUMM FOUGHT TO BREAK THE CURSE... ...YET FAILED.
THOUGH BRUMM DIED, IT IS SAID HIS SPIRIT RESTS IN THE SOULS OF KA'II CHAMPIONS.
THE TALE TEACHES US TO DEFY OUR PAIN - FOR CHAMPIONS ENDURE IN SPITE OF LOSS!

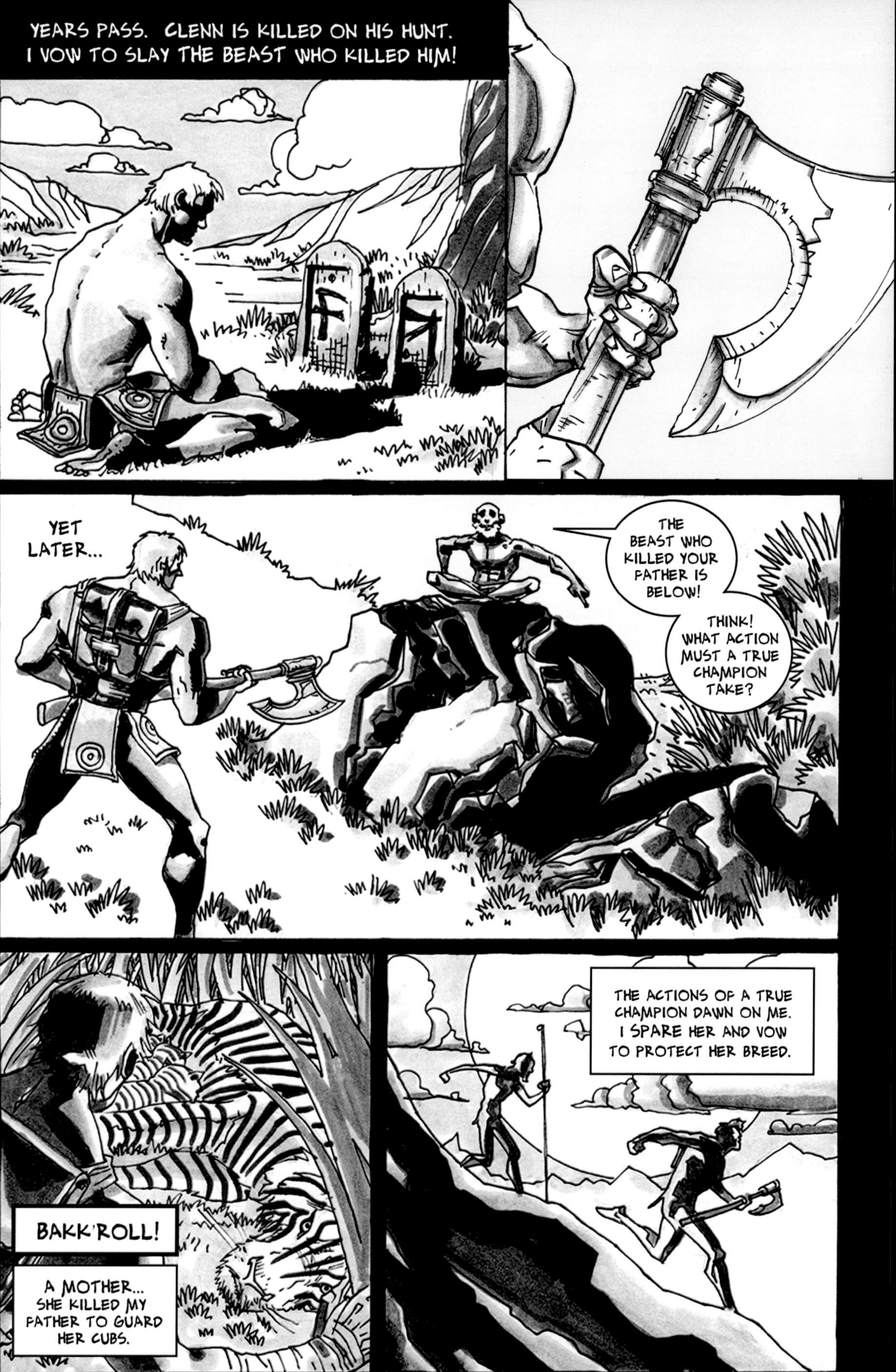
YEARS PASS. CLENN IS KILLED ON HIS HUNT. I VOW TO SLAY THE BEAST WHO KILLED HIM!
YET LATER...
THE BEAST WHO KILLED YOUR FATHER IS BELOW!
THINK! WHAT ACTION MUST A TRUE CHAMPION TAKE?
BAKK'ROLL!
A MOTHER... SHE KILLED MY FATHER TO GUARD HER CUBS.
THE ACTIONS OF A TRUE CHAMPION DAWN ON ME. I SPARE HER AND VOW TO PROTECT HER BREED.

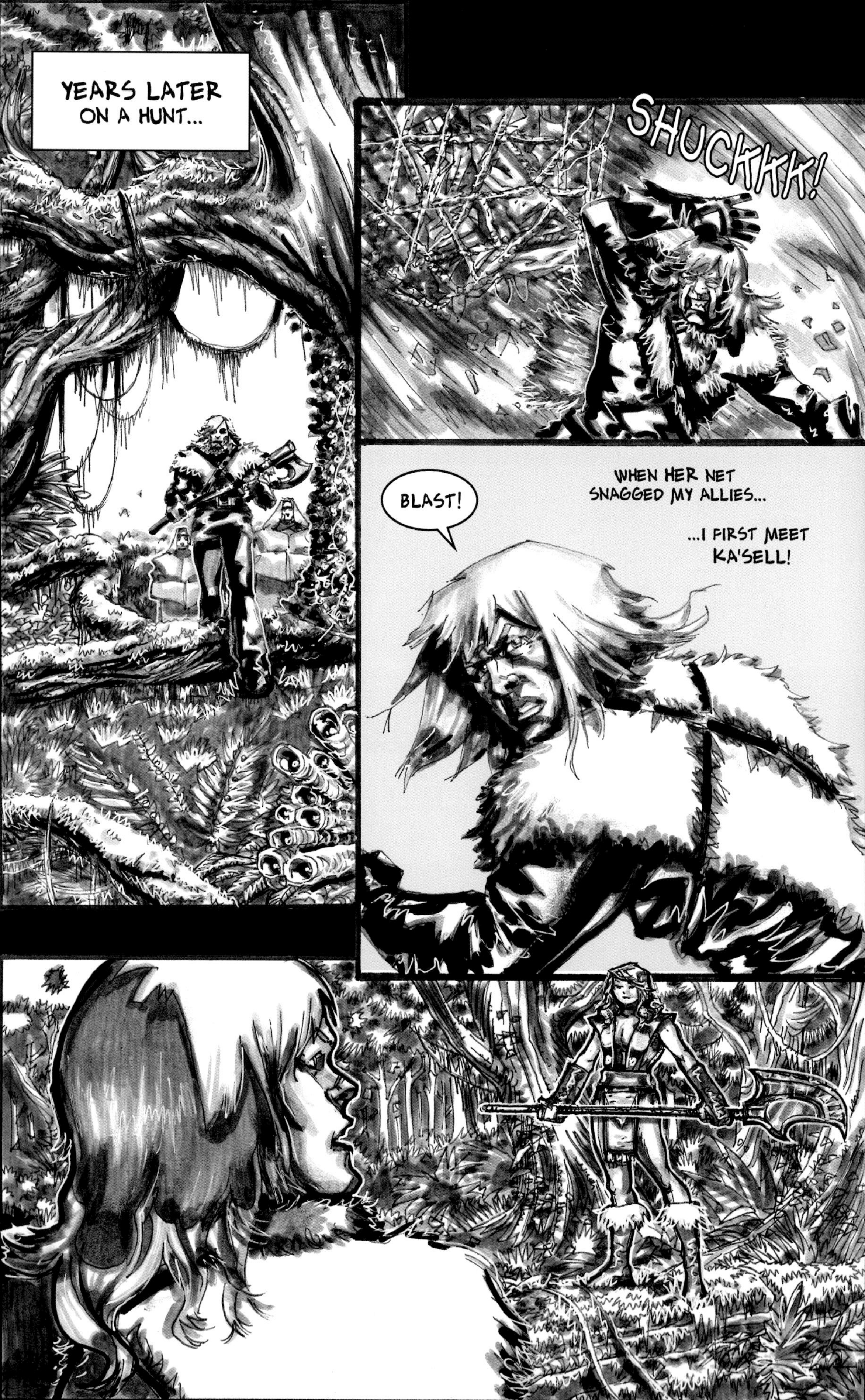
YEARS LATER ON A HUNT...
SHUCKKK!
BLAST!
WHEN HER NET SNAGGED MY ALLIES...
...I FIRST MEET KA'SELL!

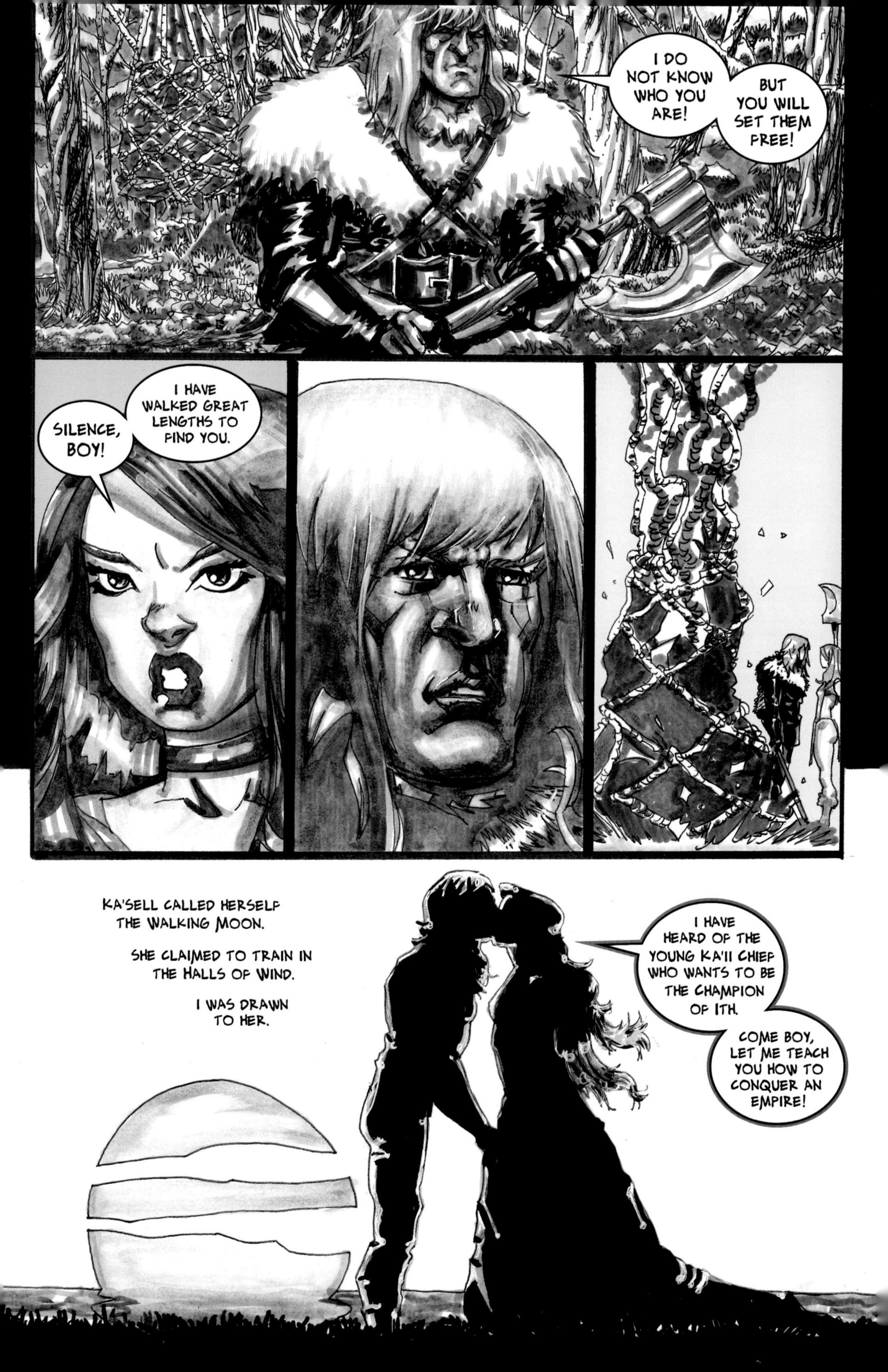
I DO NOT KNOW WHO YOU ARE!
BUT YOU WILL SET THEM FREE!
SILENCE, BOY!
I HAVE WALKED GREAT LENGTHS TO FIND YOU.
KA'SELL CALLED HERSELF THE WALKING MOON.
SHE CLAIMED TO TRAIN IN THE HALLS OF WIND.
I WAS DRAWN TO HER.
I HAVE HEARD OF THE YOUNG KA'II CHIEF WHO WANTS TO BE THE CHAMPION OF ITH.
COME BOY, LET ME TEACH YOU HOW TO CONQUER AN EMPIRE!

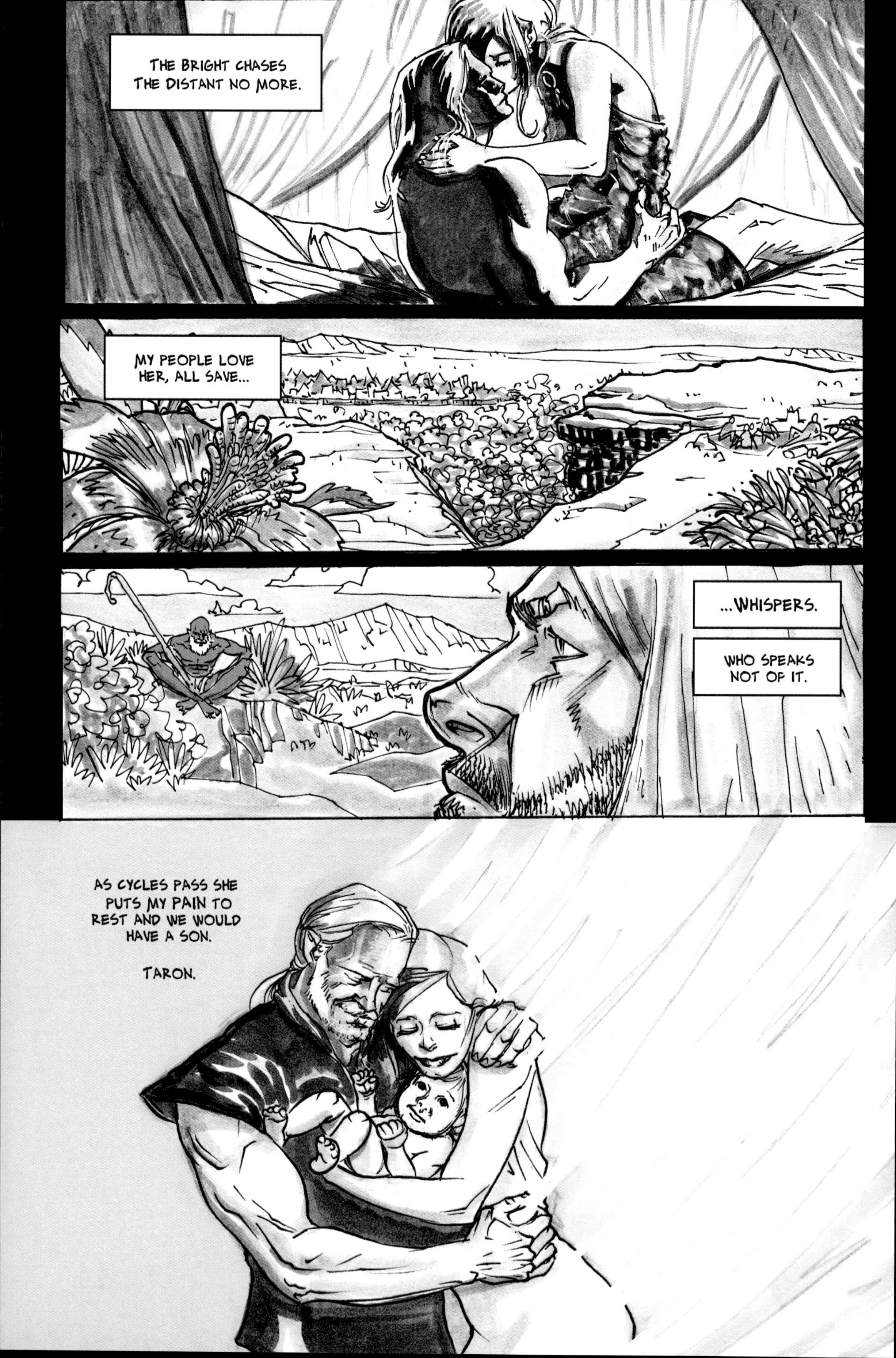

THE BRIGHT CHASES THE DISTANT NO MORE.
MY PEOPLE LOVE HER, ALL SAVE...
...WHISPERS.
WHO SPEAKS NOT OF IT.
AS CYCLES PASS SHE PUTS MY PAIN TO REST AND WE WOULD HAVE A SON.
TARON.

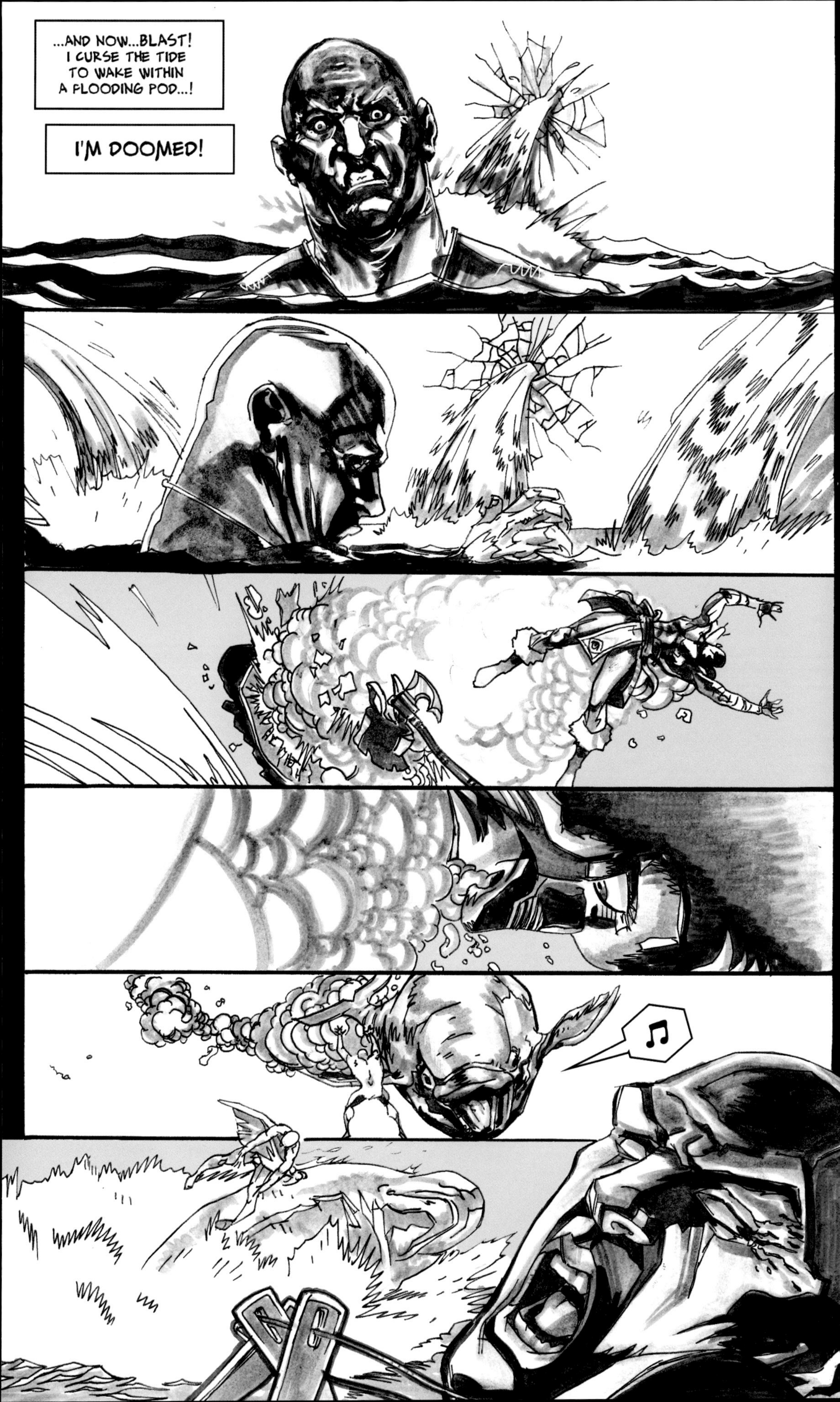
...AND NOW...BLAST! I CURSE THE TIDE TO WAKE WITHIN A FLOODING POD...!
I'M DOOMED!
♫

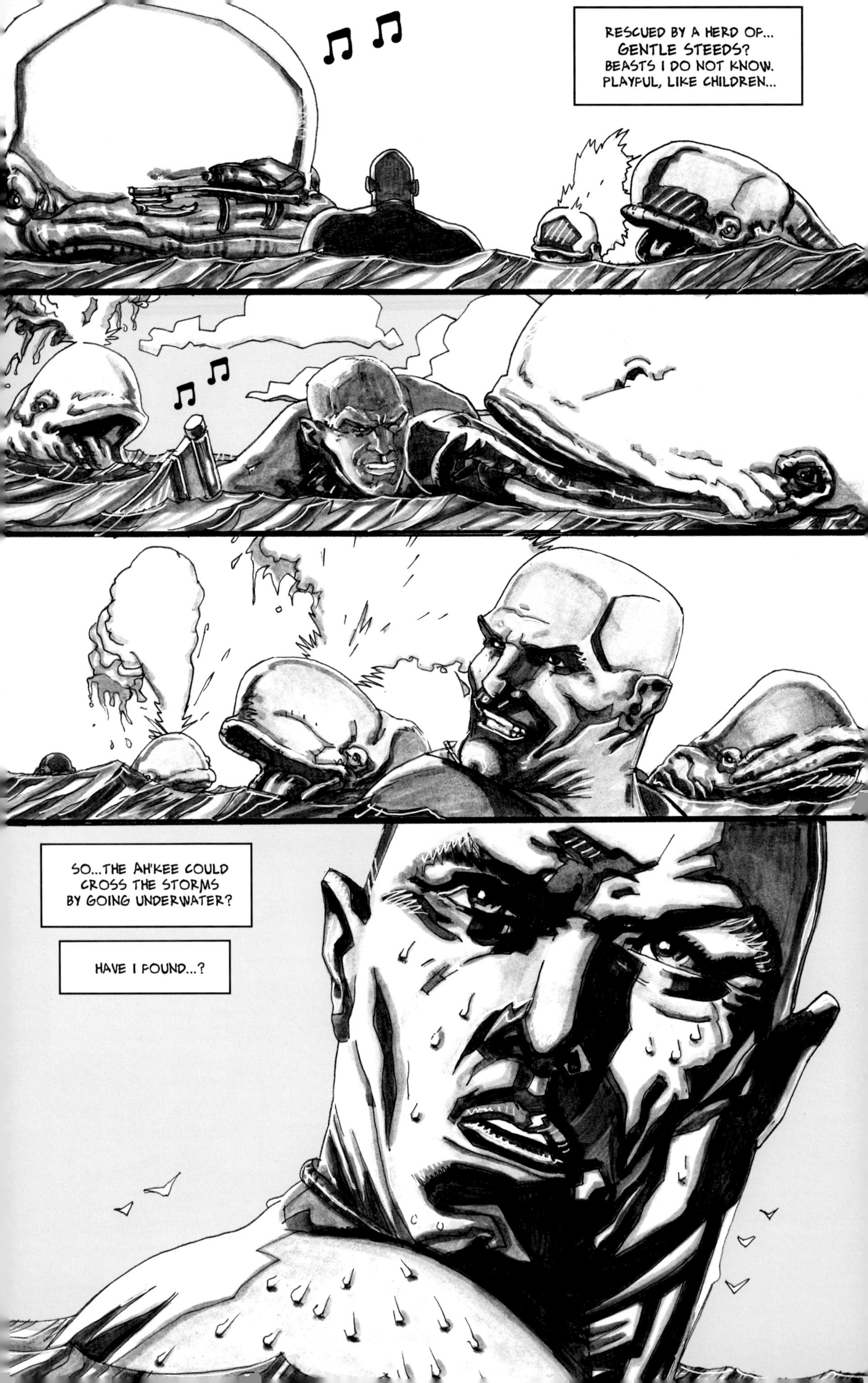
RESCUED BY A HERD OF... GENTLE STEEDS? BEASTS I DO NOT KNOW. PLAYFUL, LIKE CHILDREN...
SO...THE AH'KEE COULD CROSS THE STORMS BY GOING UNDERWATER?
HAVE I FOUND...?

CHAPTER THREE

PLATU

"IN THE FACE OF

HELL

YOU SHALL YIELD!"

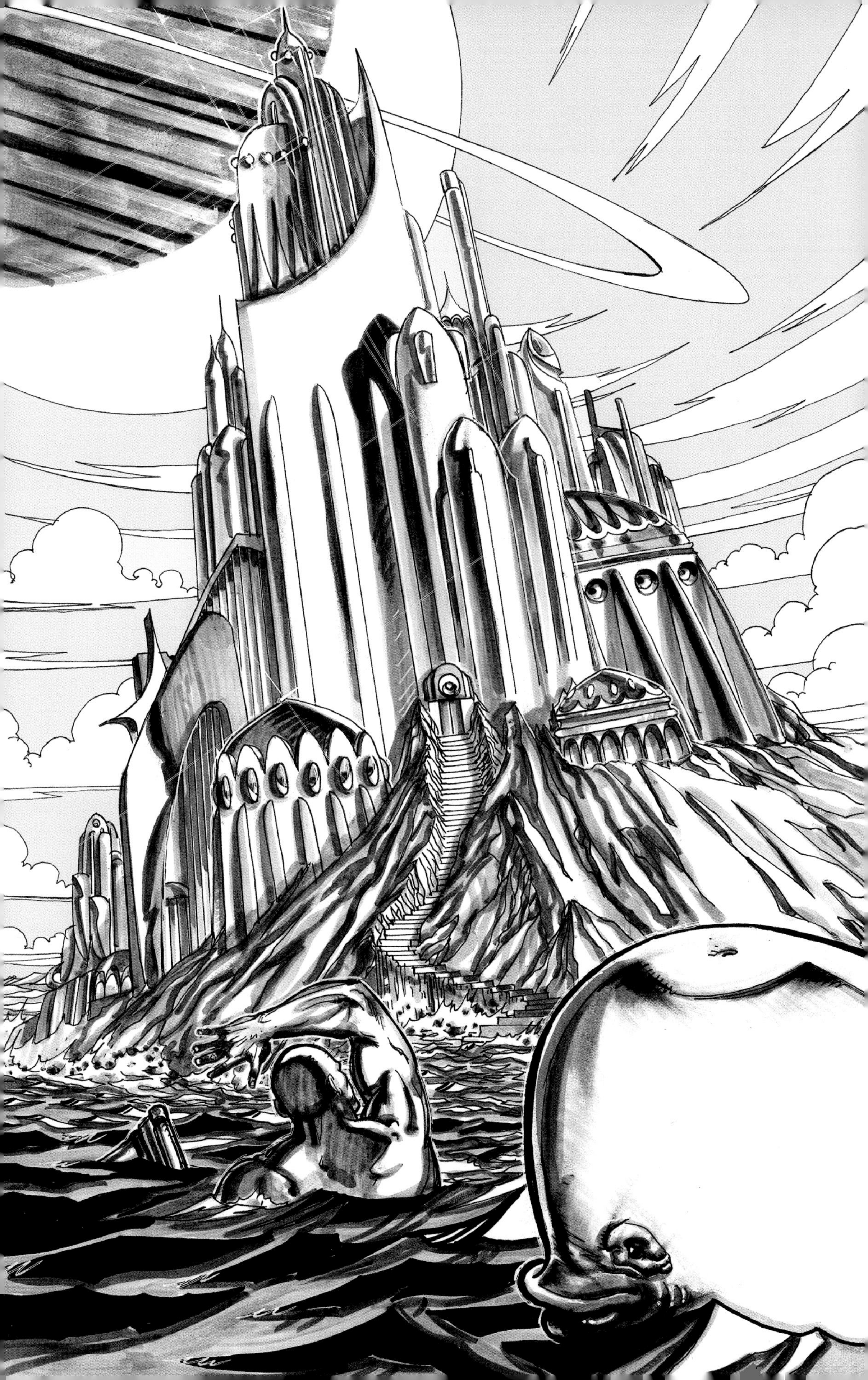

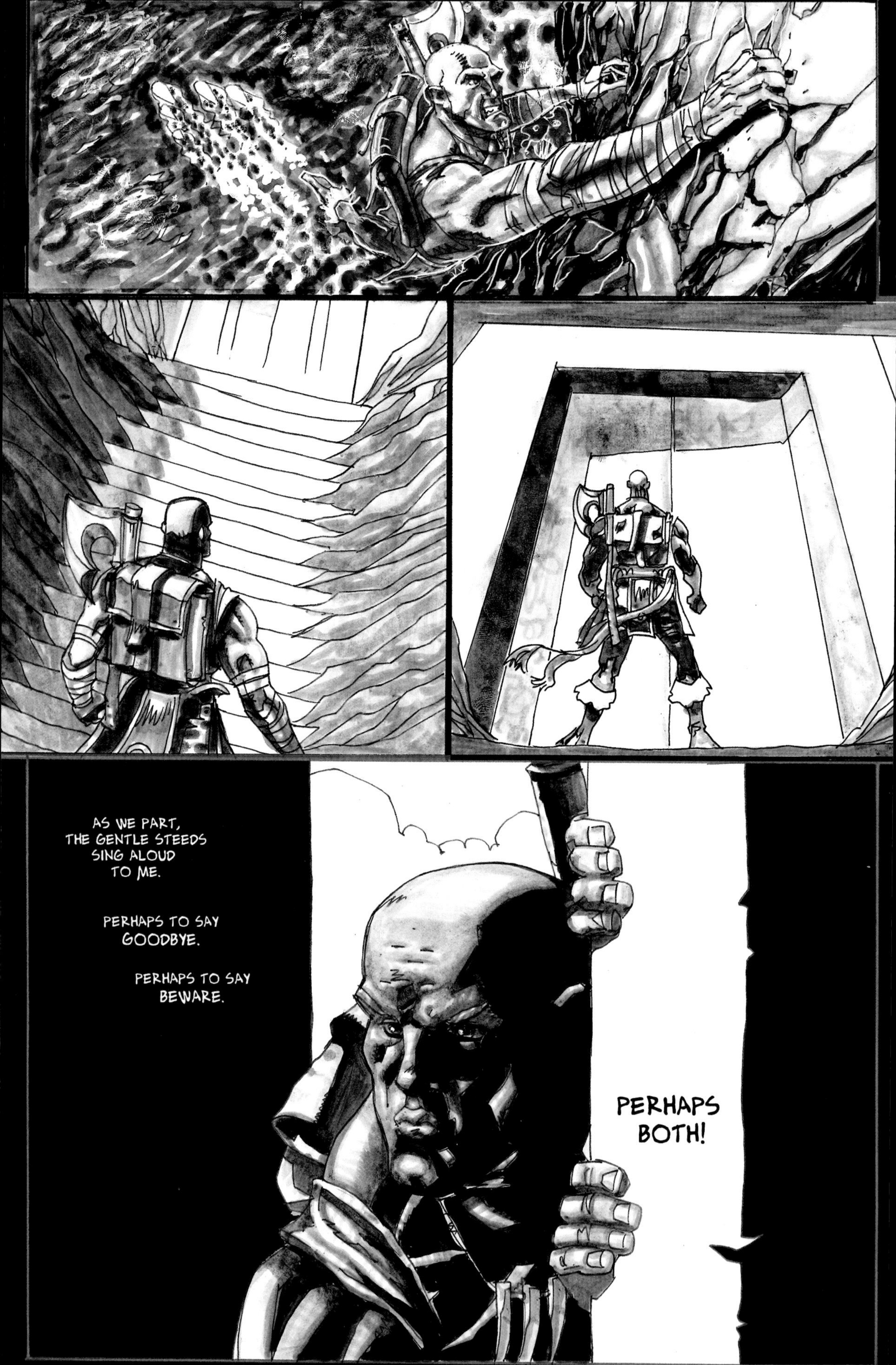

AS WE PART, THE GENTLE STEEDS SING ALOUD TO ME.
PERHAPS TO SAY GOODBYE.
PERHAPS TO SAY BEWARE.
PERHAPS BOTH!

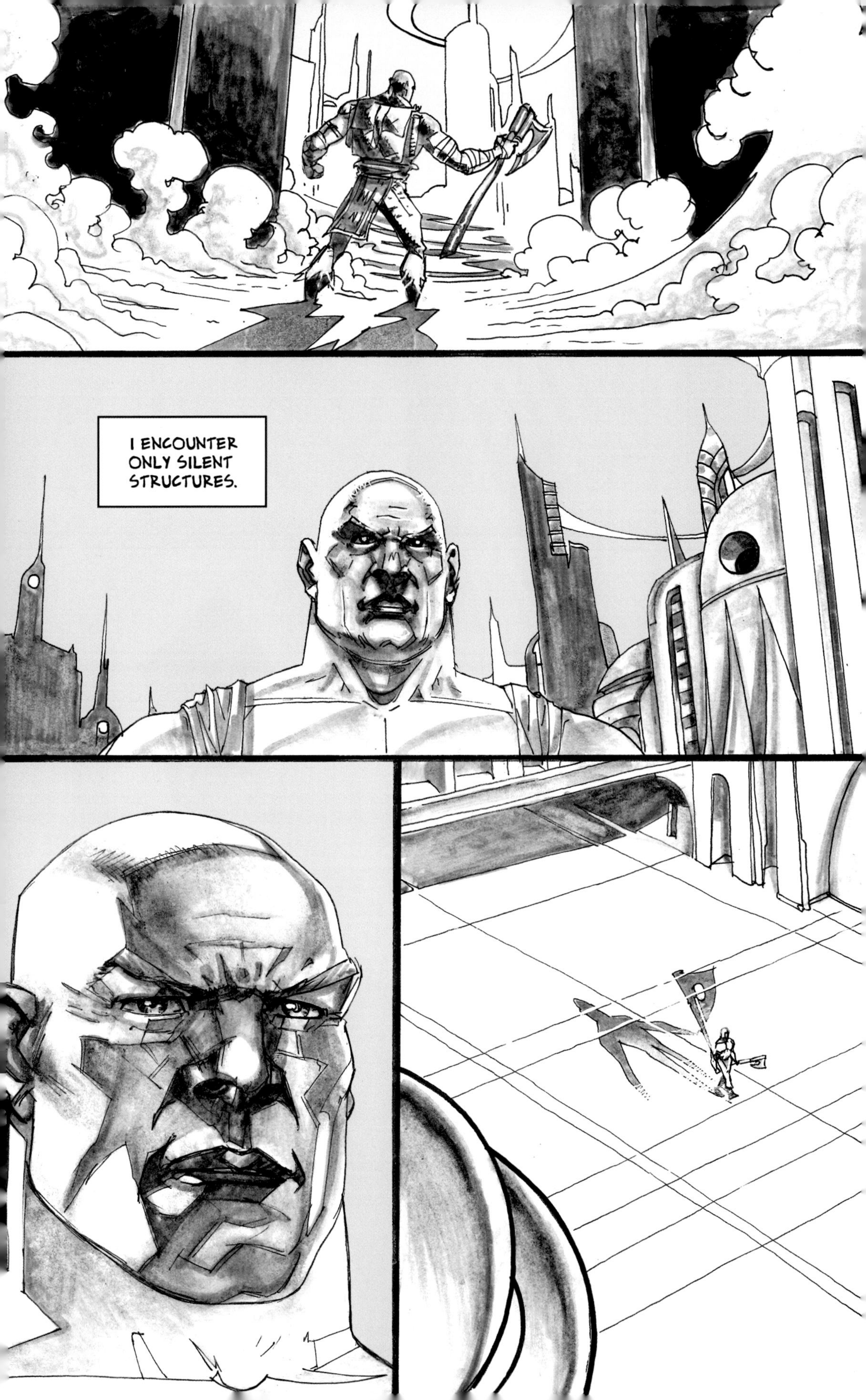
I ENCOUNTER
ONLY SILENT
STRUCTURES.

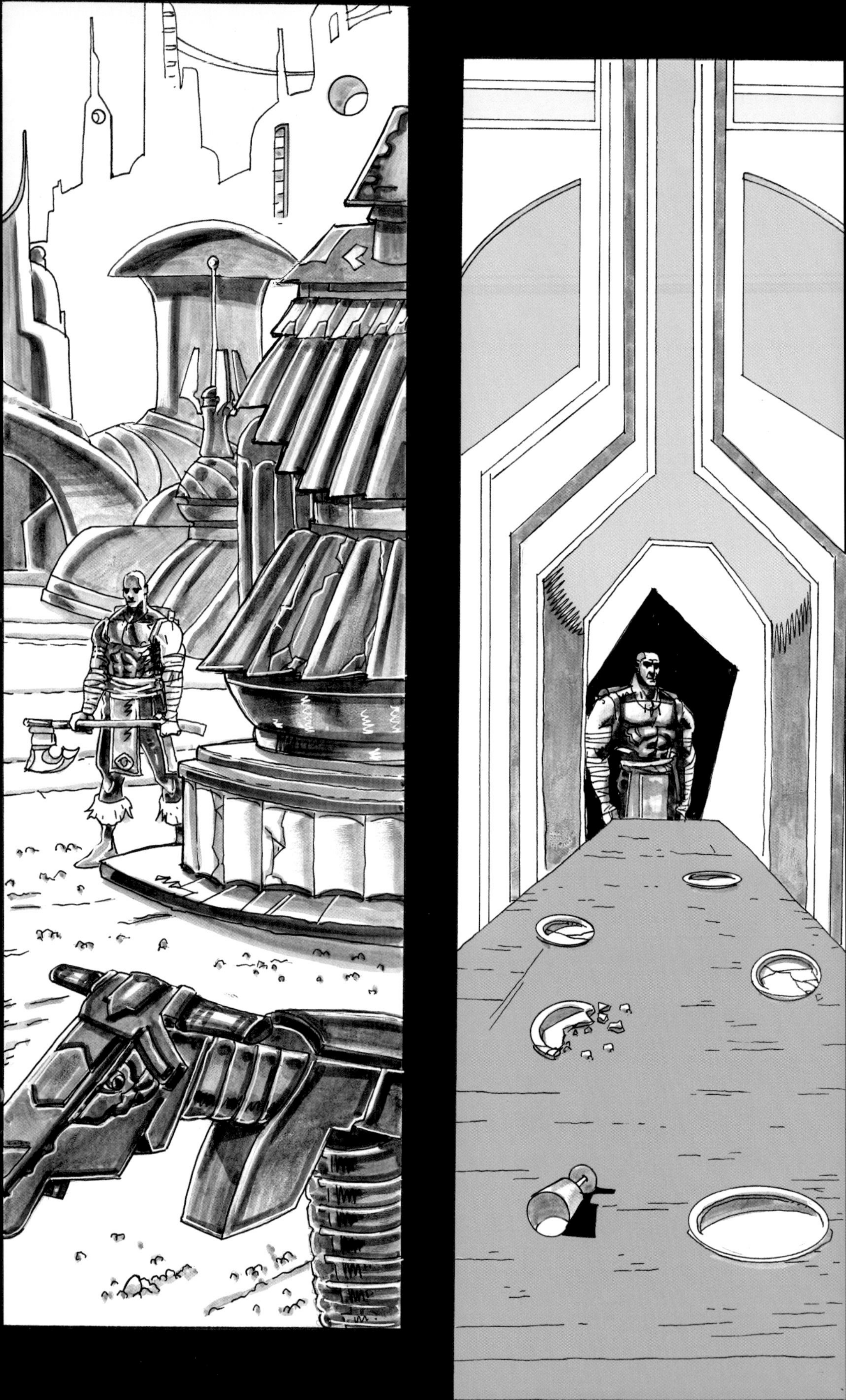

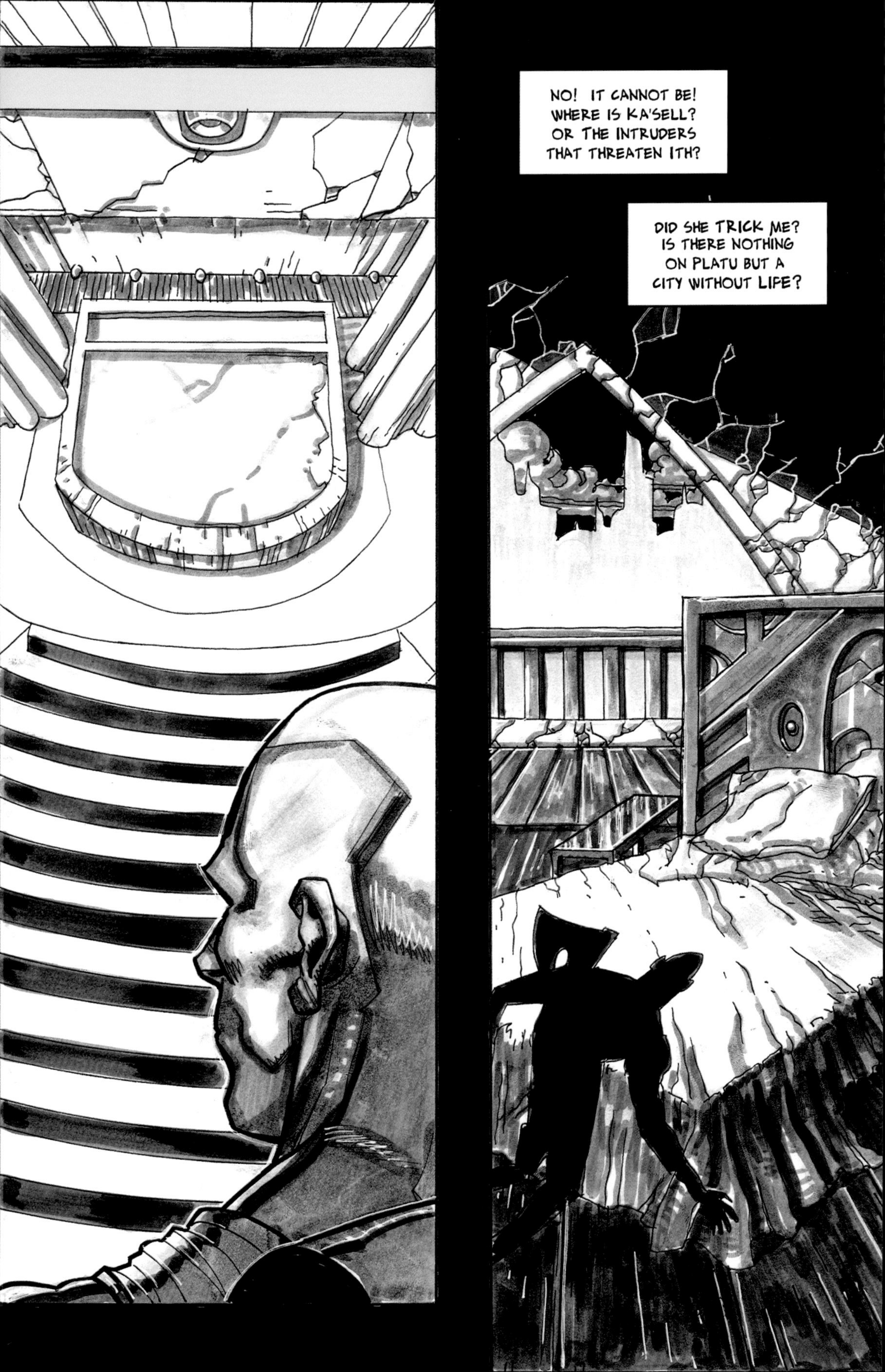
NO! IT CANNOT BE! WHERE IS KA'SELL? OR THE INTRUDERS THAT THREATEN ITH?
DID SHE TRICK ME? IS THERE NOTHING ON PLATU BUT A CITY WITHOUT LIFE?

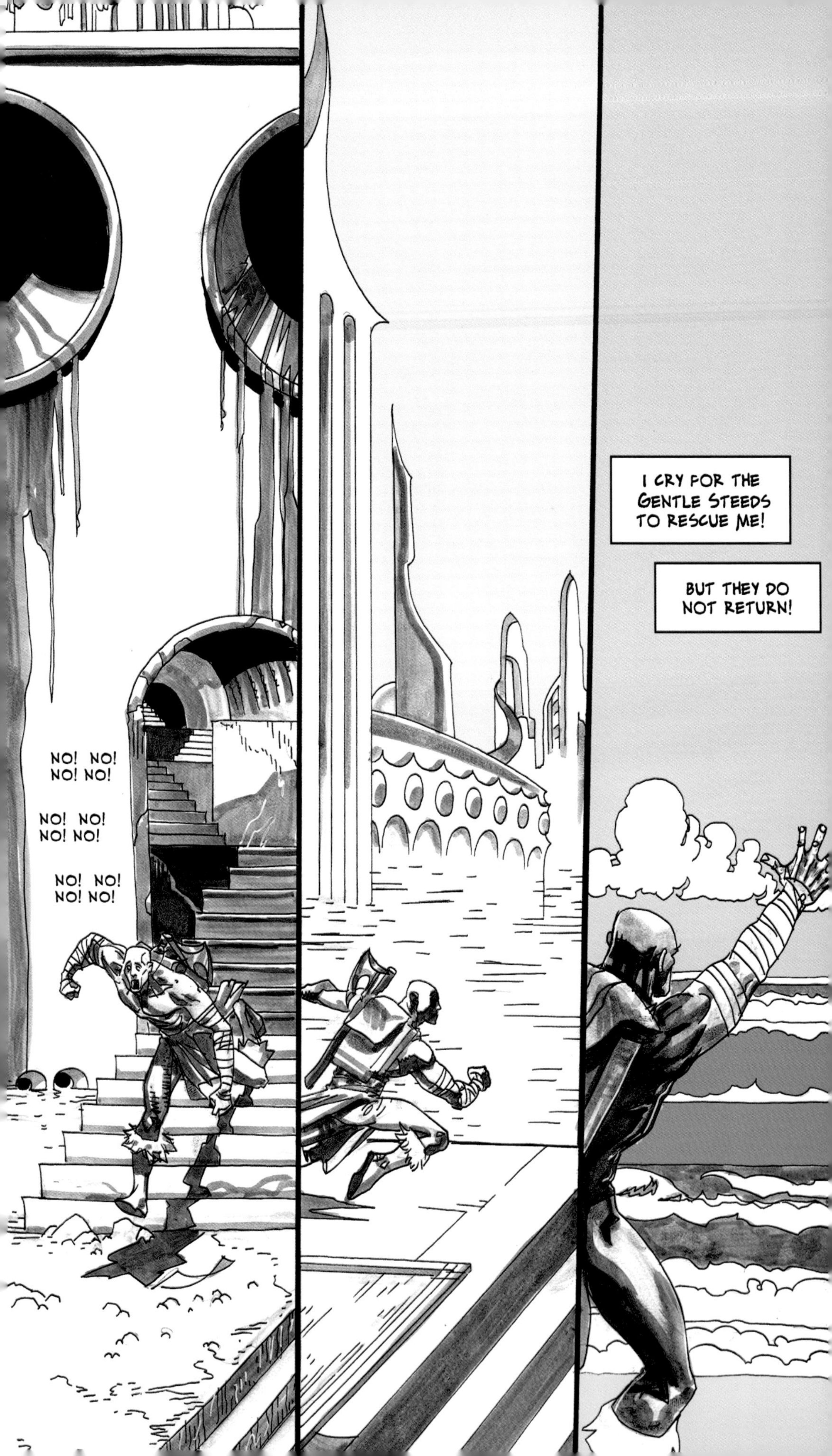
NO! NO!
NO! NO!
NO! NO!
NO! NO!
NO! NO!
NO! NO!
I CRY FOR THE GENTLE STEEDS TO RESCUE ME!
BUT THEY DO NOT RETURN!

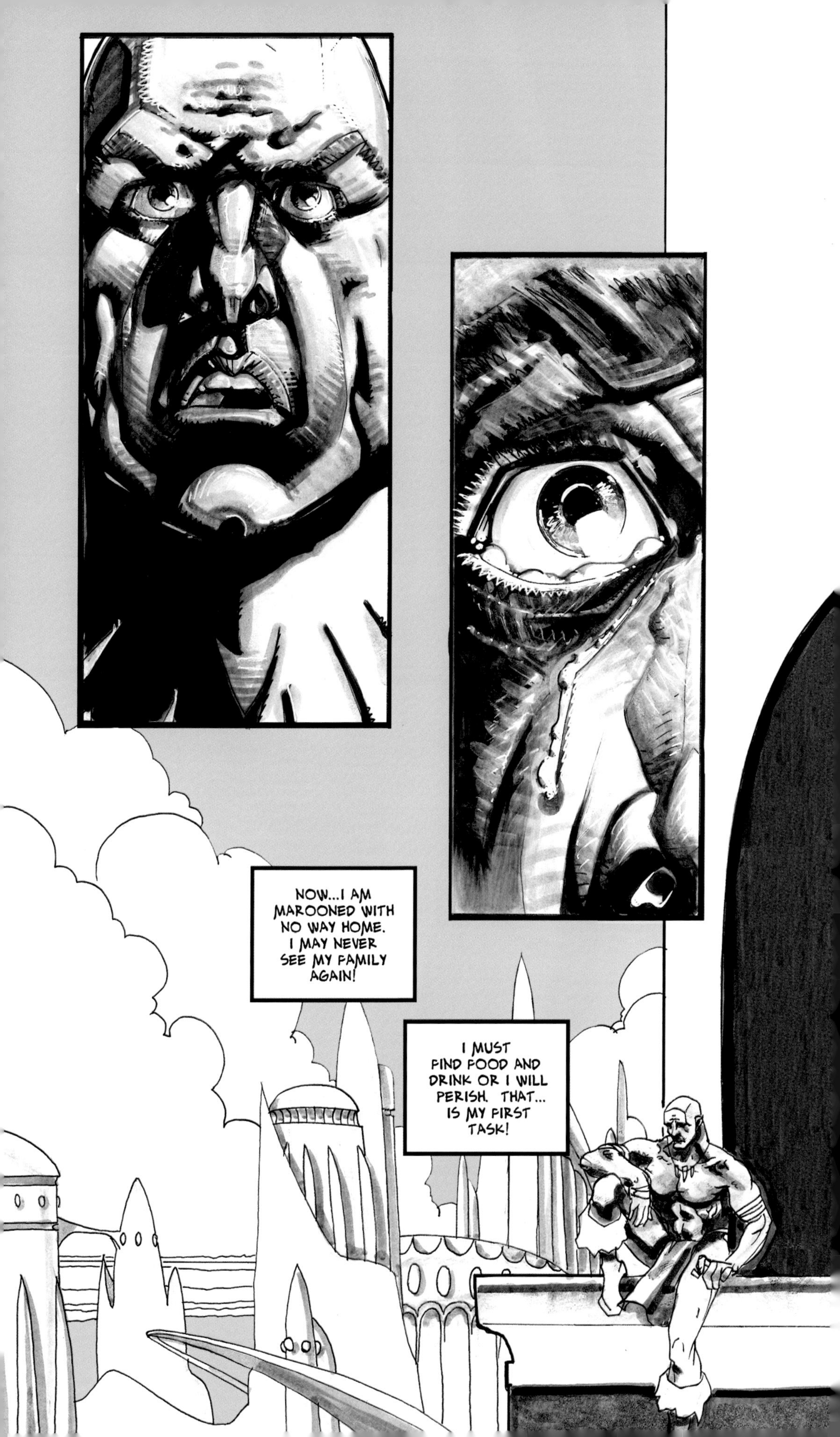
NOW...I AM MAROONED WITH NO WAY HOME. I MAY NEVER SEE MY FAMILY AGAIN!
I MUST FIND FOOD AND DRINK OR I WILL PERISH. THAT... IS MY FIRST TASK!

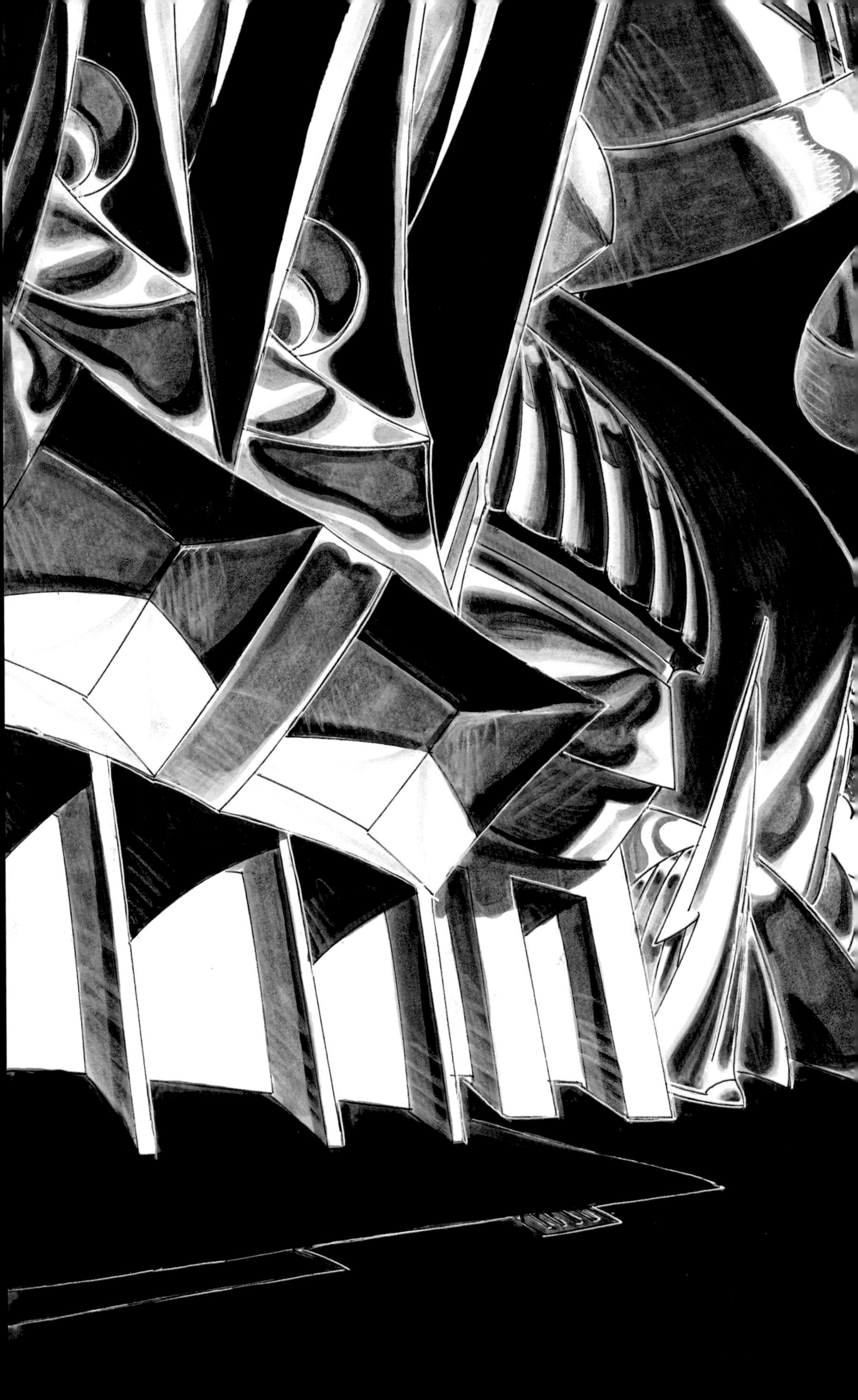

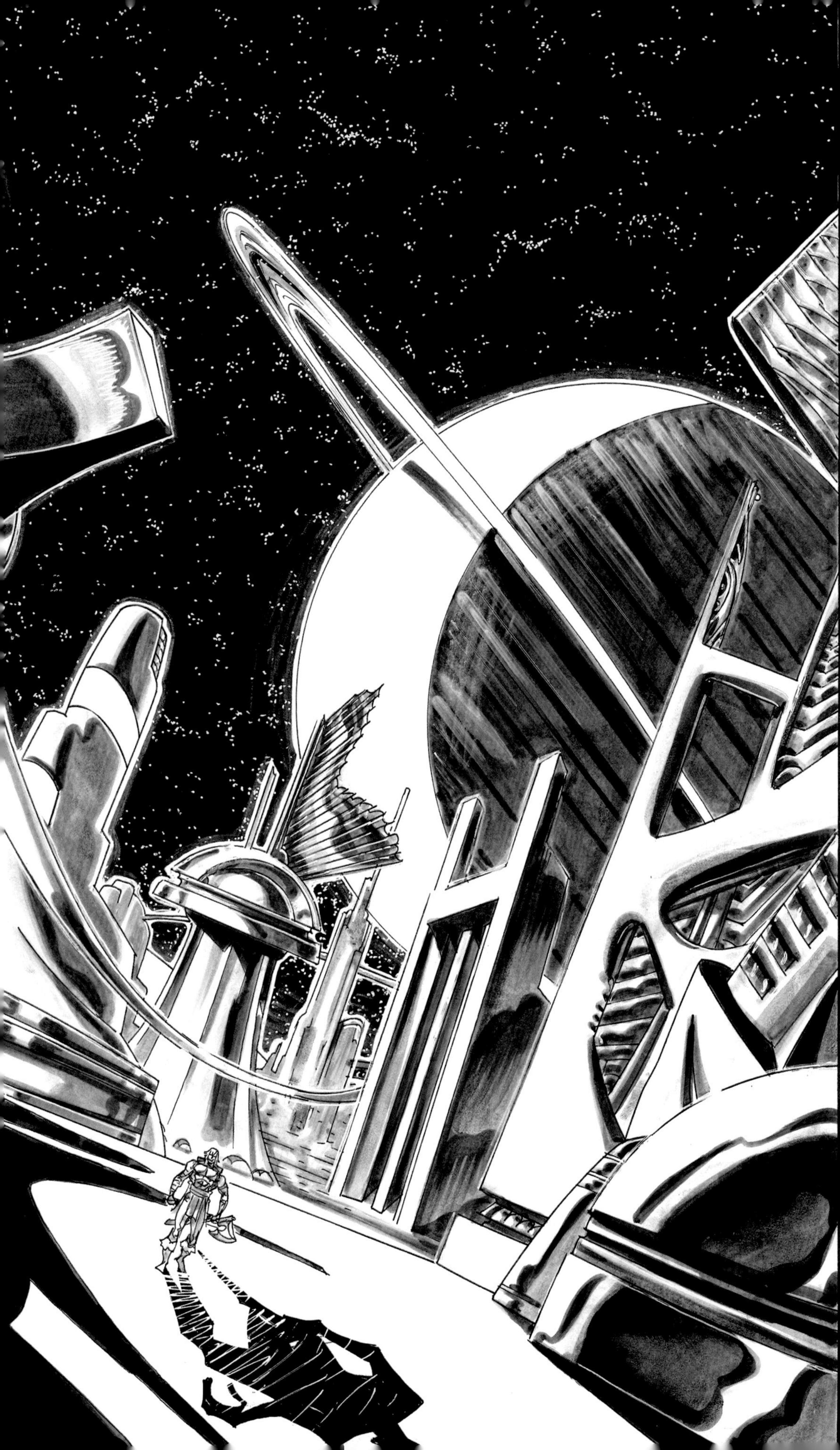

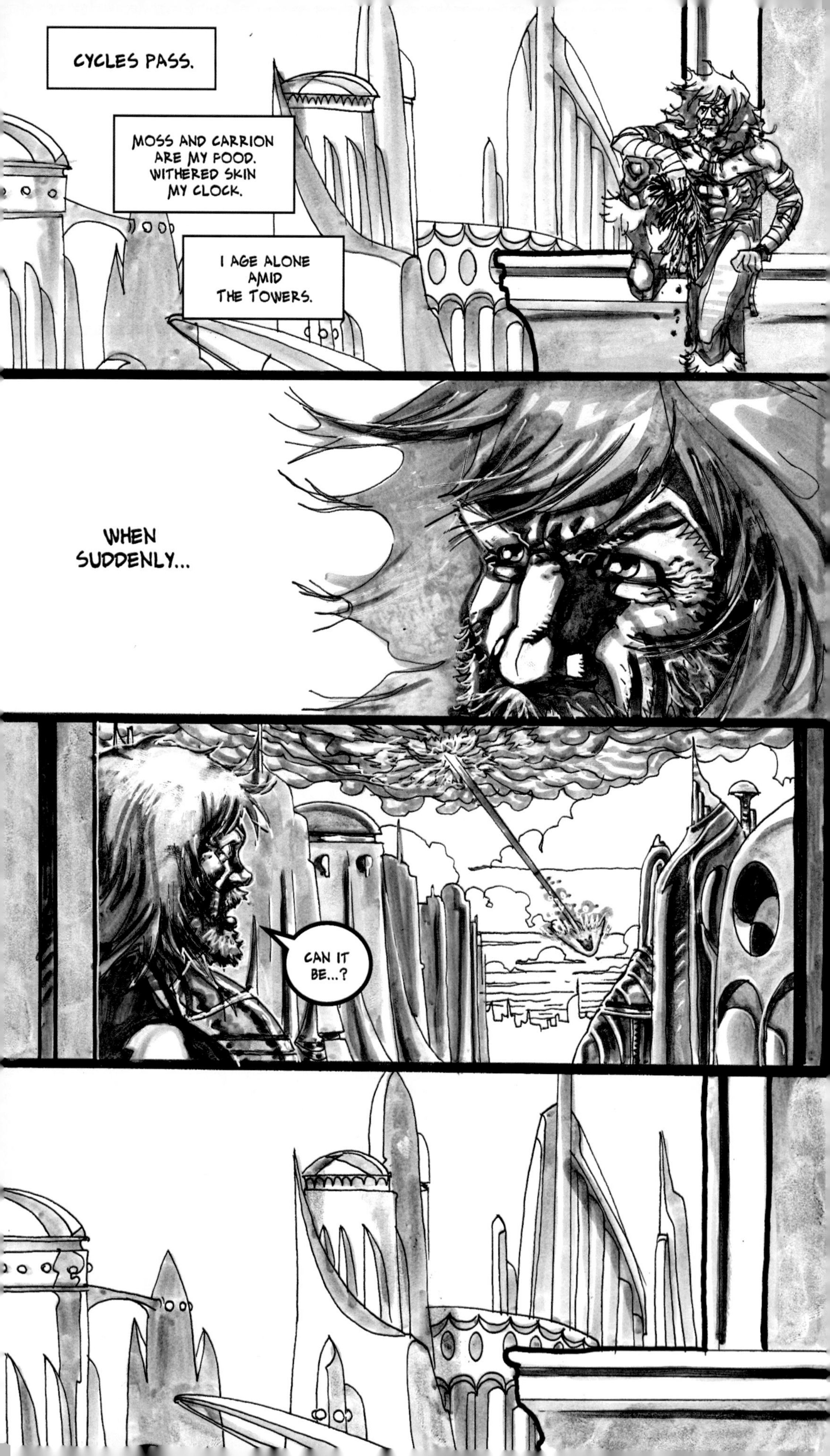
CYCLES PASS.
MOSS AND CARRION ARE MY FOOD. WITHERED SKIN MY CLOCK.
I AGE ALONE AMID THE TOWERS.
WHEN SUDDENLY...
CAN IT BE...?

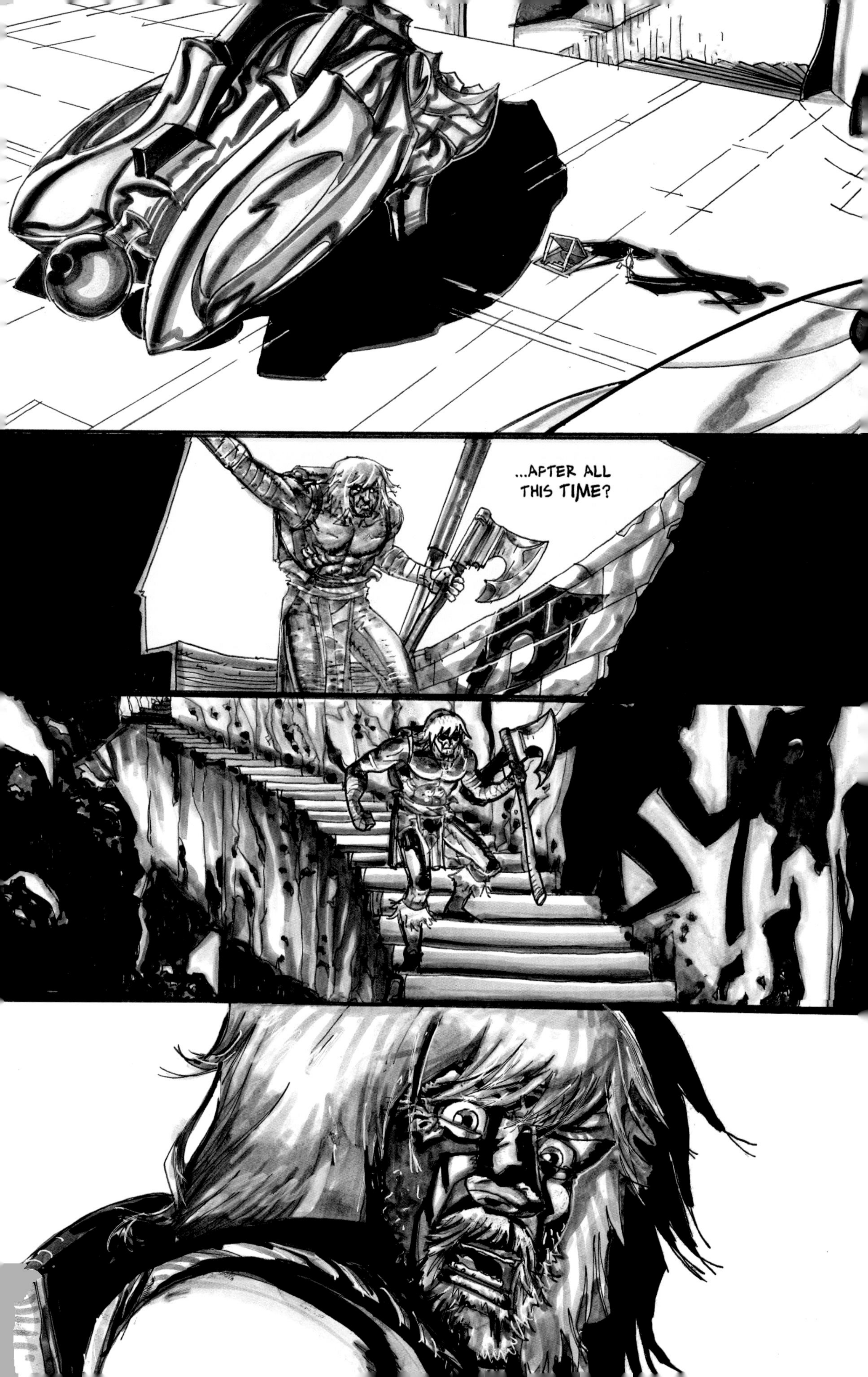
...AFTER ALL THIS TIME?

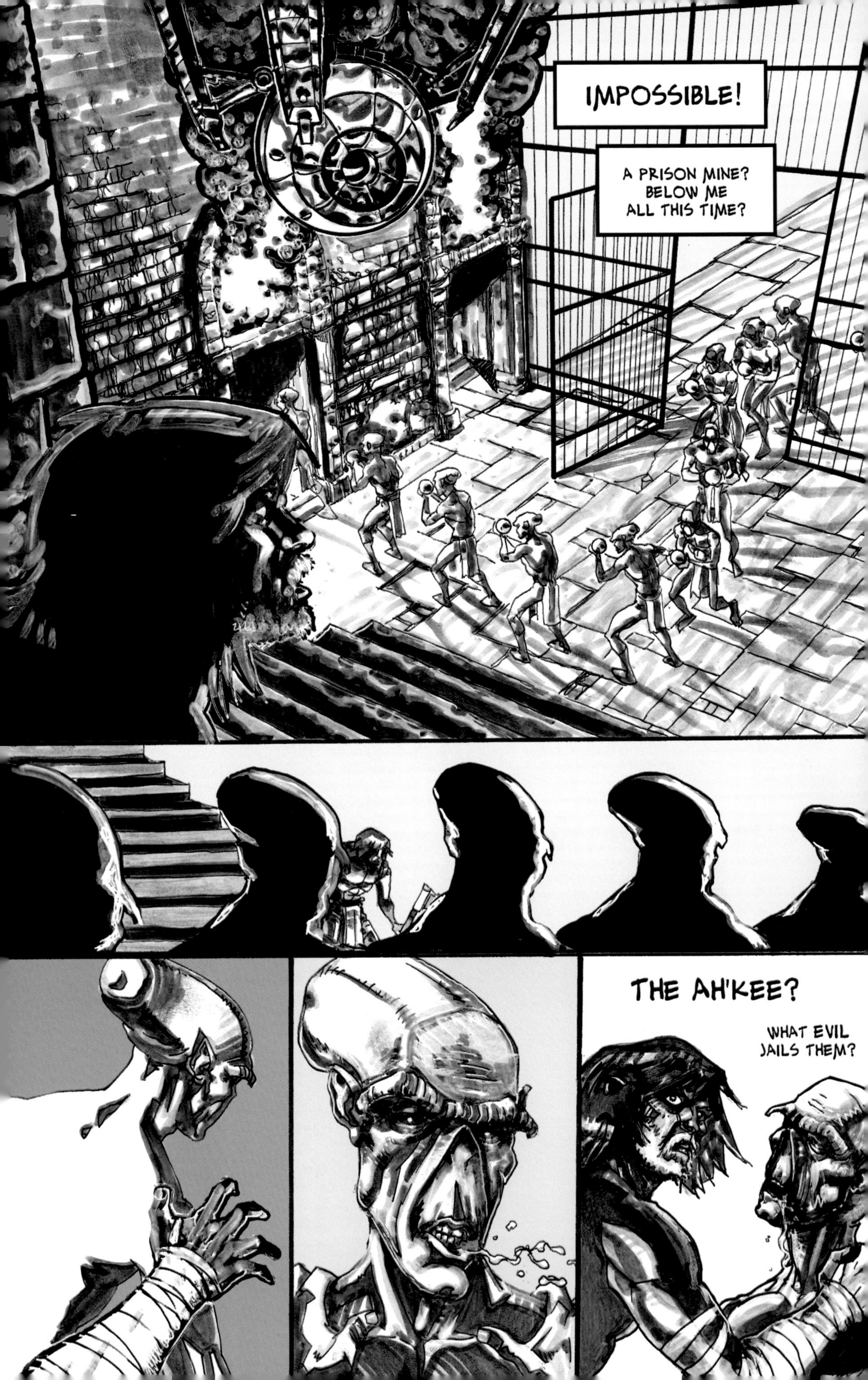
IMPOSSIBLE!
A PRISON MINE? BELOW ME ALL THIS TIME?
THE AH'KEE?
WHAT EVIL JAILS THEM?

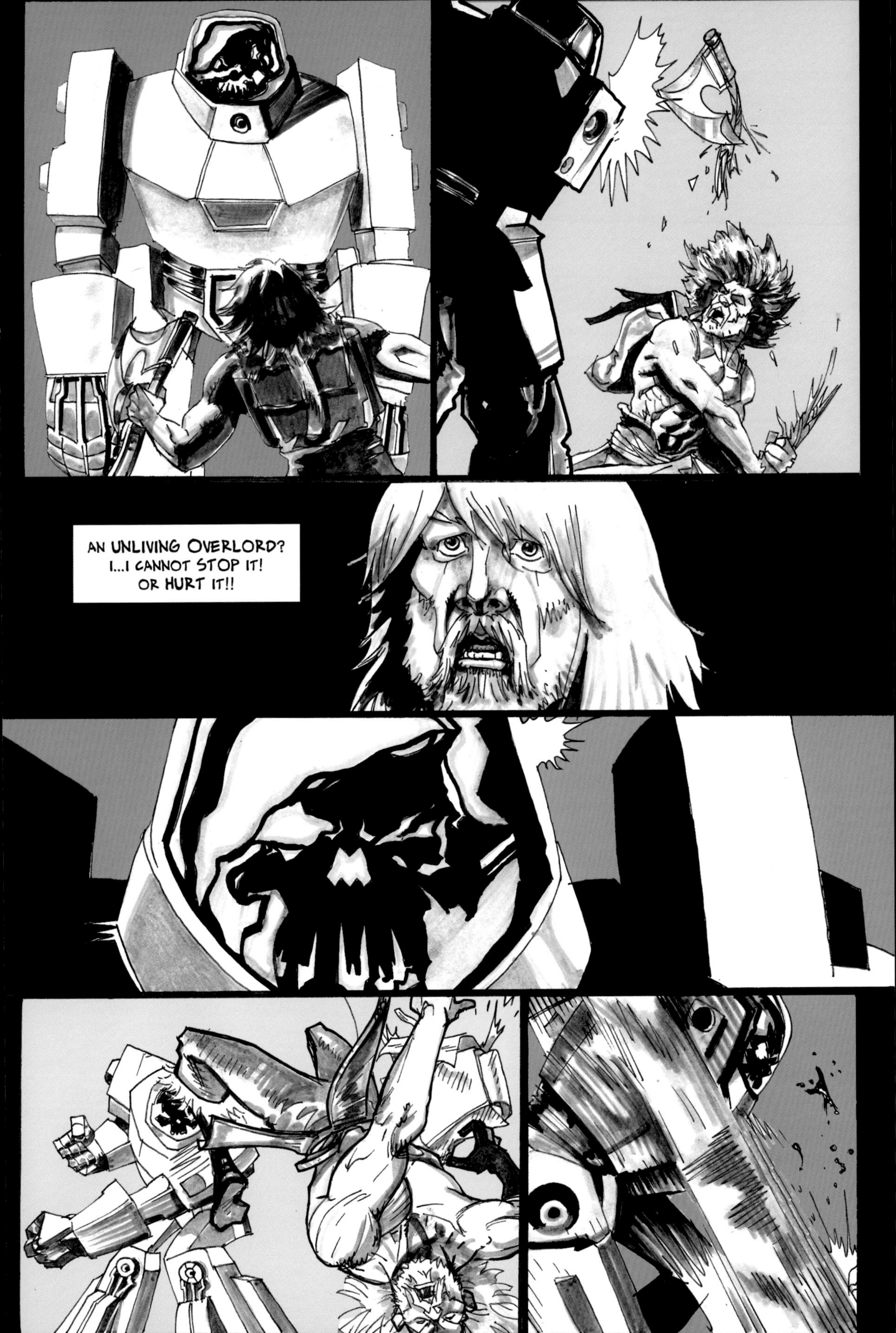
AN UNLIVING OVERLORD? I...I CANNOT STOP IT! OR HURT IT!!

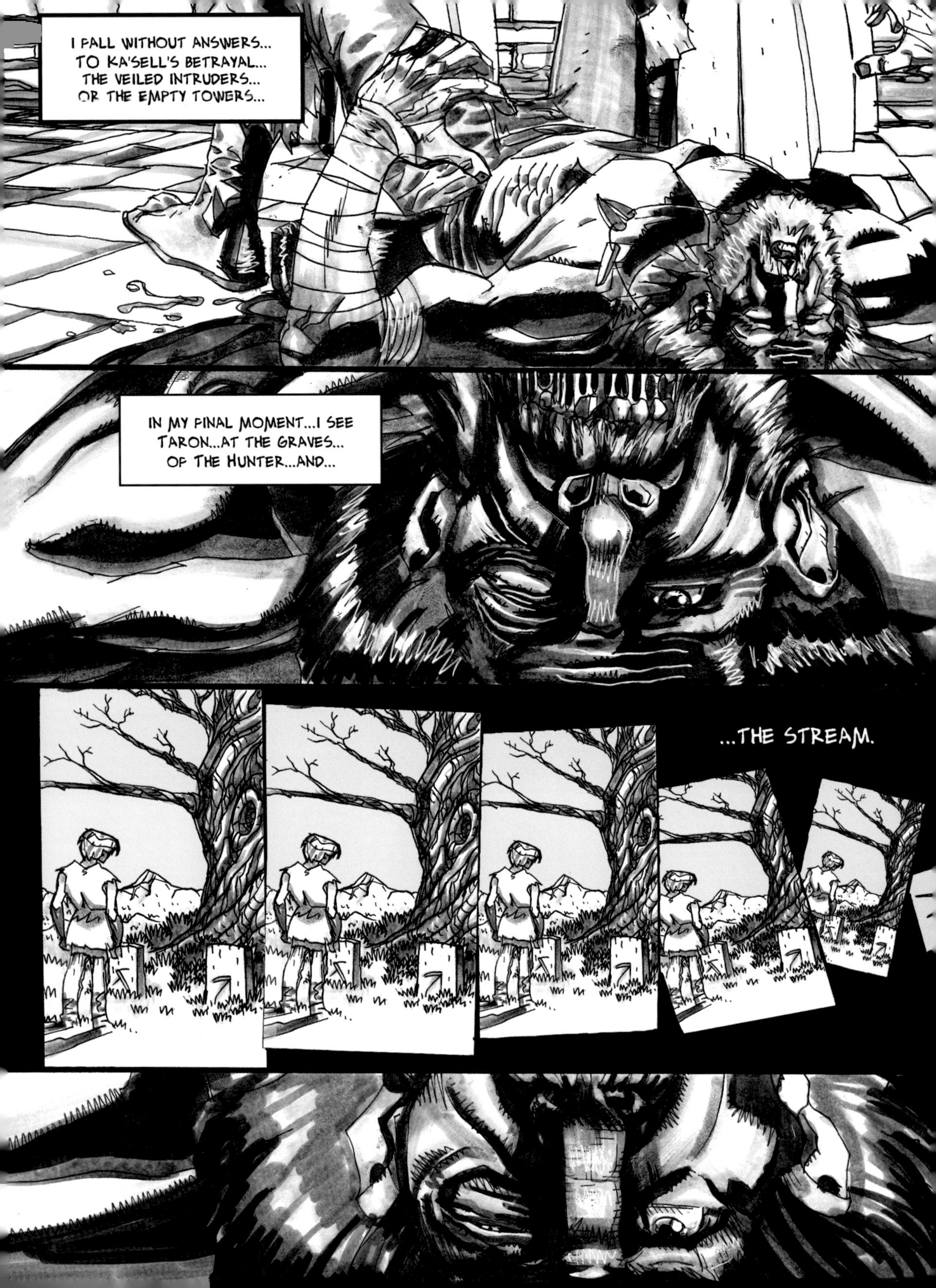
I FALL WITHOUT ANSWERS... TO KA'SELL'S BETRAYAL... THE VEILED INTRUDERS... OR THE EMPTY TOWERS...
IN MY FINAL MOMENT...I SEE TARON...AT THE GRAVES... OF THE HUNTER...AND...
...THE STREAM.

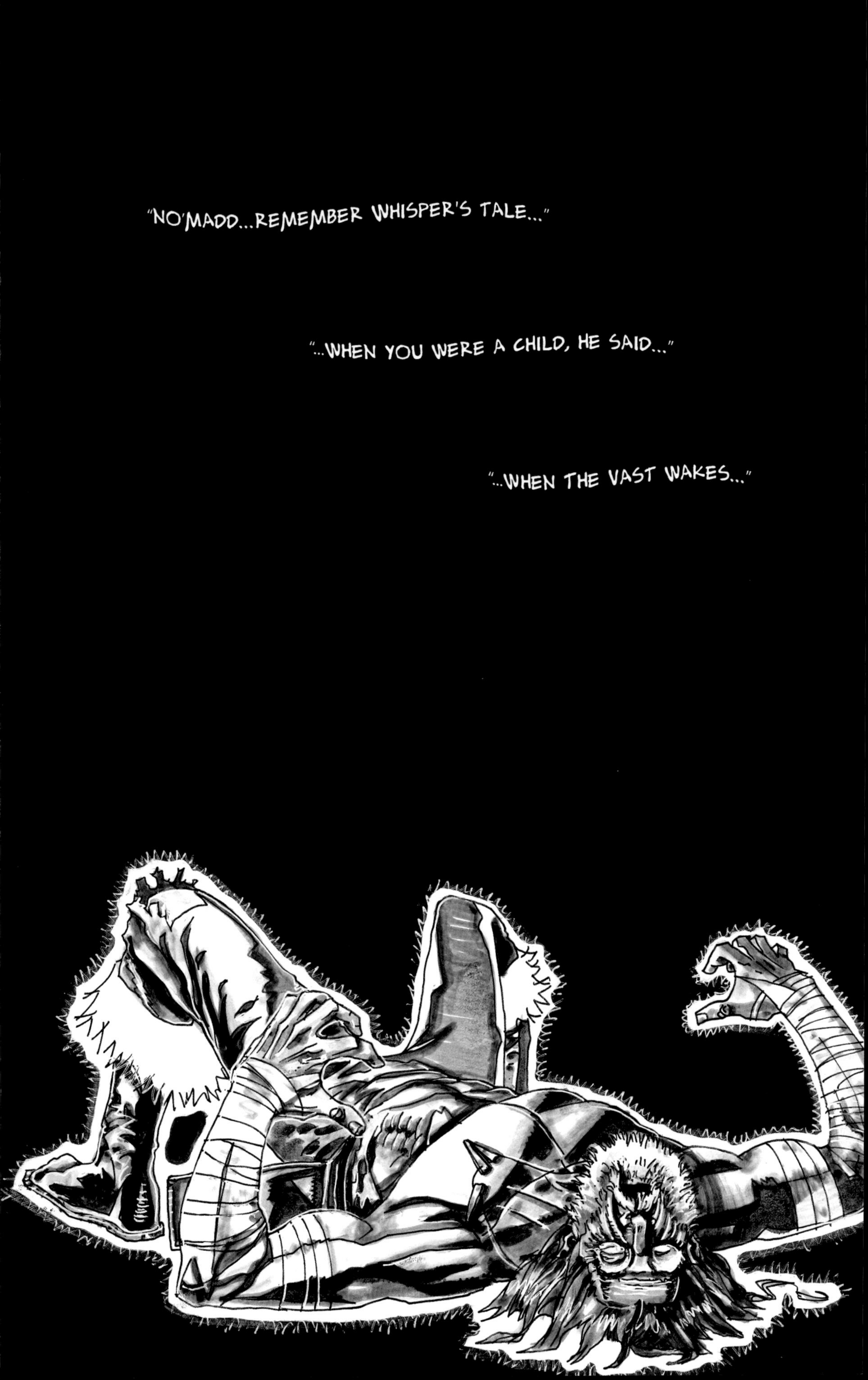
"NO'MADD...REMEMBER WHISPER'S TALE..."
"...WHEN YOU WERE A CHILD, HE SAID..."
"...WHEN THE VAST WAKES..."

"...A CHAMPION SHALL VOYAGE..."

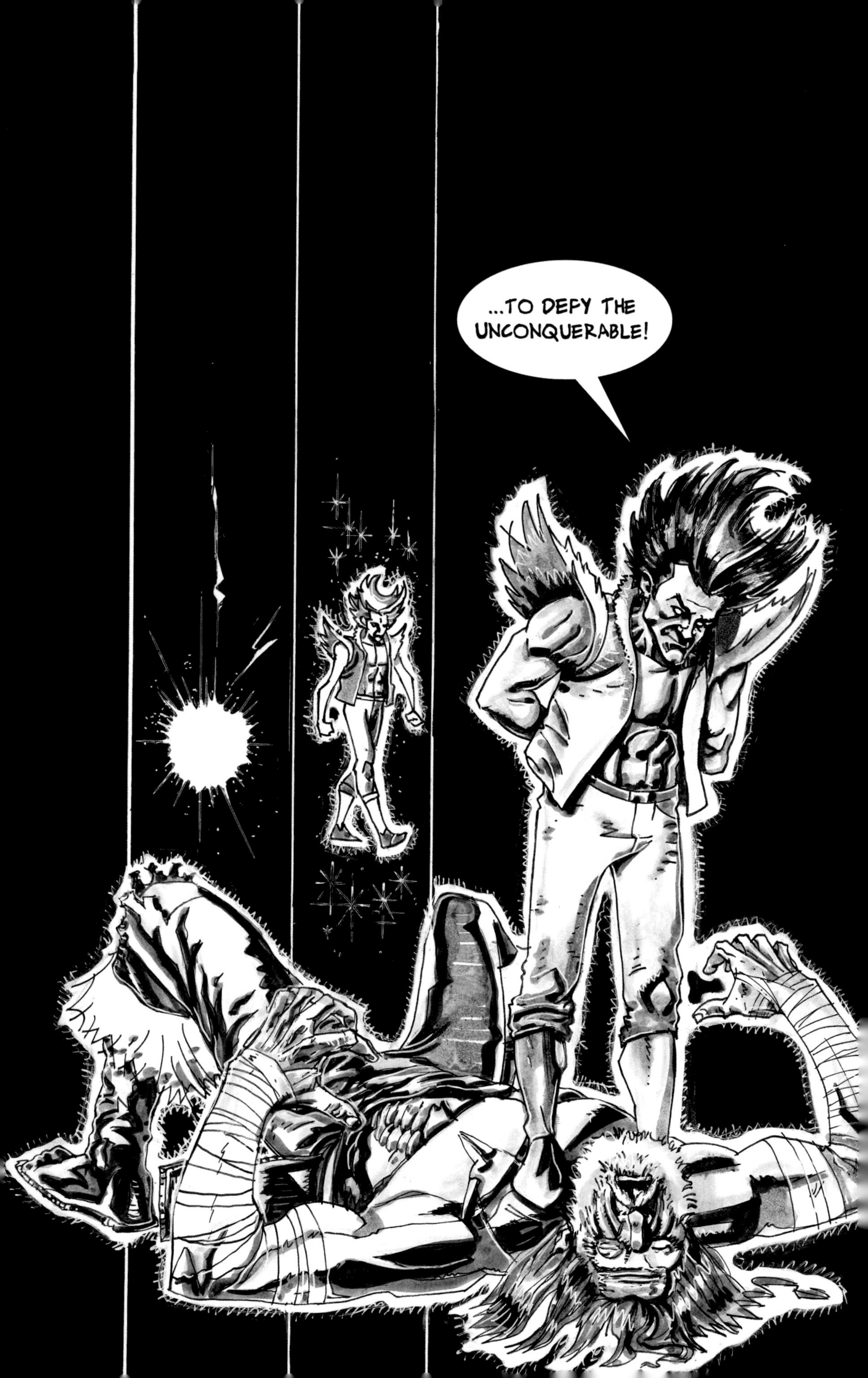
...TO DEFY THE UNCONQUERABLE!

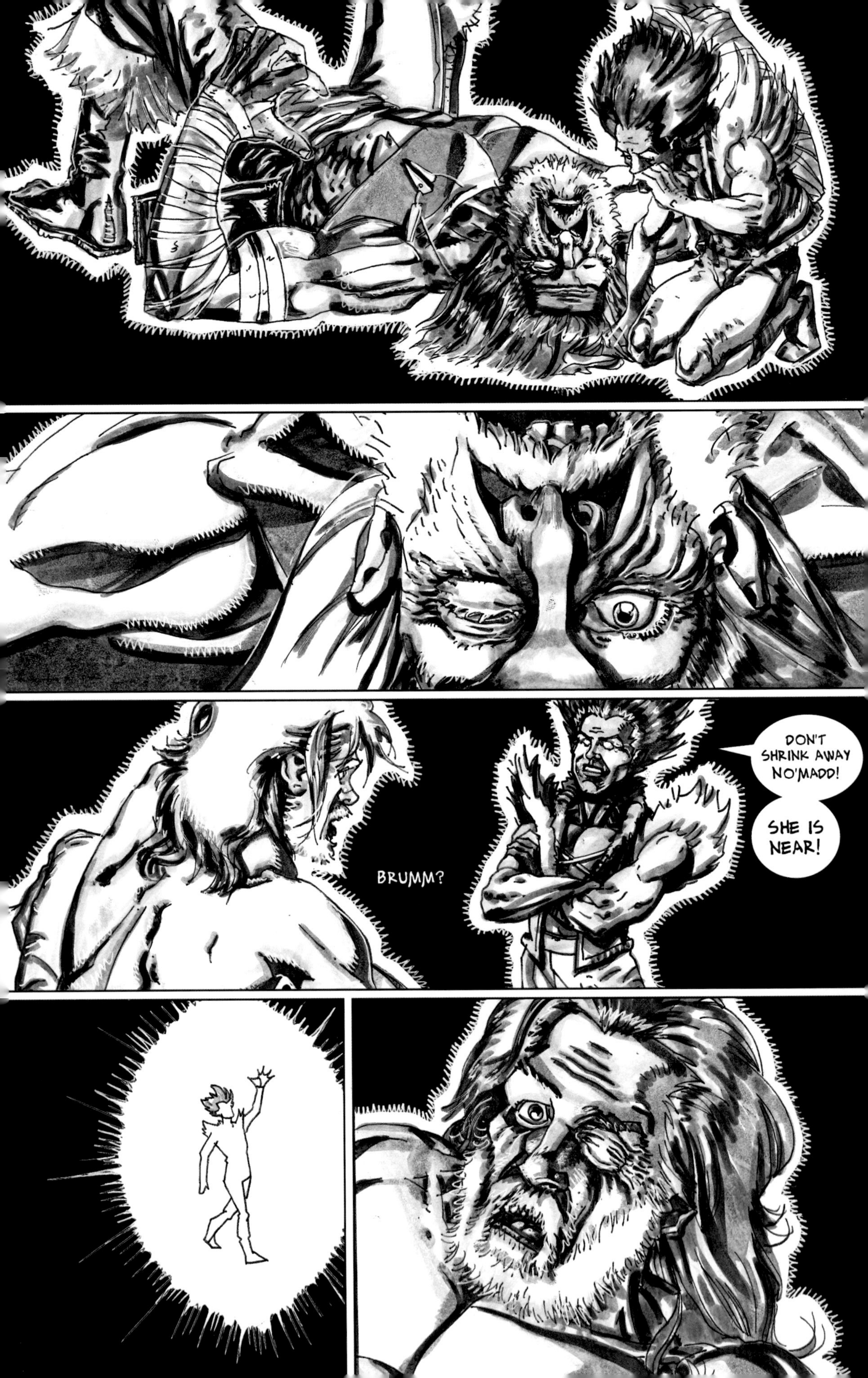
BRUMM?
DON'T SHRINK AWAY NO'MADD!
SHE IS NEAR!

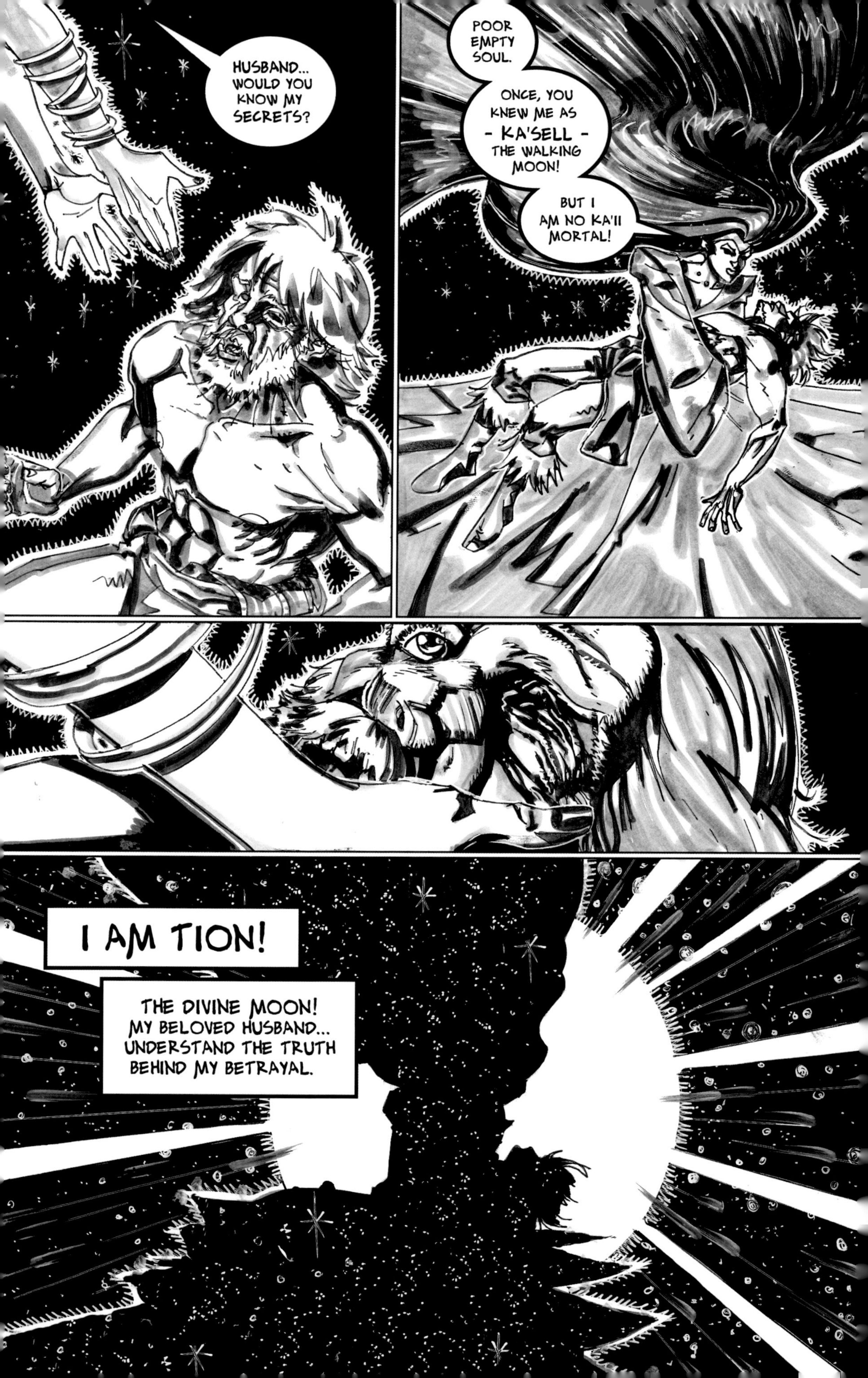
HUSBAND... WOULD YOU KNOW MY SECRETS?
POOR EMPTY SOUL.
ONCE, YOU KNEW ME AS - KA'SELL - THE WALKING MOON!
BUT I AM NO KA'II MORTAL!
I AM TION!
THE DIVINE MOON! MY BELOVED HUSBAND... UNDERSTAND THE TRUTH BEHIND MY BETRAYAL.

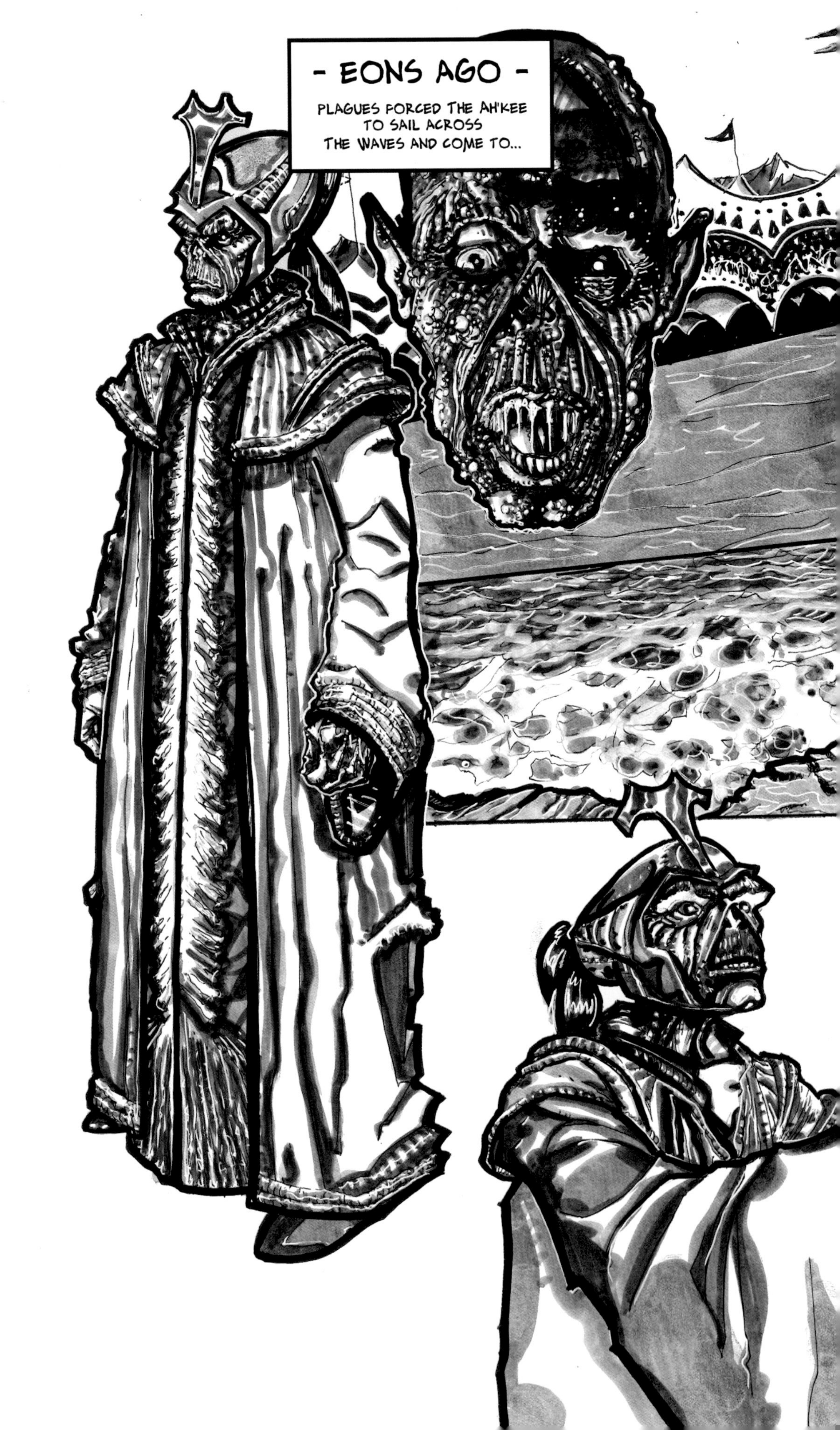
- EONS AGO -
PLAGUES FORCED THE AH'KEE TO SAIL ACROSS THE WAVES AND COME TO...

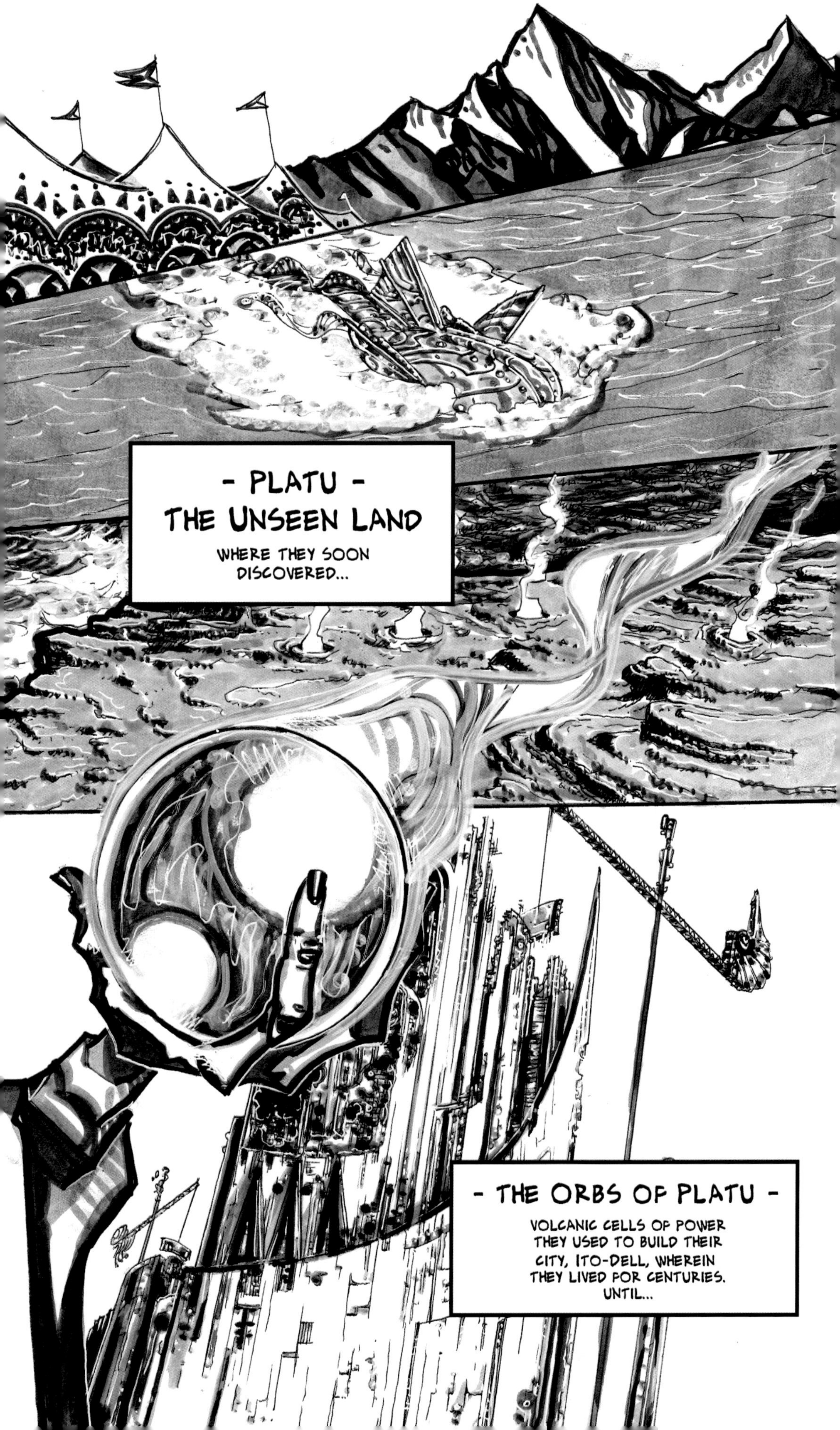
- PLATU -
THE UNSEEN LAND
WHERE THEY SOON DISCOVERED...
- THE ORBS OF PLATU -
VOLCANIC CELLS OF POWER THEY USED TO BUILD THEIR CITY, ITO-DELL, WHEREIN THEY LIVED FOR CENTURIES. UNTIL...

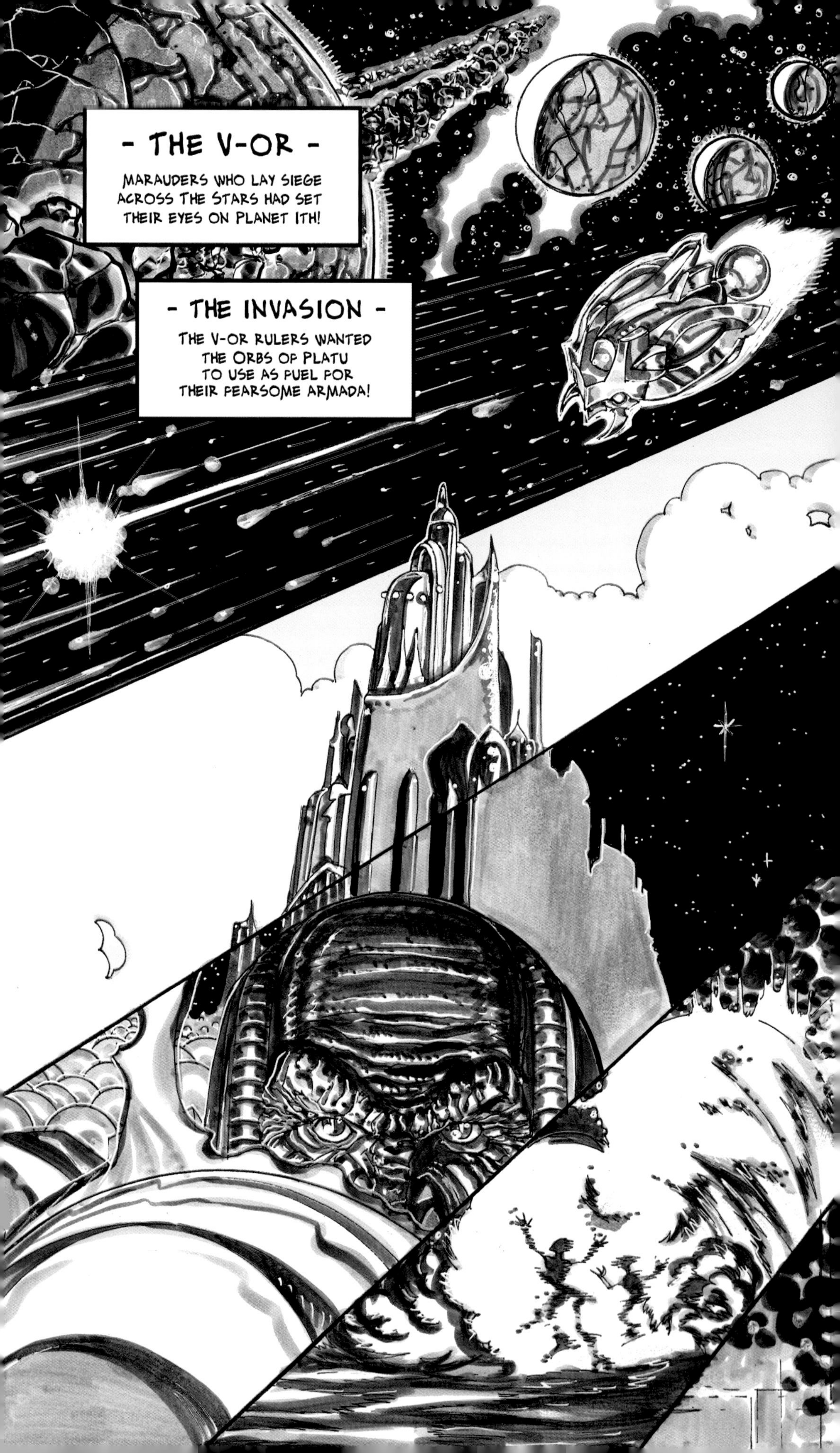
- THE V-OR -
MARAUDERS WHO LAY SIEGE ACROSS THE STARS HAD SET THEIR EYES ON PLANET ITH!
- THE INVASION -
THE V-OR RULERS WANTED THE ORBS OF PLATU TO USE AS FUEL FOR THEIR FEARSOME ARMADA!

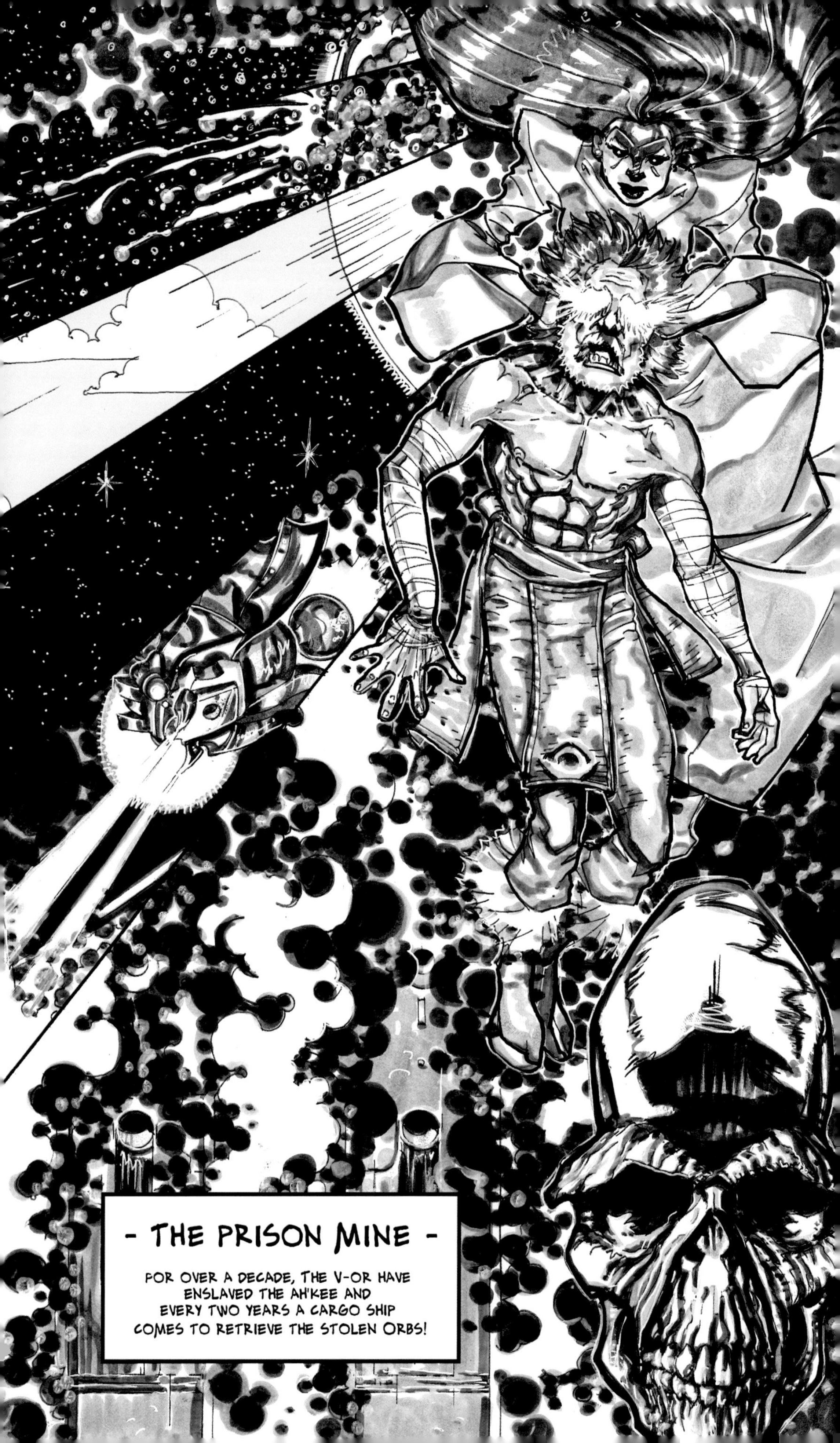
- THE PRISON MINE -
FOR OVER A DECADE, THE V-OR HAVE ENSLAVED THE AH'KEE AND EVERY TWO YEARS A CARGO SHIP COMES TO RETRIEVE THE STOLEN ORBS!

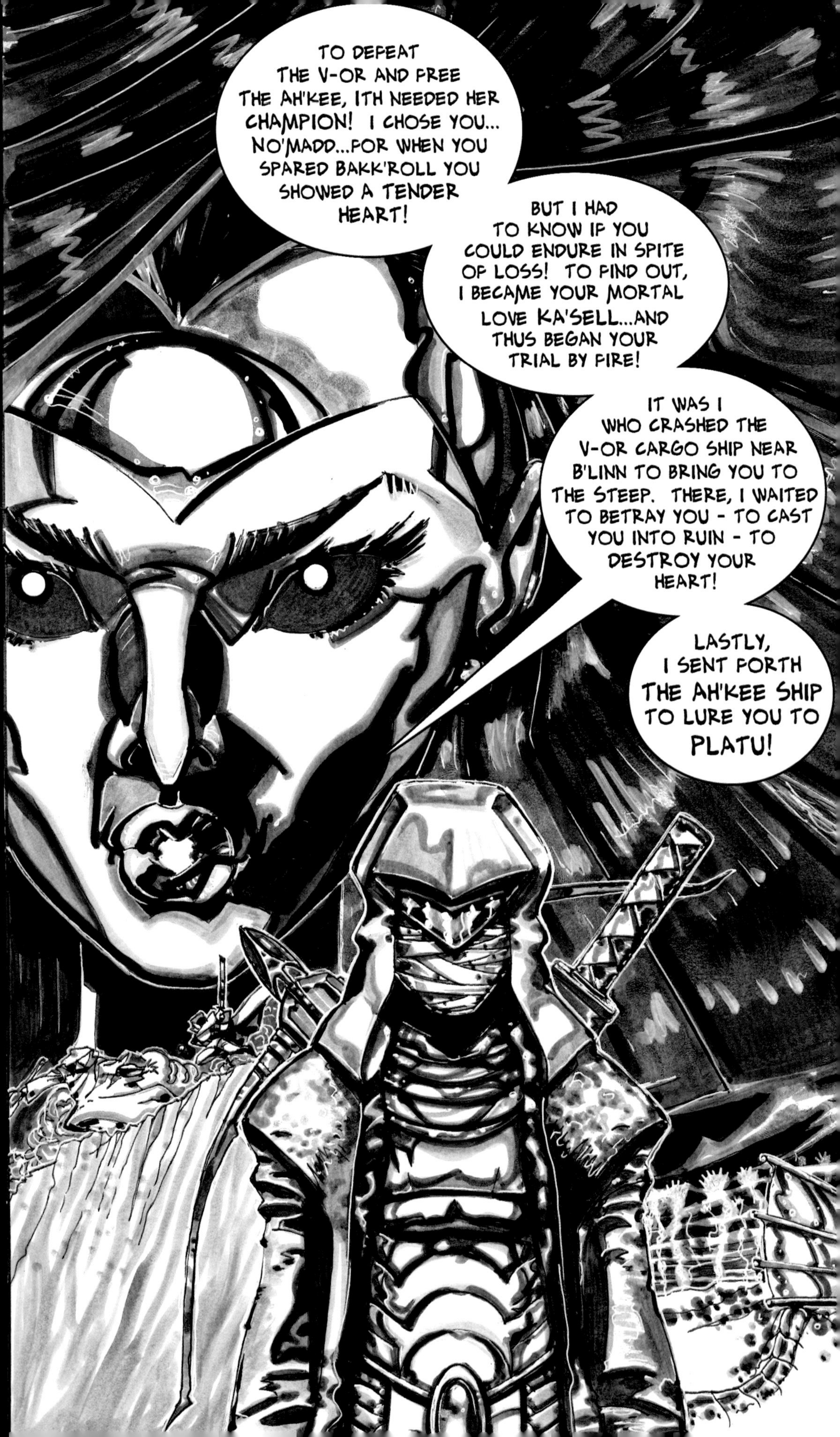

TO DEFEAT THE V-OR AND FREE THE AH'KEE, ITH NEEDED HER CHAMPION! I CHOSE YOU... NO'MADD...FOR WHEN YOU SPARED BAKK'ROLL YOU SHOWED A TENDER HEART!
BUT I HAD TO KNOW IF YOU COULD ENDURE IN SPITE OF LOSS! TO FIND OUT, I BECAME YOUR MORTAL LOVE KA'SELL...AND THUS BEGAN YOUR TRIAL BY FIRE!
IT WAS I WHO CRASHED THE V-OR CARGO SHIP NEAR B'LINN TO BRING YOU TO THE STEEP. THERE, I WAITED TO BETRAY YOU - TO CAST YOU INTO RUIN - TO DESTROY YOUR HEART!
LASTLY, I SENT FORTH THE AH'KEE SHIP TO LURE YOU TO PLATU!

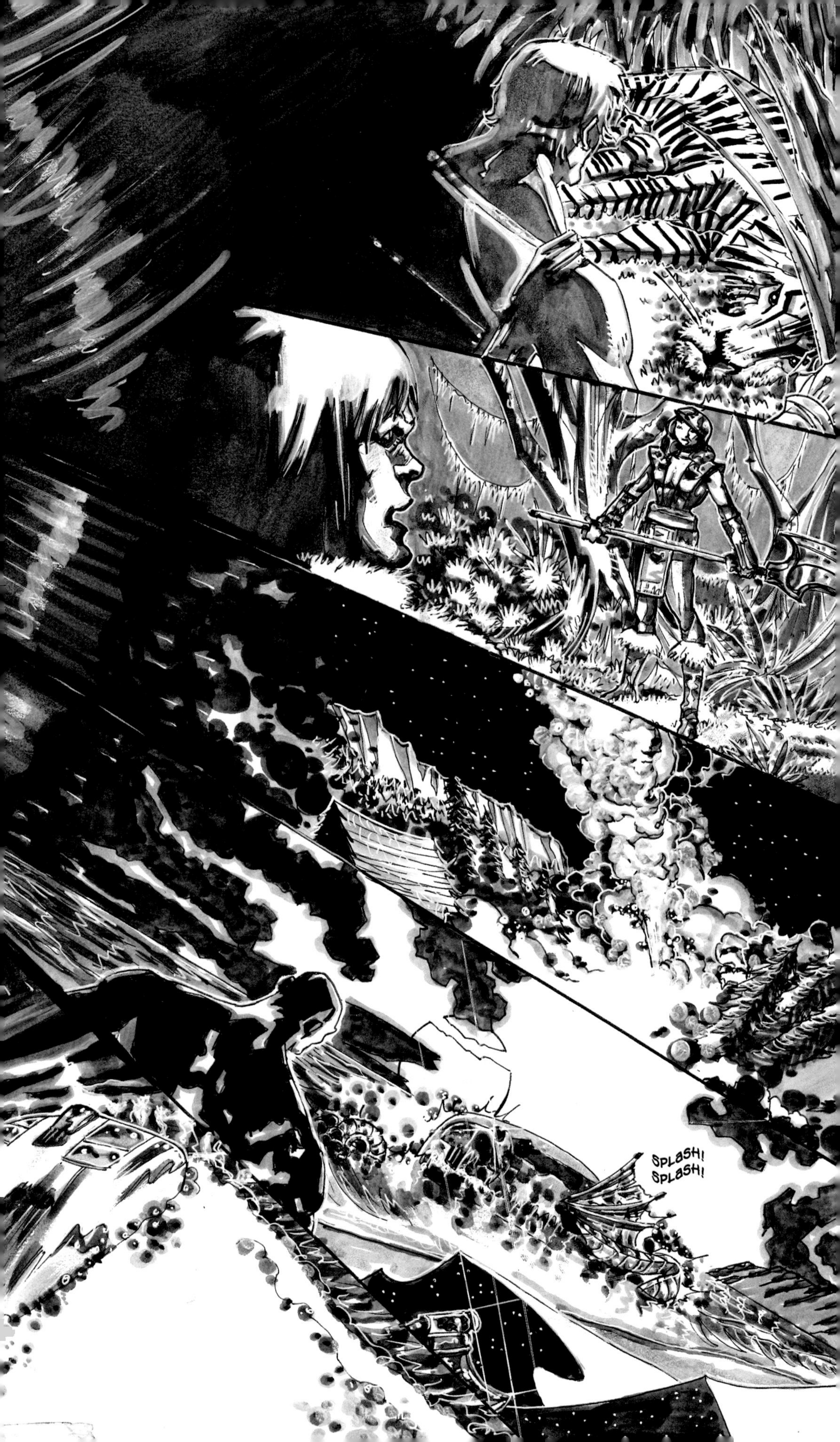
SPLASH!
SPLASH!

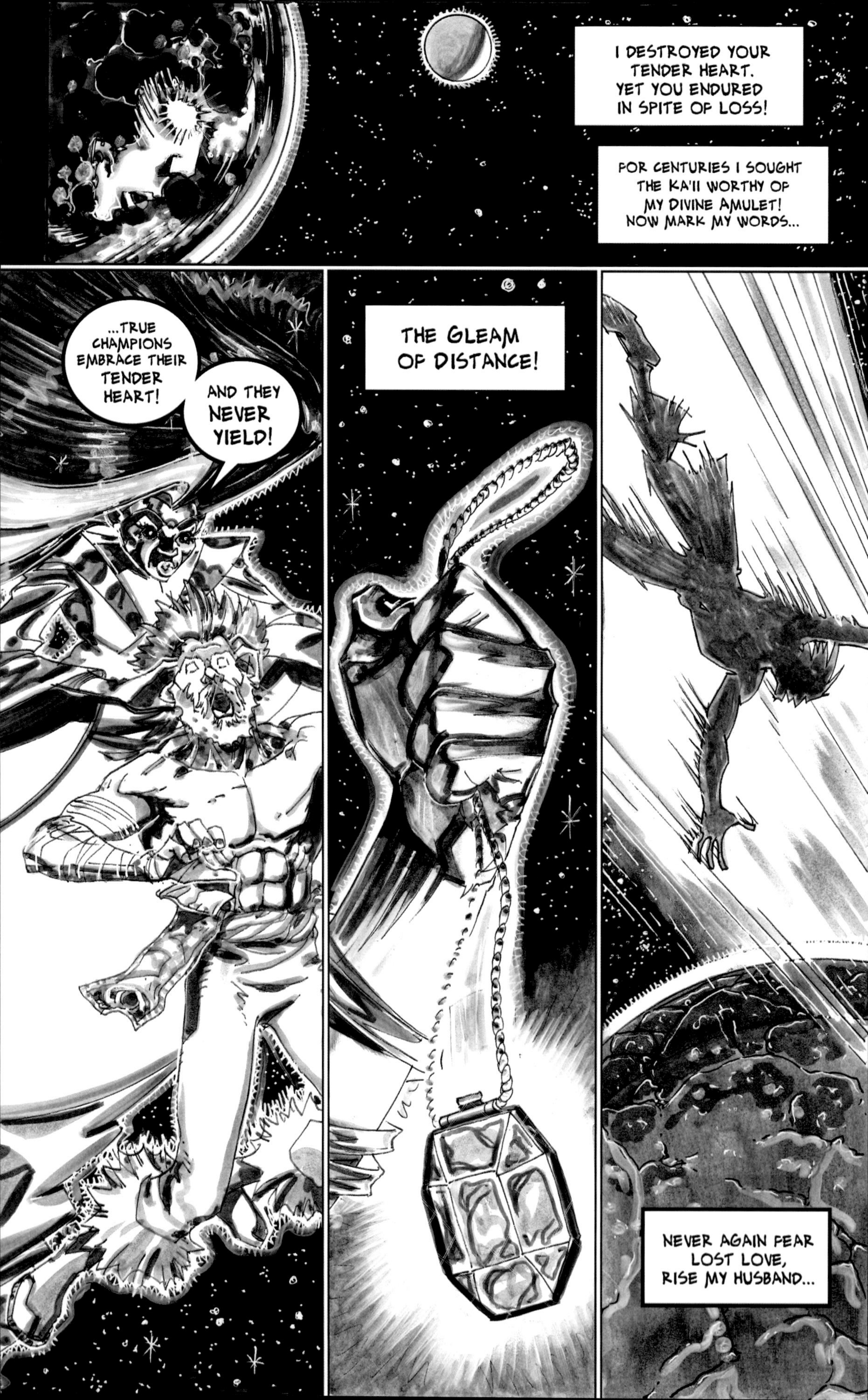
I DESTROYED YOUR TENDER HEART. YET YOU ENDURED IN SPITE OF LOSS!
FOR CENTURIES I SOUGHT THE KA'II WORTHY OF MY DIVINE AMULET! NOW MARK MY WORDS...
...TRUE CHAMPIONS EMBRACE THEIR TENDER HEART!
AND THEY NEVER YIELD!
THE GLEAM OF DISTANCE!
NEVER AGAIN FEAR LOST LOVE, RISE MY HUSBAND...

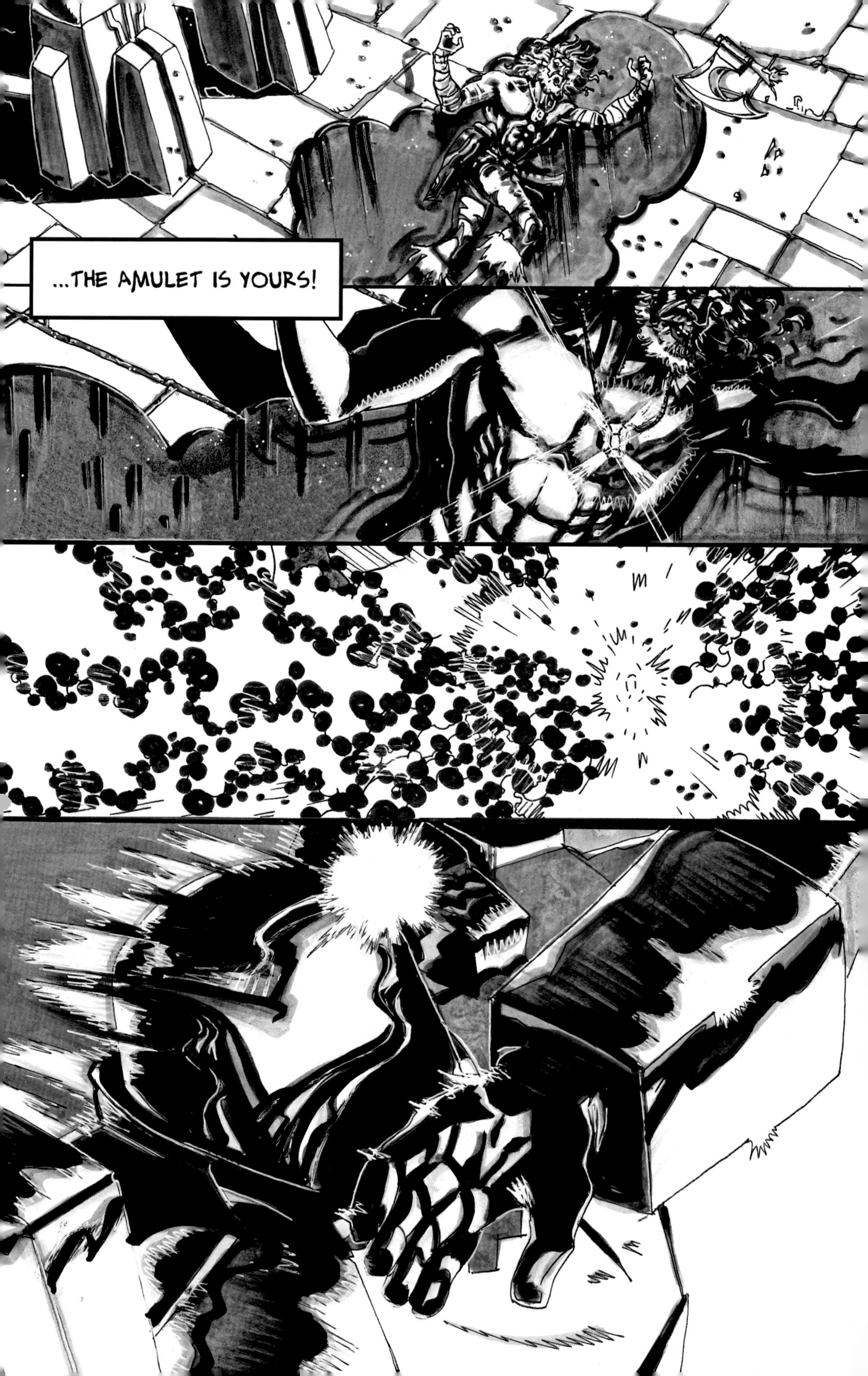
...THE AMULET IS YOURS!

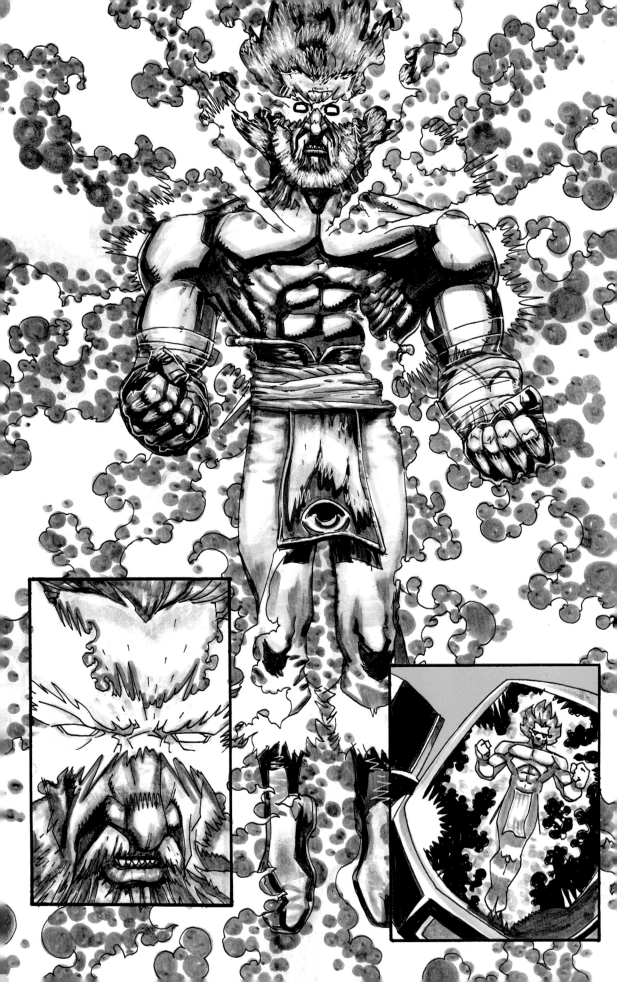

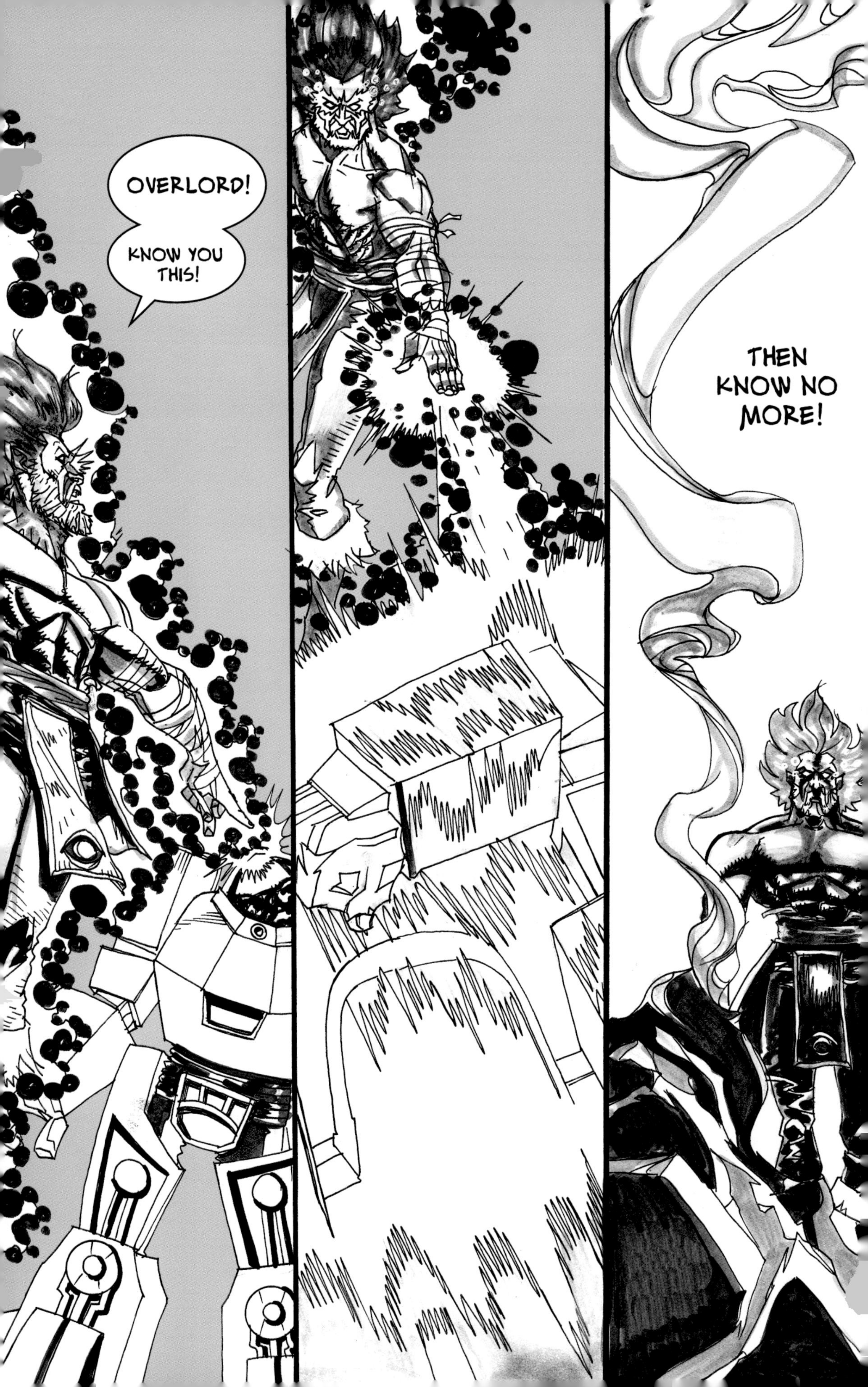
OVERLORD!
KNOW YOU THIS!
THEN KNOW NO MORE!

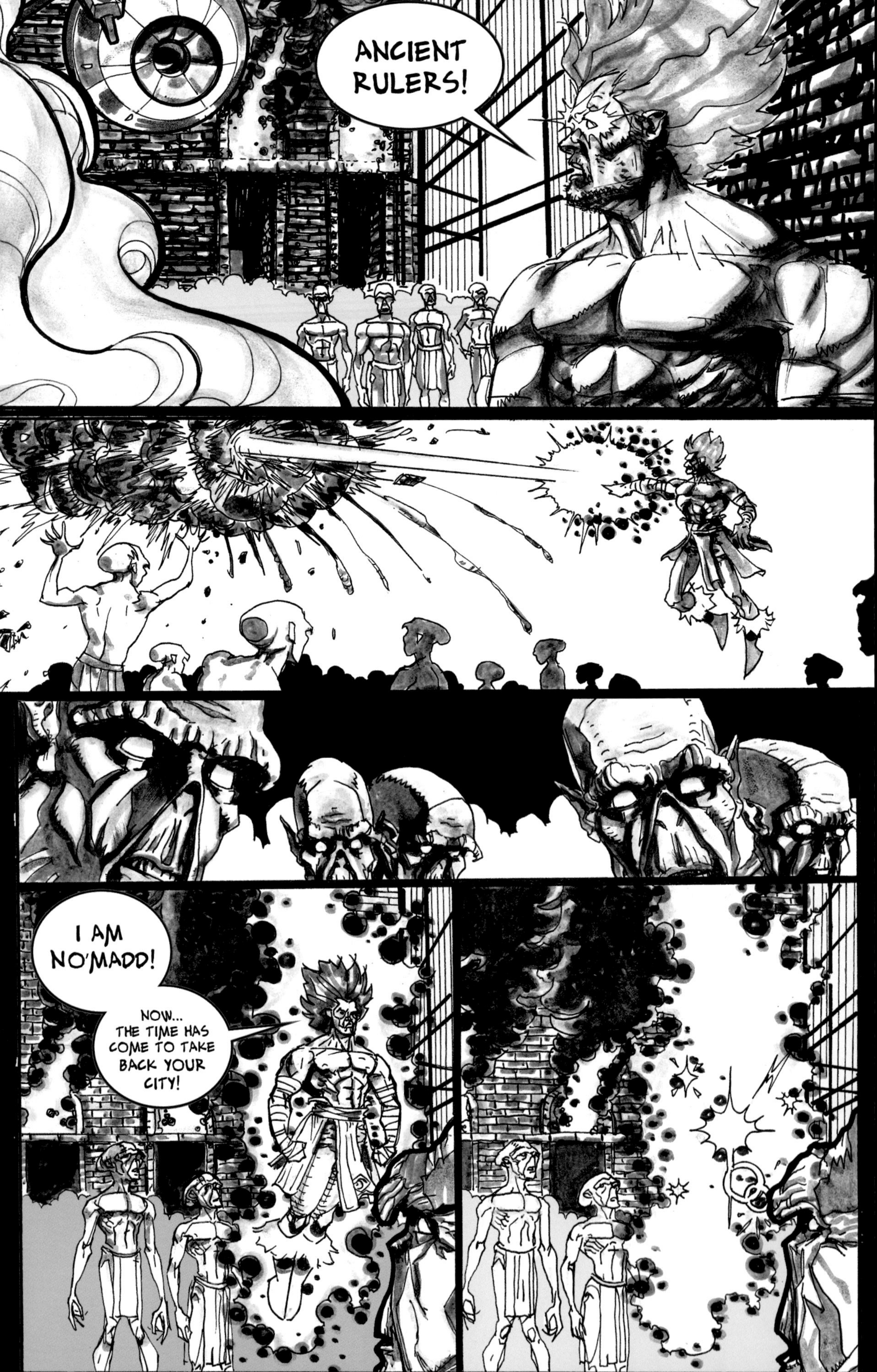
ANCIENT RULERS!
I AM NO'MADD!
NOW... THE TIME HAS COME TO TAKE BACK YOUR CITY!

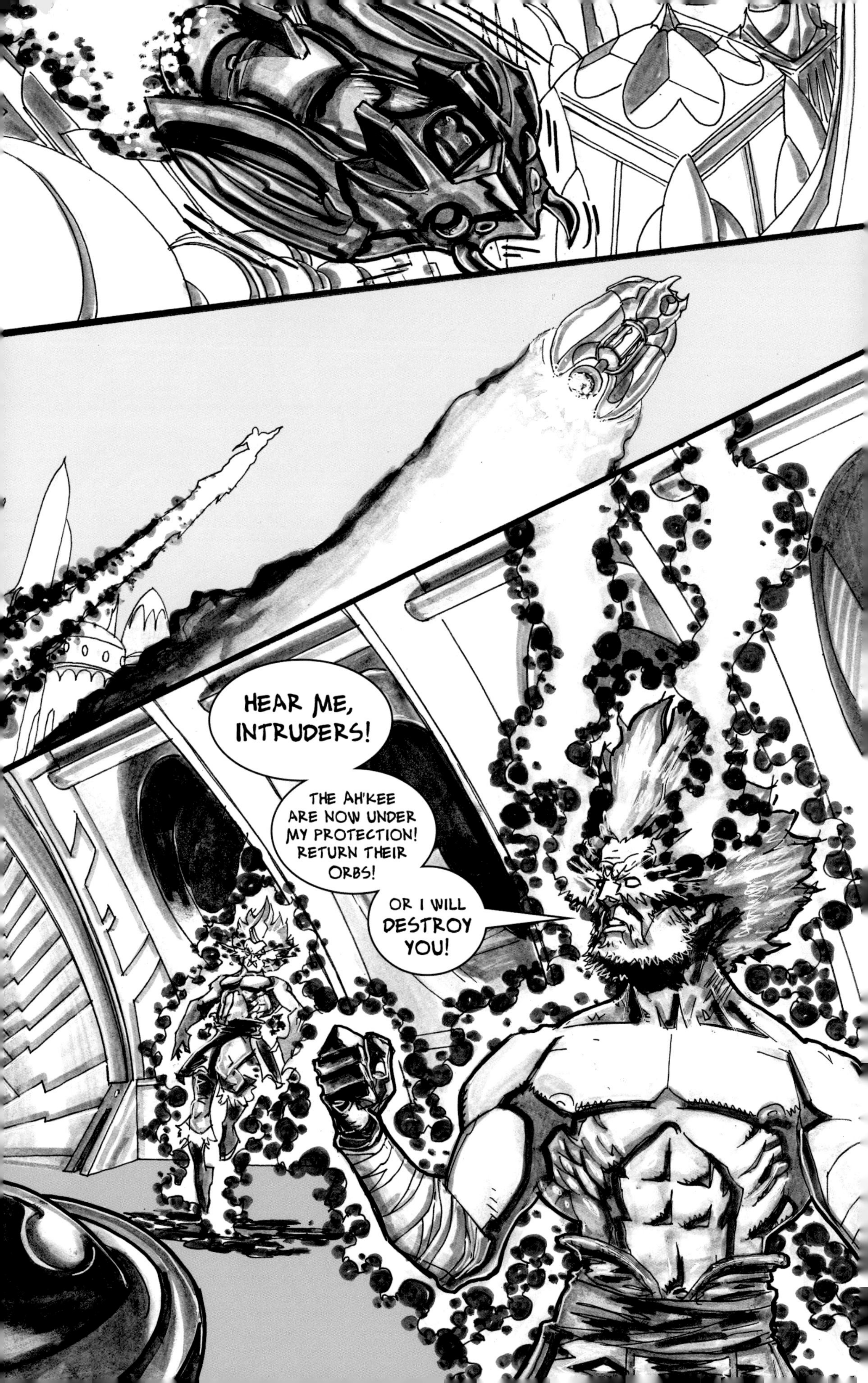
HEAR ME, INTRUDERS!
THE AH'KEE ARE NOW UNDER MY PROTECTION! RETURN THEIR ORBS!
OR I WILL DESTROY YOU!

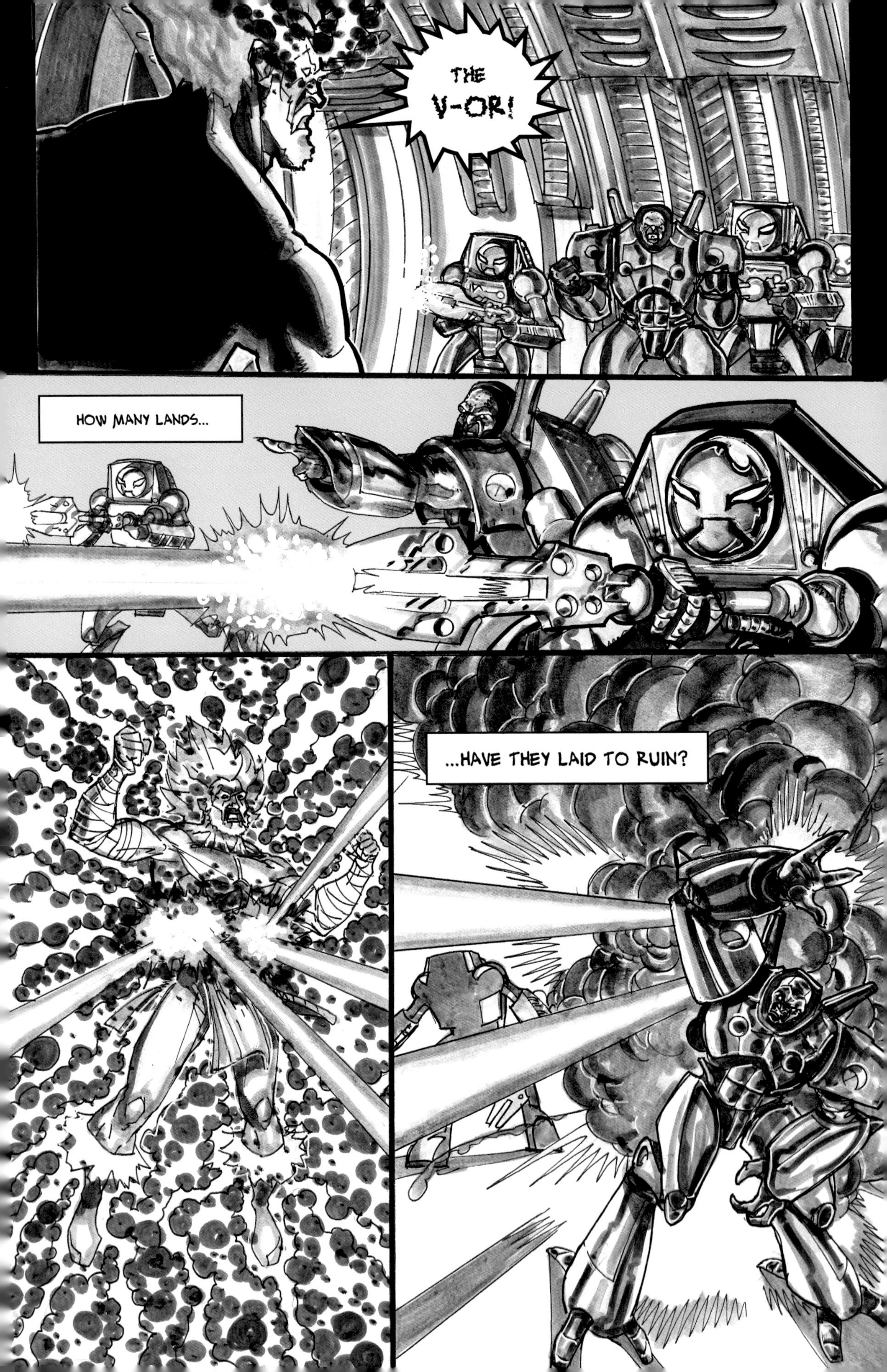
THE V-OR!
HOW MANY LANDS...
...HAVE THEY LAID TO RUIN?

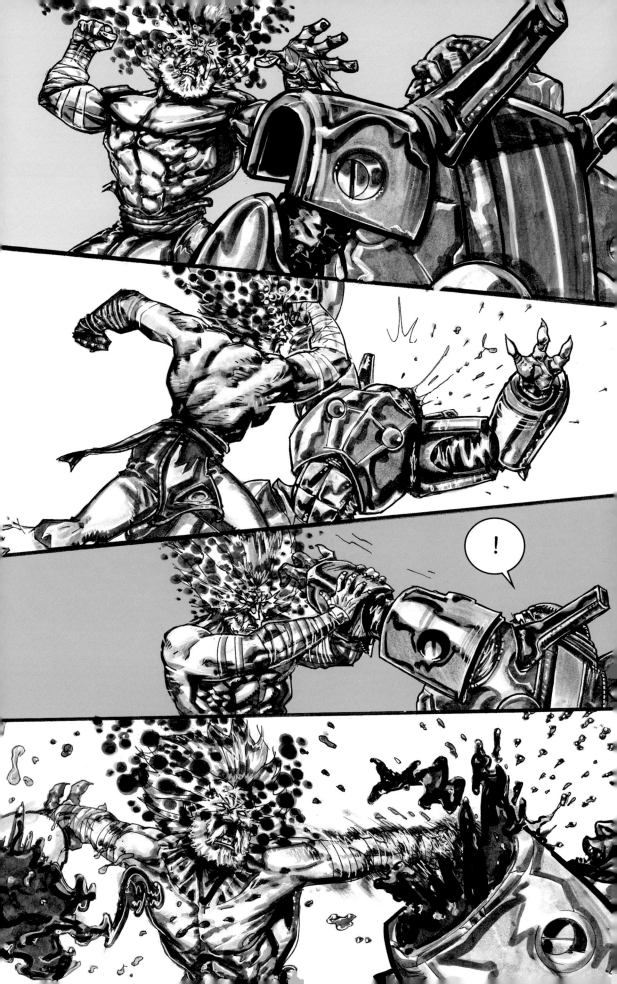

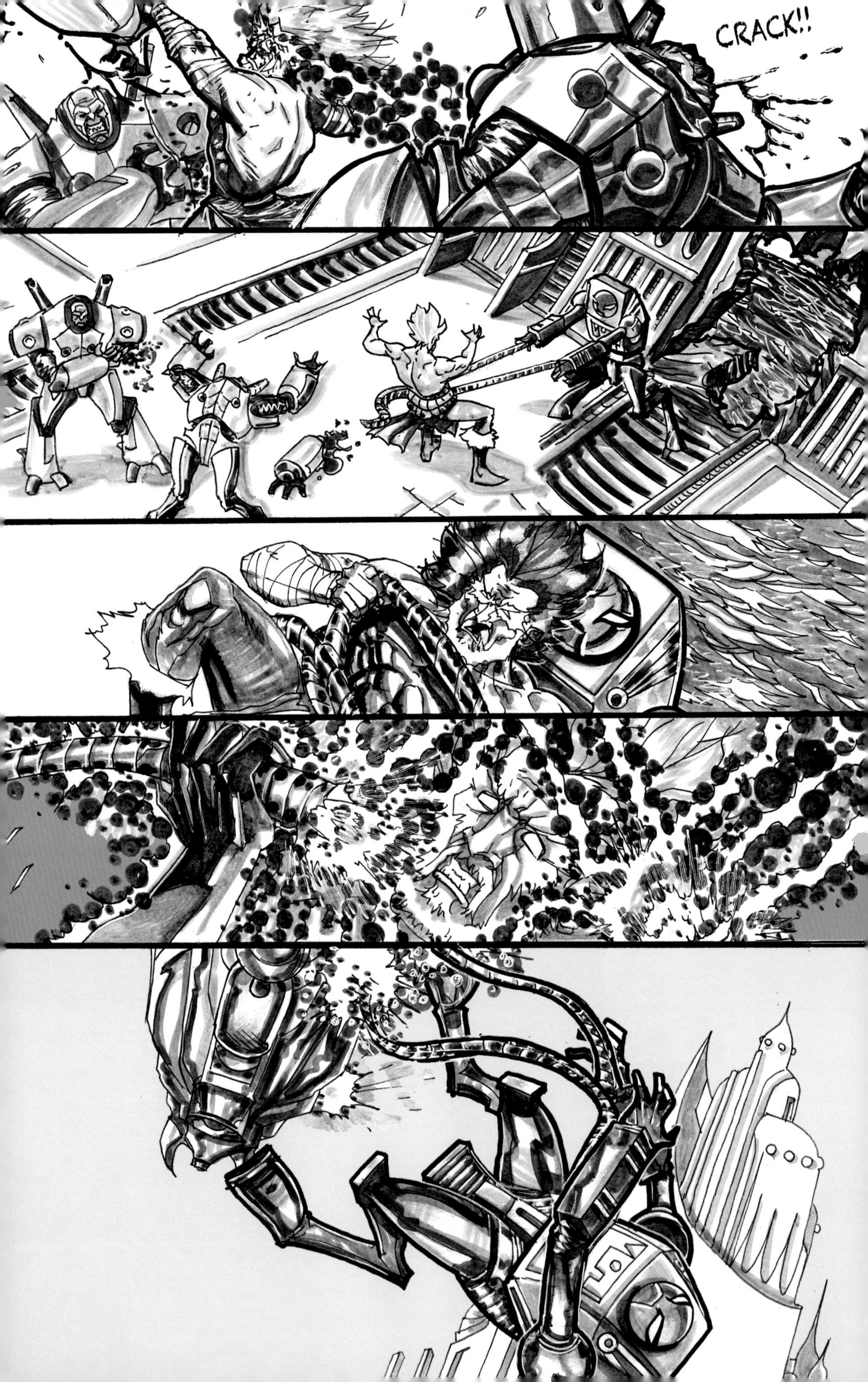
CRACK!!

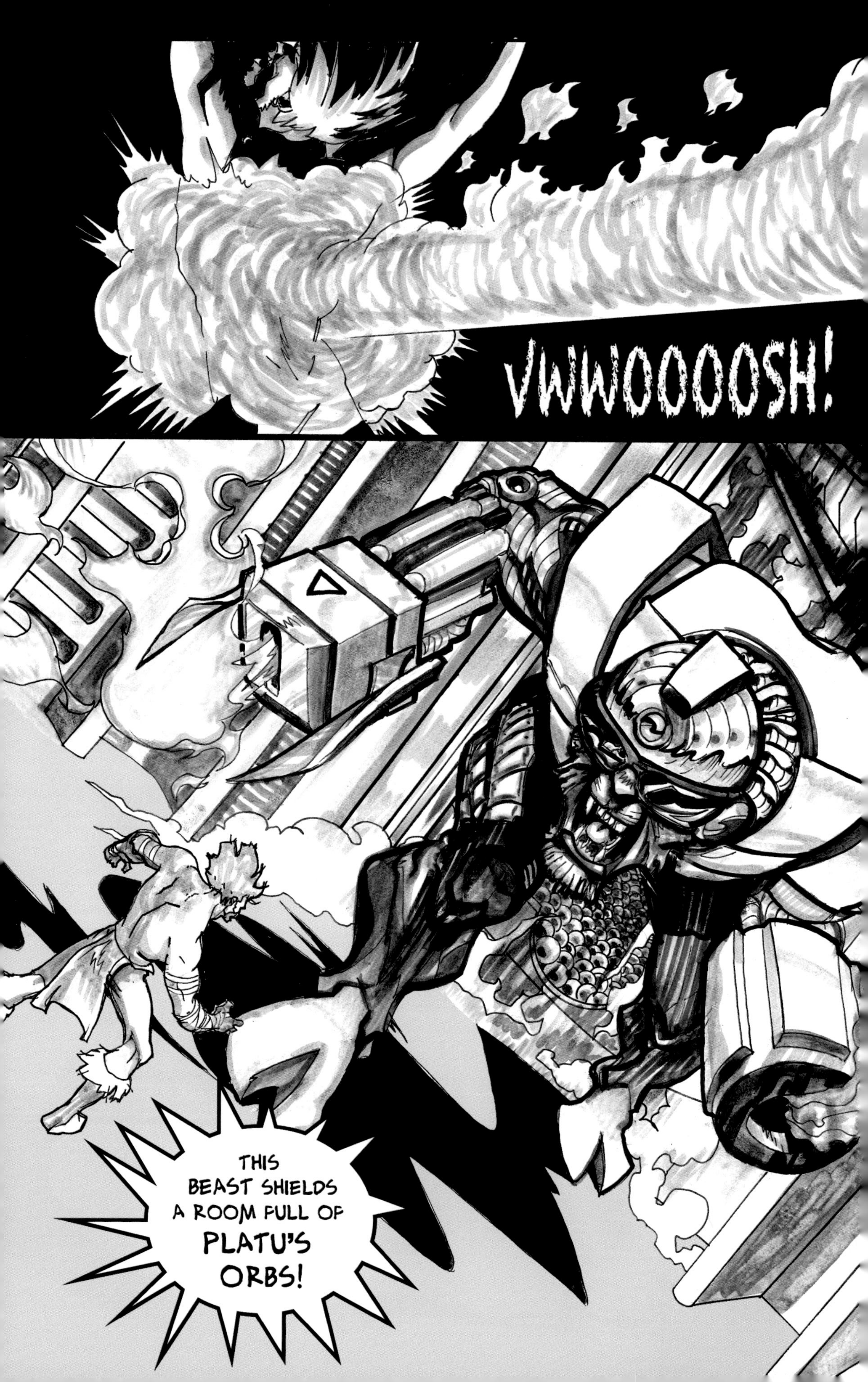
VWWOOOOSH!
THIS BEAST SHIELDS A ROOM FULL OF PLATU'S ORBS!

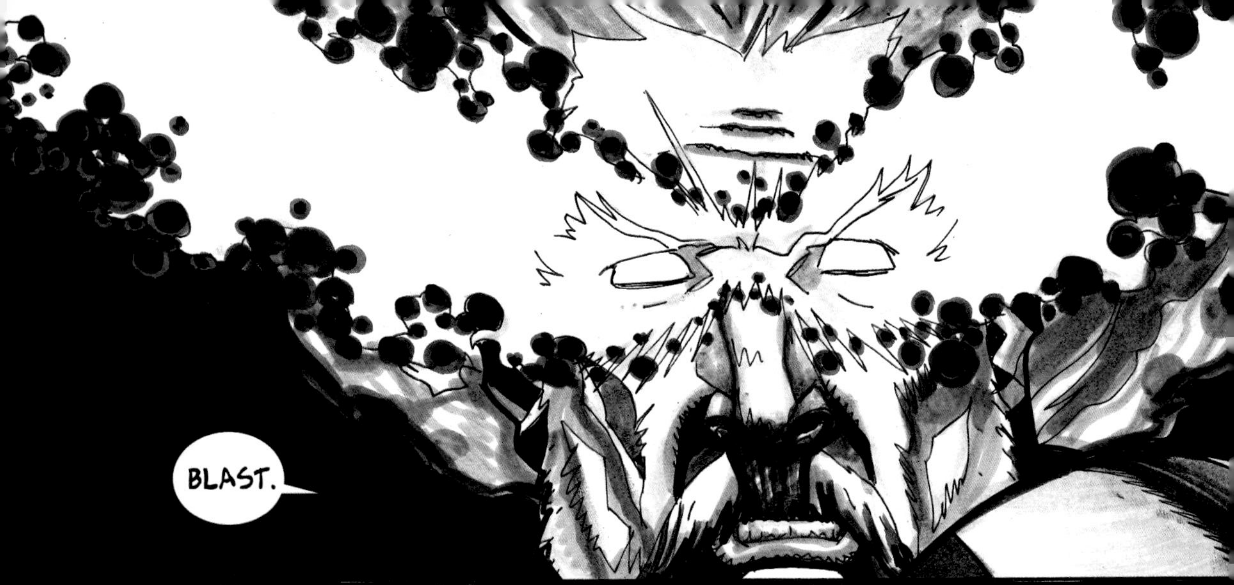
BLAST.

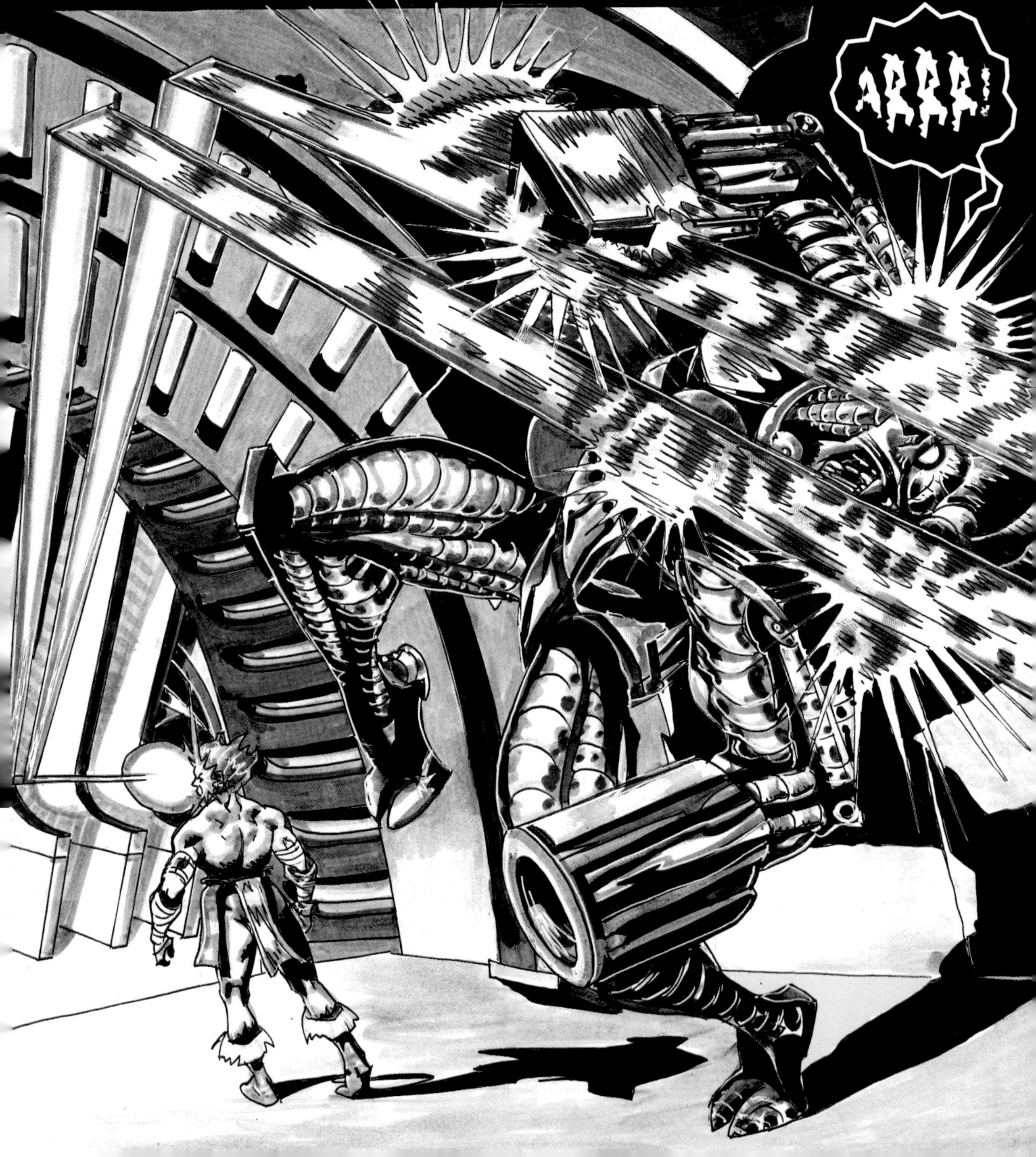
ARRR!

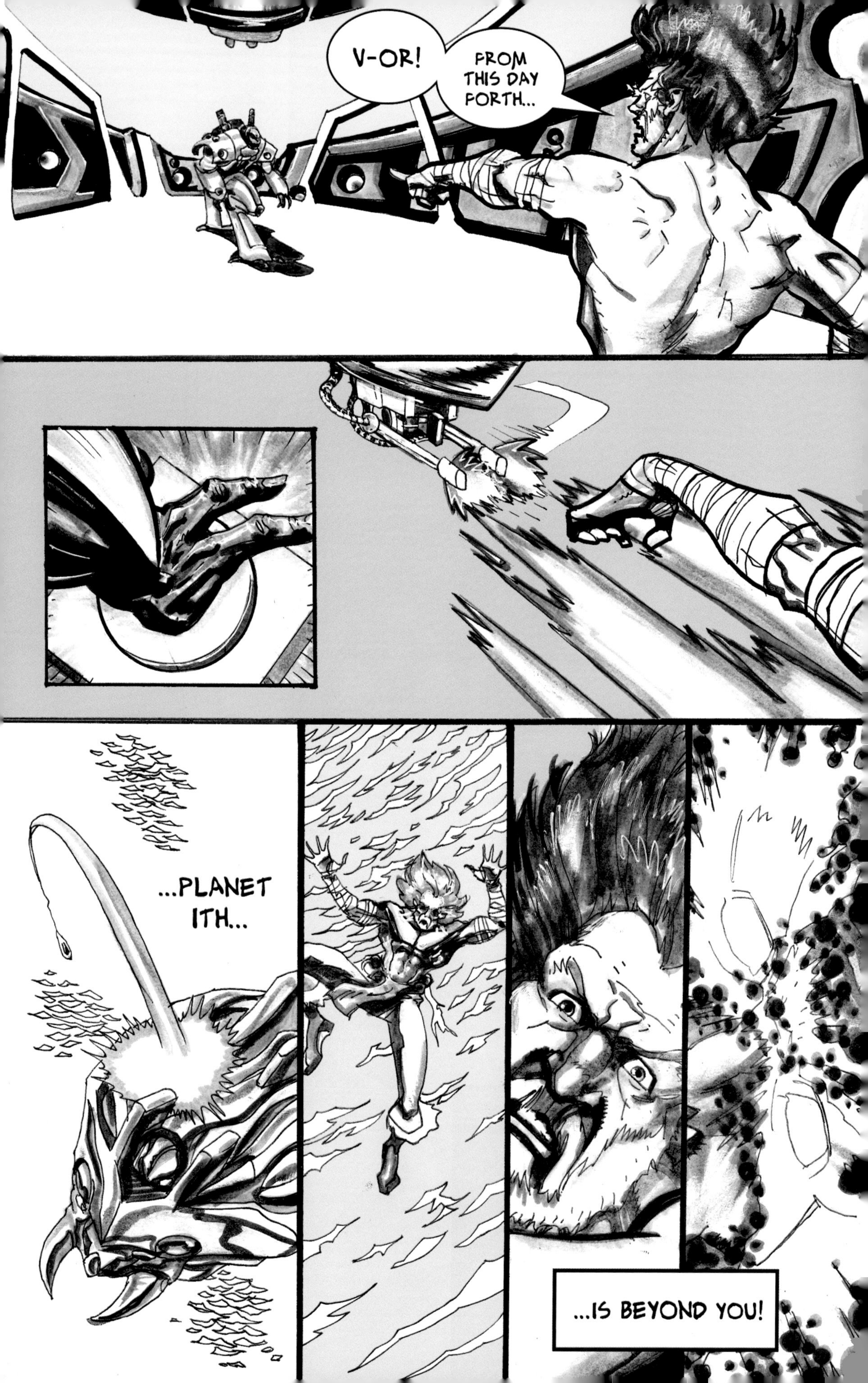
V-OR!
FROM THIS DAY FORTH...
...PLANET ITH...
...IS BEYOND YOU!

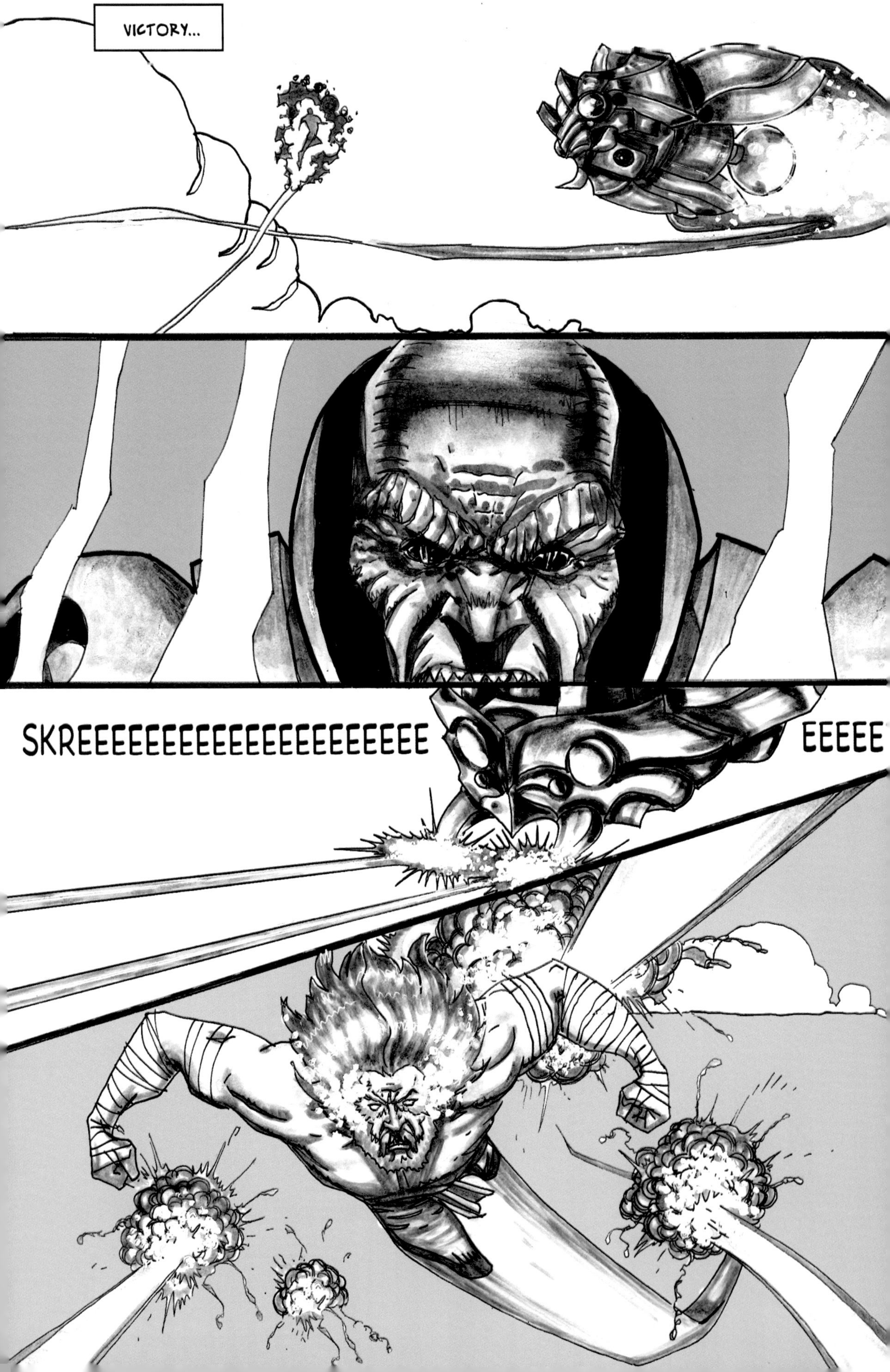
VICTORY...
SKREEEEEEEEEEEEEEEEEEEEEE
EEEEE

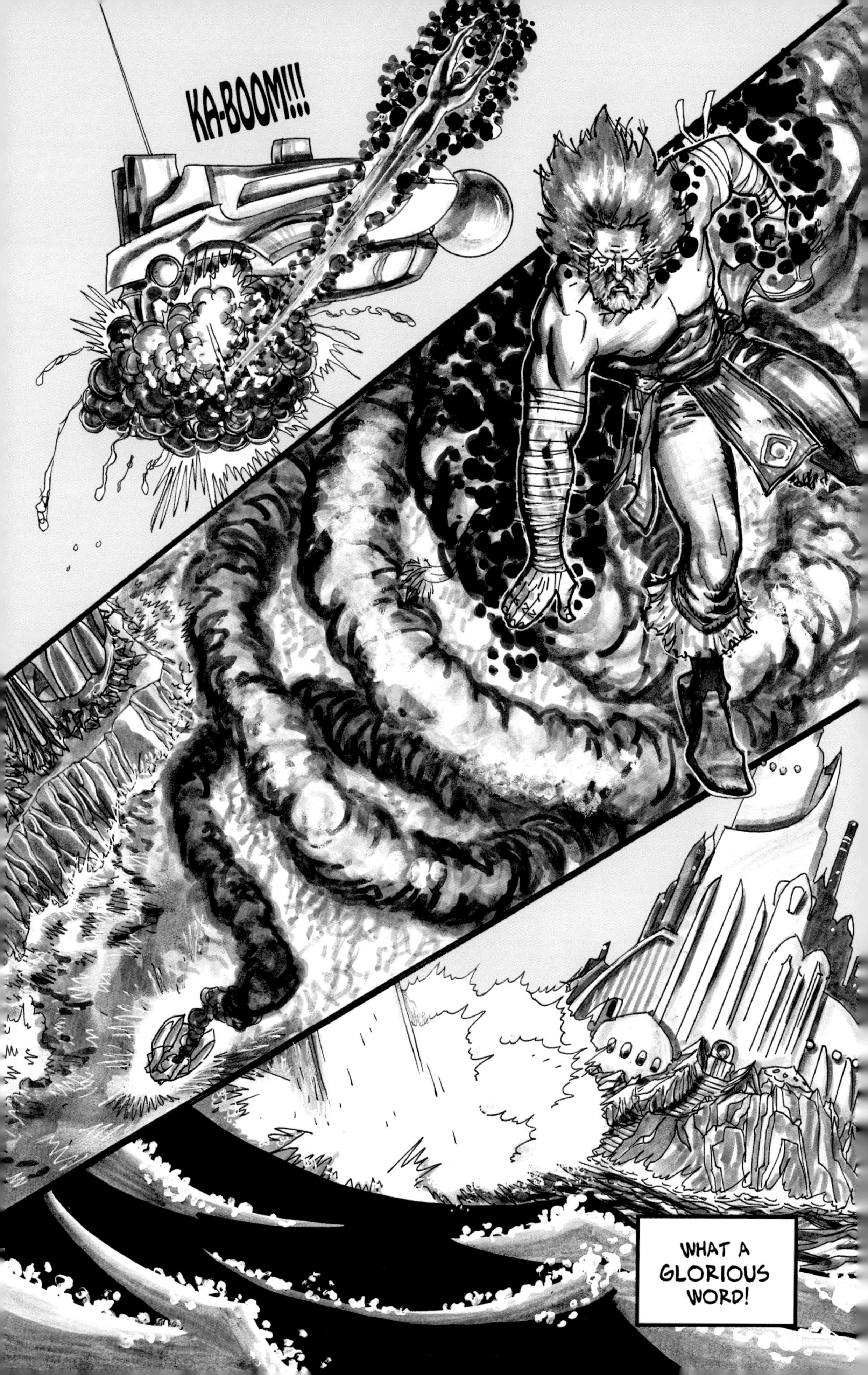
KA-BOOM!!!
WHAT A GLORIOUS WORD!

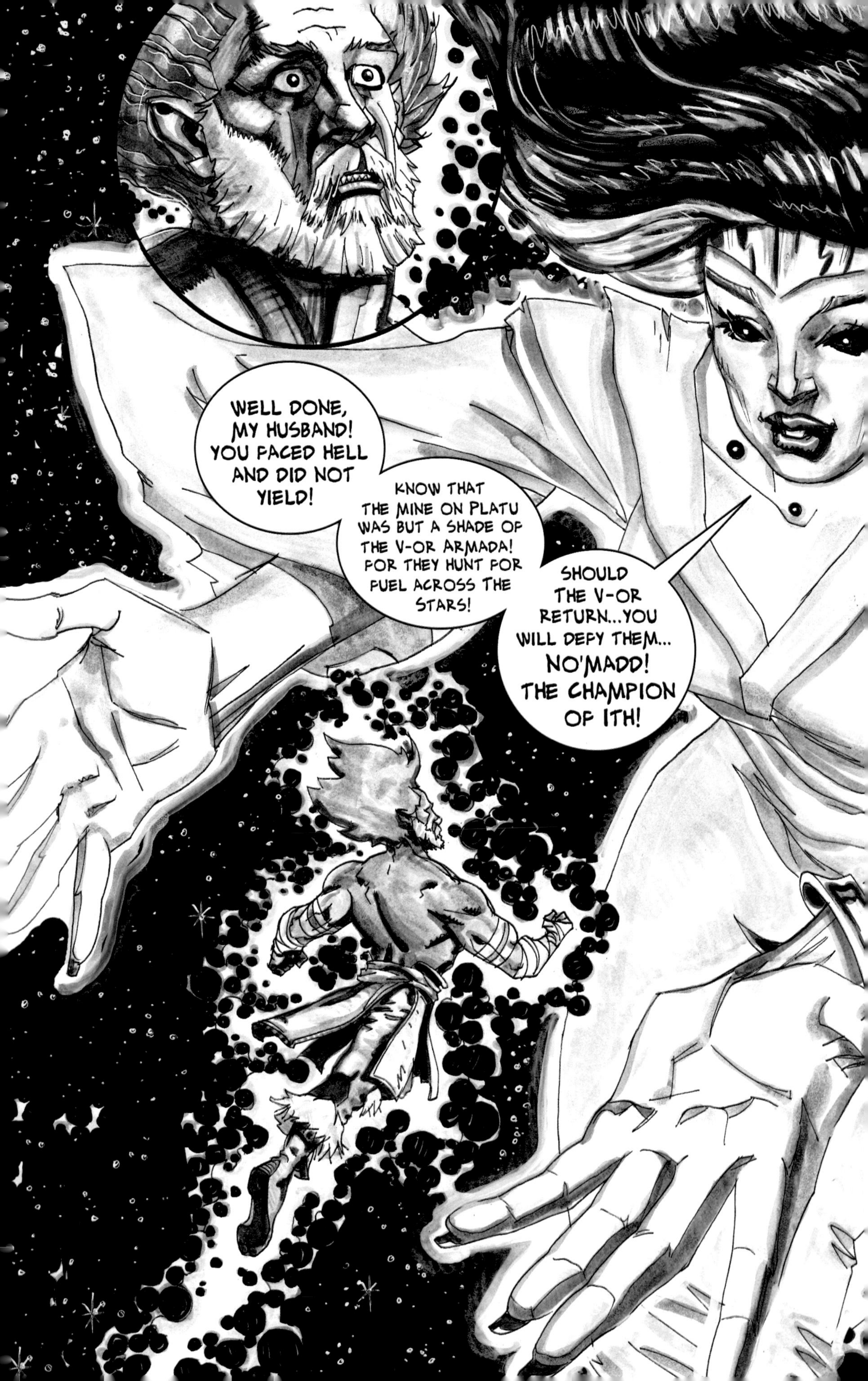
WELL DONE, MY HUSBAND! YOU FACED HELL AND DID NOT YIELD!
KNOW THAT THE MINE ON PLATU WAS BUT A SHADE OF THE V-OR ARMADA! FOR THEY HUNT FOR FUEL ACROSS THE STARS!
SHOULD THE V-OR RETURN...YOU WILL DEFY THEM... NO'MADD! THE CHAMPION OF ITH!

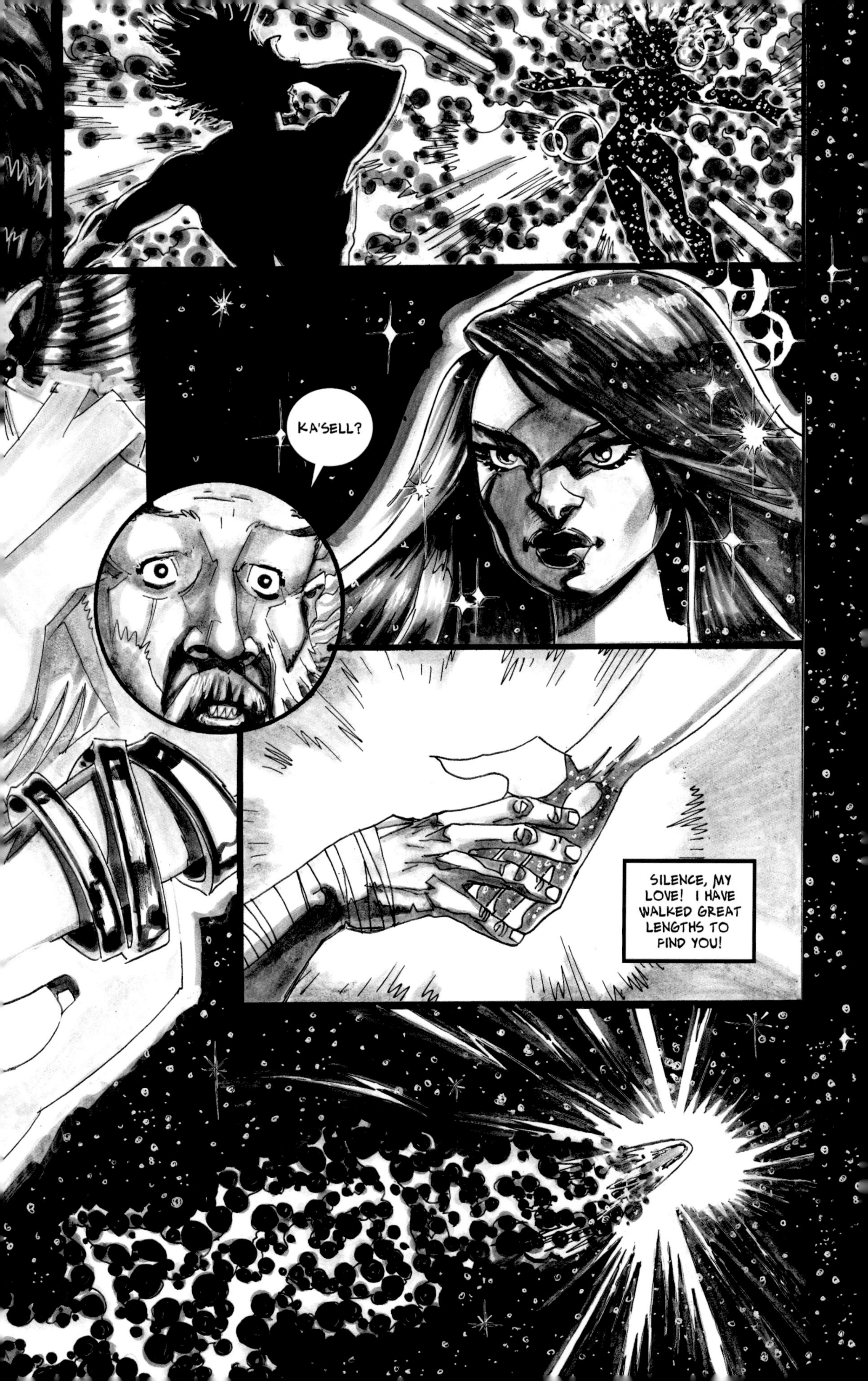
KA'SELL?
SILENCE, MY LOVE! I HAVE WALKED GREAT LENGTHS TO FIND YOU!

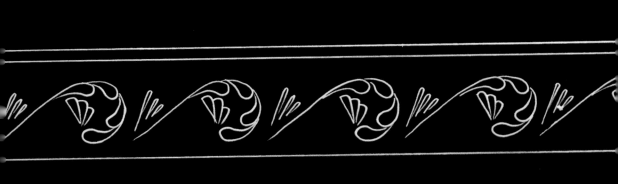

EPILOGUE

TION

"HUSBAND...

...WOULD YOU
KNOW MY SECRETS?"

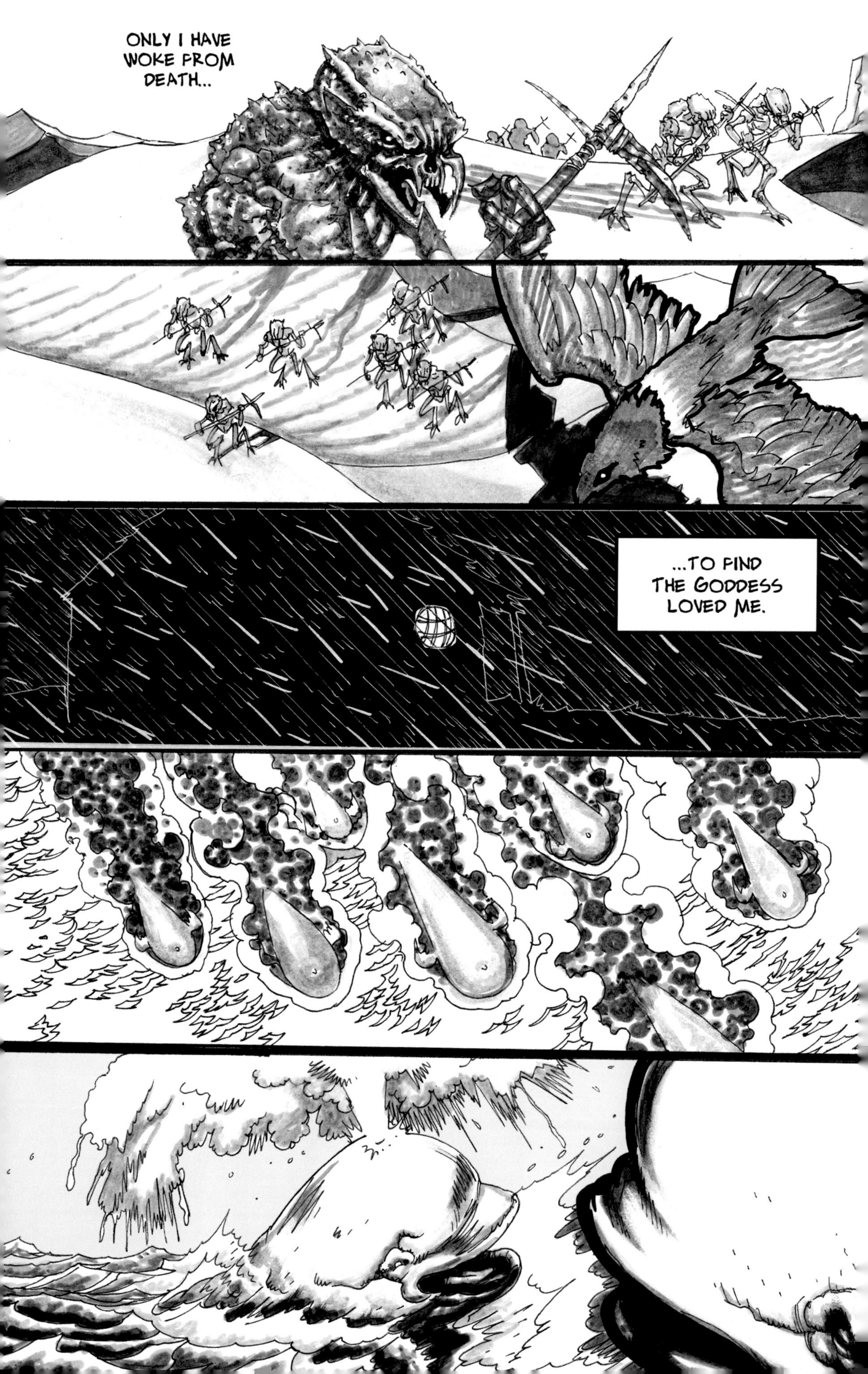
ONLY I HAVE WOKE FROM DEATH...
...TO FIND THE GODDESS LOVED ME.

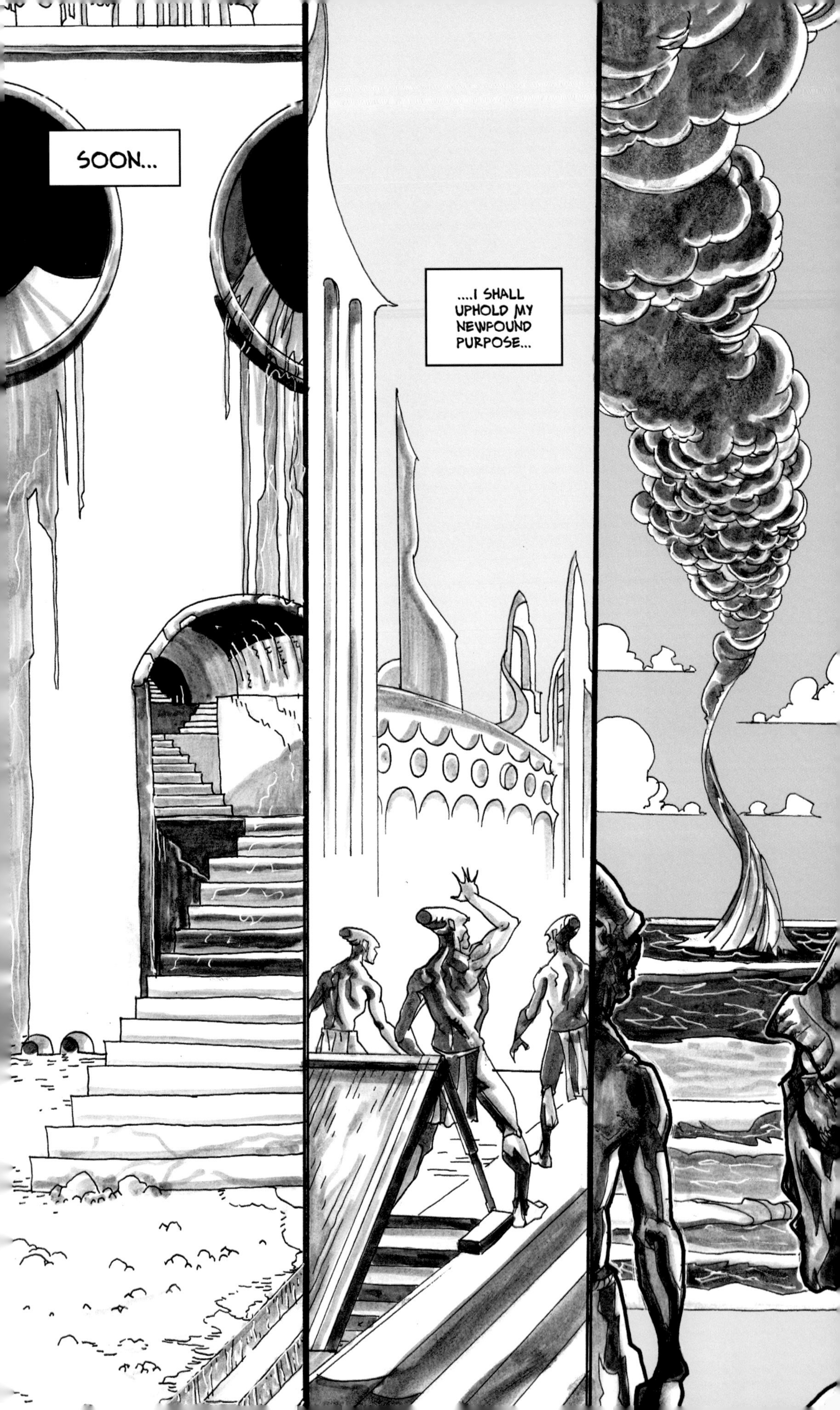
SOON...
....I SHALL UPHOLD MY NEWFOUND PURPOSE...

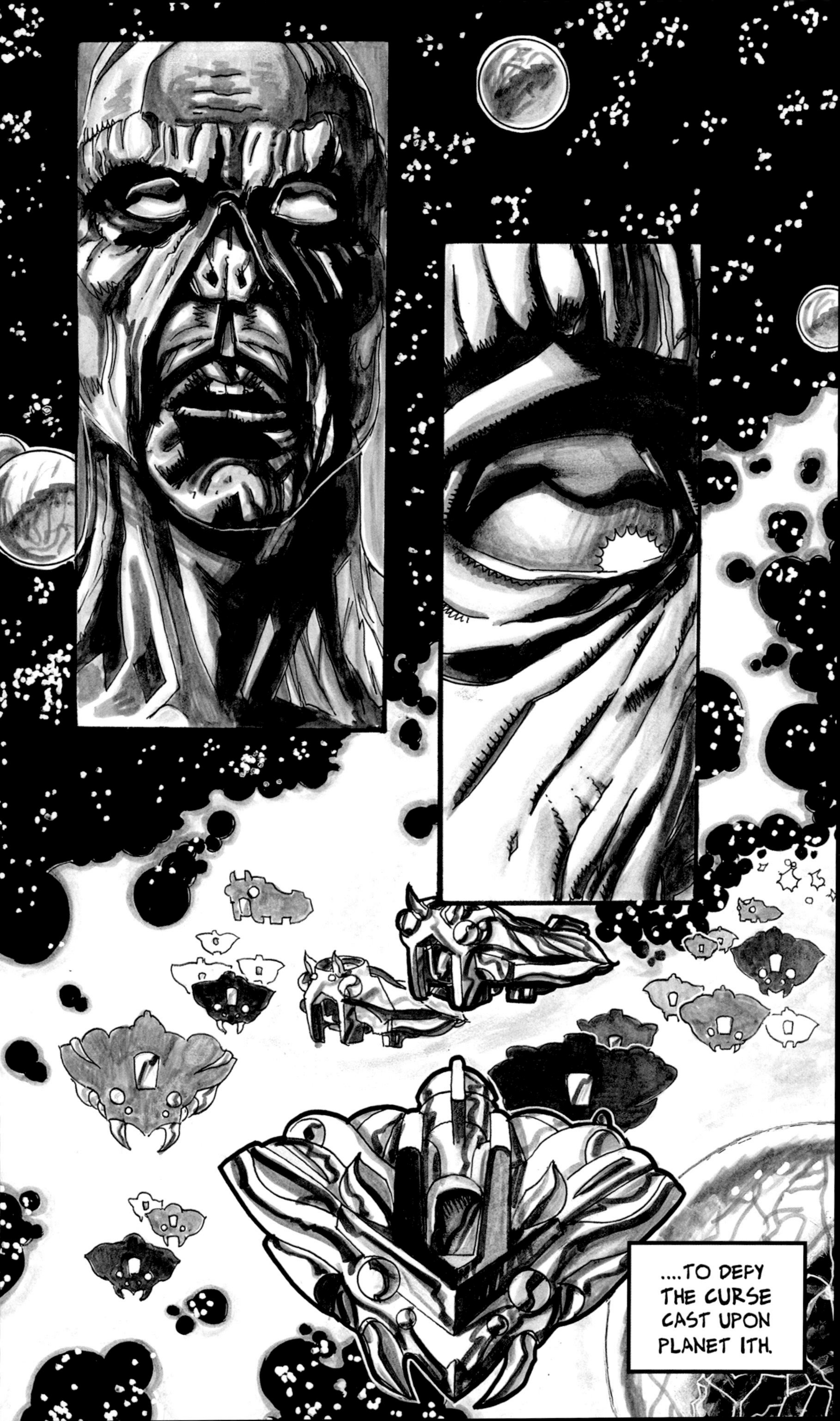
....TO DEFY THE CURSE CAST UPON PLANET ITH.

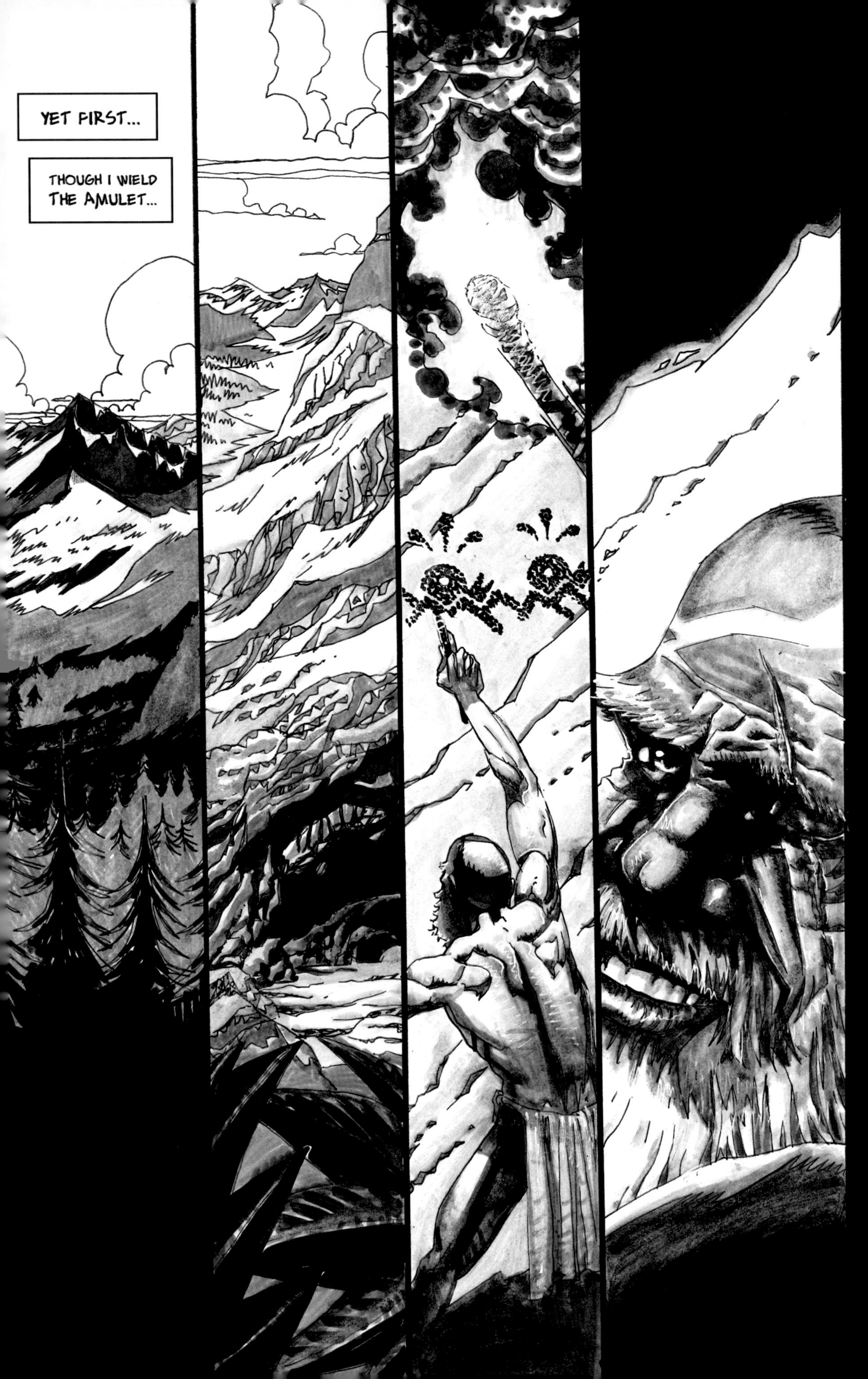
YET FIRST...
THOUGH I WIELD THE AMULET...

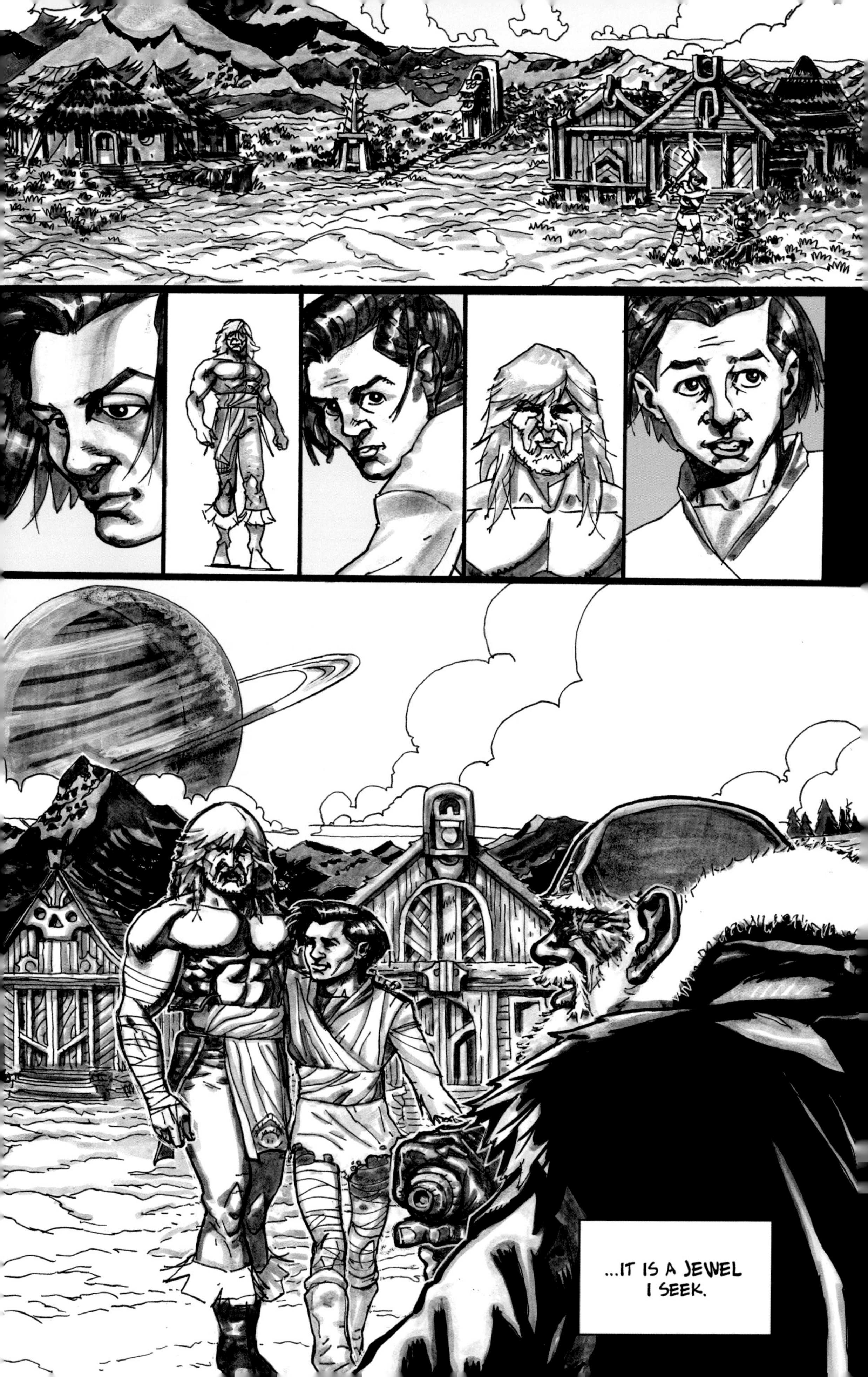
...IT IS A JEWEL I SEEK.

NOTE FROM THE AUTHOR

THANK YOU FOR READING THIS FAR!

THE NO'MADD WORLD IS ONE OF
GIANT BEASTS, VAST RUINS, EPIC BATTLES,
DISTANT LOVE, AND HEROIC DEEDS.

I TRY TO WEAVE A DREAMLIKE NARRATIVE
FOR ALL AGE READERS.

MY INTENTION IS TO CREATE A GRAPHIC NOVEL
TRILOGY OUT OF THIS WORLD.

FOLLOW US ON SOCIAL MEDIA OR FIND US AT:

NOMADD.NET

DREW

CREATOR BIOS

ANDREW KAFOURY

ANDREW IS FROM PORTLAND, OR.
HE GREW UP READING BATMAN, X-MEN, AND
TMNT. NO'MADD IS HIS FIRST
GRAPHIC NOVEL.

AKAFOURY@HOTMAIL.COM

TODD HERMAN

TODD HAS DRAWN FOR DARK HORSE,
TOP SHELF, DYNAMITE, AND NUMEROUS
OTHER PUBLISHERS THIS IS
HIS FIRST FULL BOOK DESIGN.

JEFFERSONHOUSE@YAHOO.COM

CHRIS FACCONE

CHRIS IS A PROFESSIONAL ILLUSTRATOR
WHO LIVES IN NEW JERSEY. HE IS
THE CREATOR OF SAVAGE CONQUEST.

CHRISFACCONEART.COM

ITH - A SMALL PLANET WITH TWO LANDS. THE LANDS OF ITH ARE
SEPARATED BY AN UNCONQUERABLE WALL OF STORMS AT SEA
KNOWN AS " THE CHAIN OF WRATH."

BARROX - A LAND OF WILD BEASTS AND DIVERSE TERRAIN -
IT WAS HOME TO THE AH'KEE - AND LATER THE KA'II.
IT IS OFTEN CALLED "THE ARM."

PLATU - A LAND OF JAGGED ROCKS AND PERILOUS MOUNTAINS.
DEEP UNDERGROUND ARE VOLCANIC
CELLS OF POWER - KNOWN AS "THE ORBS OF PLATU."

THE CHAIN OF WRATH - AN UNCONQUERABLE WALL OF STORMS
AT SEA - IT IS THE BARRIER THAT DIVIDES THE LANDS OF ITH.

ARIZ - THE GOD OF THE SUN - KNOWN AS "THE BRIGHT."
IT IS SAID THAT ARIZ CHASES TION - THE MOON -
IN QUEST OF HER LOVE.

TION - THE GODDESS OF THE MOON - KNOWN AS "THE DISTANT."
WORSHIPPED BY ALL - BUT ONLY A HEARTFELT
CHAMPION CAN EARN HER LOVE.

THE GLEAM OF DISTANCE - TION'S DIVINE AMULET - A WEAPON
MADE UP OF HER ESSENCE - FORGED FROM THE SURFACE
OF THE MOON. IT IS SAID: "WHOEVER WIELDS THE GLEAM
WILL RISE AS THE CHAMPION OF ITH!"

THE AH'KEE - THE ANCIENT RULERS OF PLANET ITH,
ONCE A RACE OF THINKERS WHO LIVED ALONG THE SEA.
THEY WERE LED BY KINGS - BUT SWAYED BY SORCERERS
KNOWN AS "THE MYYS."

THE STRETCH - A TIME OF PLAGUES - BROUGHT ON BY
WHAT WAS SAID TO BE THE SORCERY OF "THE MYYS."
THE AH'KEE WERE THOUGHT TO HAVE PERSIHED.
BUT IN TRUTH - THEY SAILED BENEATH THE SEA - TO PLATU.

THE ORBS OF PLATU - VOLCANIC CELLS OF POWER THAT
THE AH'KEE DISCOVERED AND USED TO
BUILD THEIR CITY - "ITO-DELL".

THE KA'II - A TRIBAL RACE WHO INHERITED PLANET ITH
AFTER THE AH'KEE DISAPPEARED. THEY
WOULD SEEK THE LOVE OF TION - AND WOULD
GO TO WAR TO EARN HER LOVE.

THE AGE OF BLOOD - WARS THAT RAGED FOR CENTURIES.
KA'II WARLORDS FOUGHT TO EARN THE LOVE OF TION,
IN ORDER TO WIELD HER DIVINE AMULET,
"THE GLEAM OF DISTANCE."

THE STEEP - A WARLORD PALACE BUILT INTO REMOTE DESERT CLIFFS.
THE WARLORDS WHO LIVED THERE DIED UNLOVED AND IN DESPAIR.
IT IS SAID TO BE HAUNTED.

THE DAYS OF CALM - WHEN THE WARS ENDED -
THE KA'II PUT DOWN THEIR BLADES TO LIVE IN PEACE,
A PEACE THAT LASTED FOR A THOUSAND YEARS.

CLENN AND YU - THE PARENTS OF NO'MADD LIVED IN A VILLAGE
CALLED "B'LINN," NEAR MOUNTAINS KNOWN AS
"THE HILLS OF STONE."

NO'MADD - HIS MOTHER DIED WHEN HE WAS AN INFANT.
LEAVING HIM WITH A WOUND THAT HE LONGED TO HEAL.
HE IS A HEARTFELT SOUL, WHO HOPES TO PROVE
WORTHY OF TION'S LOVE.

BAKK'ROLL - A RARE BEAST WHO KILLED NO'MADD'S FATHER.
WHEN NO'MADD SAW THAT SHE SOUGHT ONLY TO PROTECT HER CUBS,
HE SPARED HER, AND VOWED TO PROTECT HER BREED.
BY THIS HEARTFELT DEED, HE EARNED TION'S LOVE.

KA'SELL - TION CAME TO NO'MADD IN MORTAL FORM,
AS A WARRIOR NAMED "KA'SELL."
SHE LOVED HIM, AND CREATED A FAMILY.
YEARS LATER, TO TEST HIS WORTH,
SHE TOOK AWAY EVERYTHING THAT HE LOVED.

THE V-OR - MARAUDERS FROM A DEAD WORLD WHO LAY SIEGE
ACROSS THE STARS. THEIR RULERS SEEK
"THE ORBS OF PLATU" TO FUEL THEIR FEARSOME ARMADA.

THE MINE ON PLATU - AFTER THE V-OR INVADE THE AH'KEE CITY,
THEY BUILD A PRISON MINE, WHERE THE AH'KEE DIG FOR ORBS.
THE MINE ON PLATU IS ONE OF MANY PRISON MINES
MAINTAINED BY THE V-OR ACROSS THE GALAXY.

THE CHAMPION OF ITH - NO'MADD IS CHOSEN BY TION TO PROTECT
PLANET ITH FROM THE DREADED V-OR ARMADA.
SHE GRANTS HIM "THE GLEAM OF DISTANCE"
THAT HE MAY RISE TO PROTECT HIS WORLD.

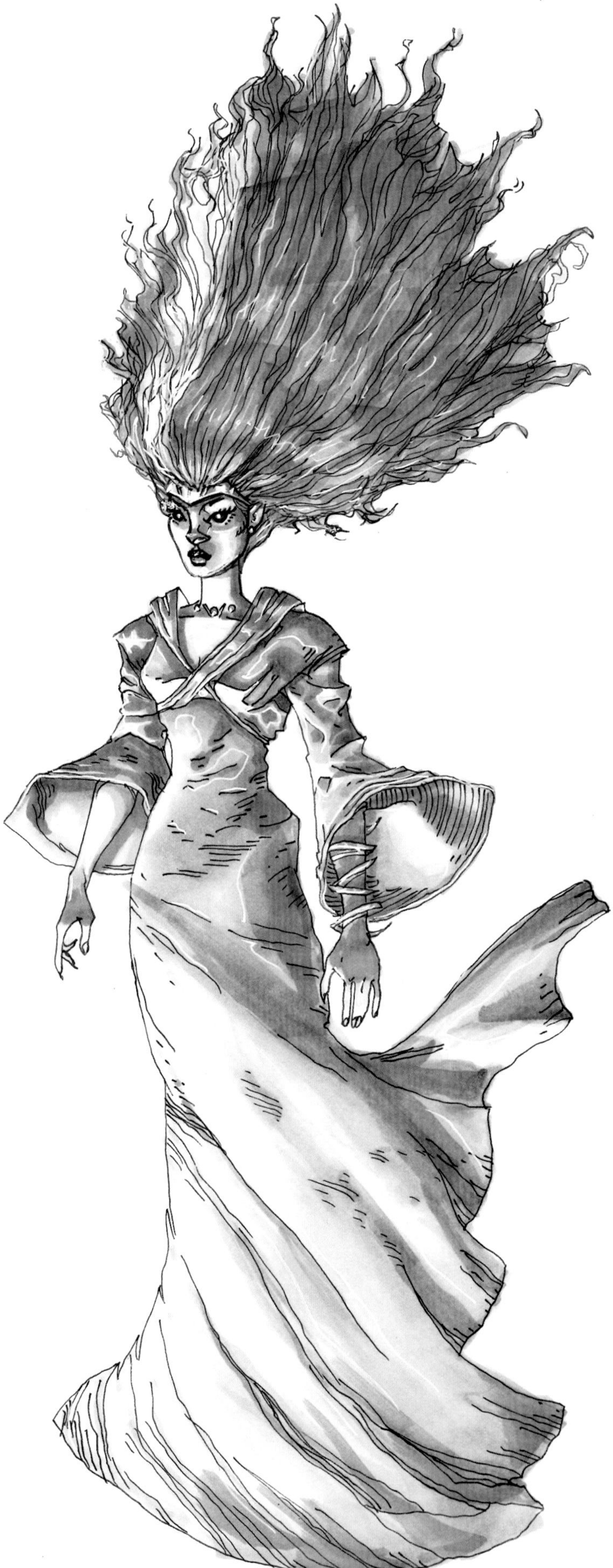

TION: THE DISTANT

SHE IS THE GODDESS OF THE MOON ~ KNOWN AS "THE DISTANT."
MORTALS SEEK HER LOVE ~ BUT SHE SHINES
JUST OUT OF THEIR REACH.

TION IS EVEN SOUGHT BY ARIZ, THE GOD OF THE SUN,
WHO IS KNOWN AS "THE BRIGHT."
BUT SHE REJECTS HIM.

MUCH OF KA'II CULTURE CENTERS AROUND TION.
THE GOAL OF KA'II WARRIORS IS TO
EARN HER LOVE.

THERE WAS ONCE A TIME KNOWN AS "THE AGE OF BLOOD"
WHERE KA'II WARLORDS WAGED WAR
TO IMPRESS HER.

TION IGNORED THEM ~ FOR ONLY A HEARTFELT
CHAMPION COULD EARN
HER LOVE.

TION HAS A DIVINE AMULET KNOWN AS
"THE GLEAM OF DISTANCE."

HER AMULET IS A WEAPON, MADE UP OF HER ESSENCE,
FORGED FROM THE SURFACE OF THE MOON.

SHOULD TION LOVE A CHAMPION, SHE WILL TEST
HIS WORTH WITH A HEART~SHATTERING
CHALLENGE.

SHOULD THE CHAMPION PASS ~ SHE WILL BESTOW UPON HIM
THE GLEAM OF DISTACE AND HE WILL RISE AS
THE CHAMPION OF ITH!

NO'MADD IS HER CHOSEN CHAMPION,
AND SHE LOVES HIM BUT
MUST DESTROY HIM.

TION COMES TO NO'MADD DISGUISED AS A MORTAL,
GIVES HIM A FAMILY, THEN SHATTERS
HIS HEART SO HE CAN CREATE
HIS DESTINY.

THROUGHOUT THE STORY THE IMAGE OF THE MOON
LOOKS DOWN ON PLANET ITH,
FOR TION WATCHES.
ALWAYS.

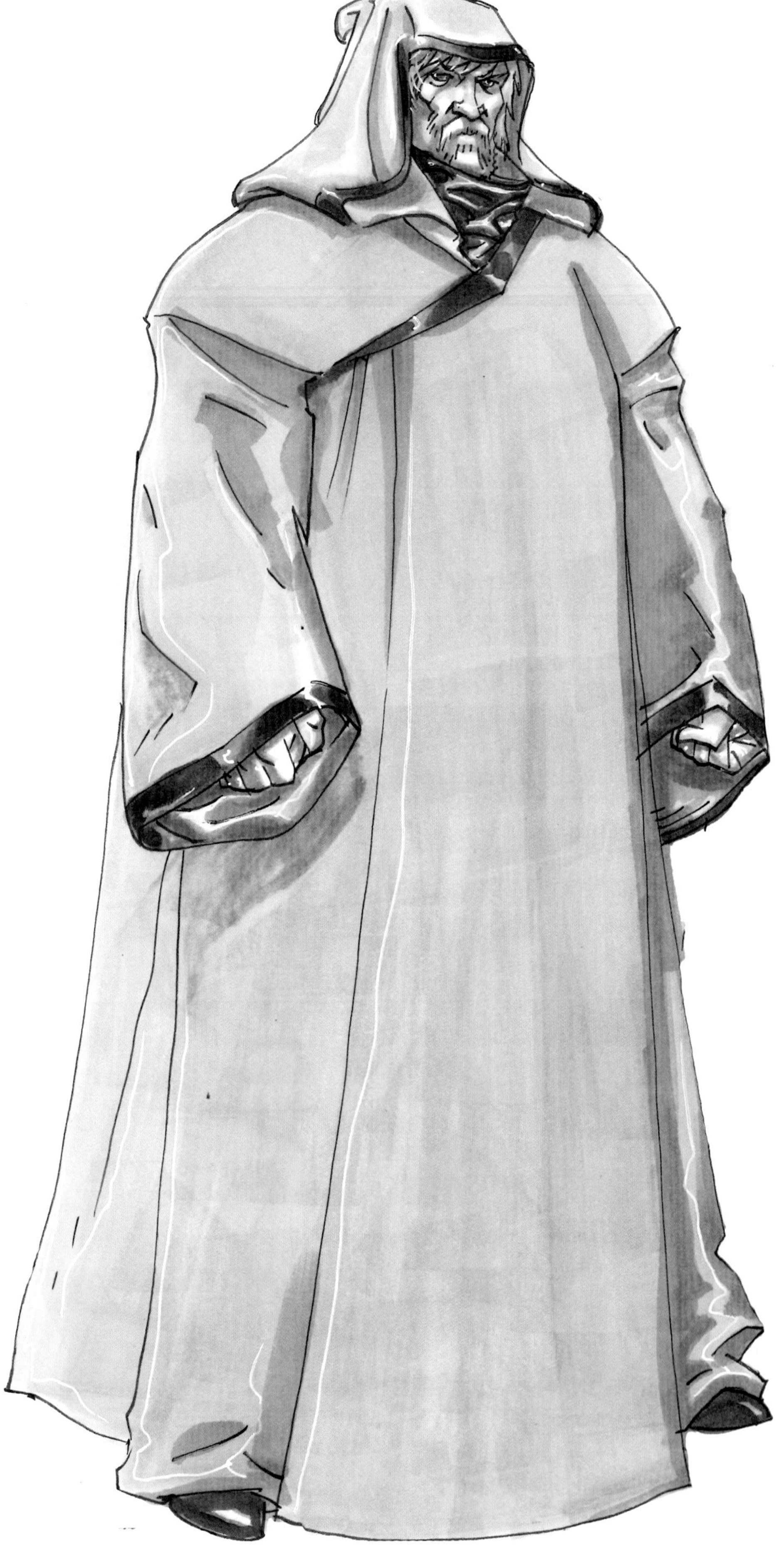

NO'MADD: LOST IN SHADOWS

IN CHAPTER ONE - OUR HERO IS SET FORTH ON A JOURNEY
ACROSS HIS PLANET IN SEARCH OF ALIEN INTRUDERS,
WHO ARE MYSTERIOUS AND TECHNOLOGICALLY ADVANCED.

UNKNOWN TO NO'MADD, HIS JOURNEY IS A TEST BY THE
GODDESS TION - TO SEE IF OUR HERO CAN
ENDURE IN SPITE OF LOSS, TO RISE AS
THE CHAMPION OF ITH.

LOST, ALONE, AND FRIGHTENED, NO'MADD IS
UNAWARE THAT HE IS BEING WATCHED
OVER BY TION.

WHEN WE FIRST MEET NO'MADD, HE IS COVERED IN A HOODED CLOAK.
THROUGHOUT THE STORY, HE "SHEDS LAYERS,"
PHYSICALLY AND MENTALLY.

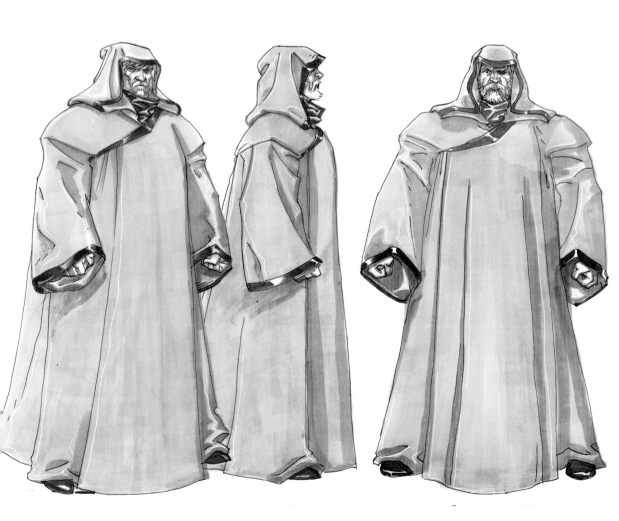

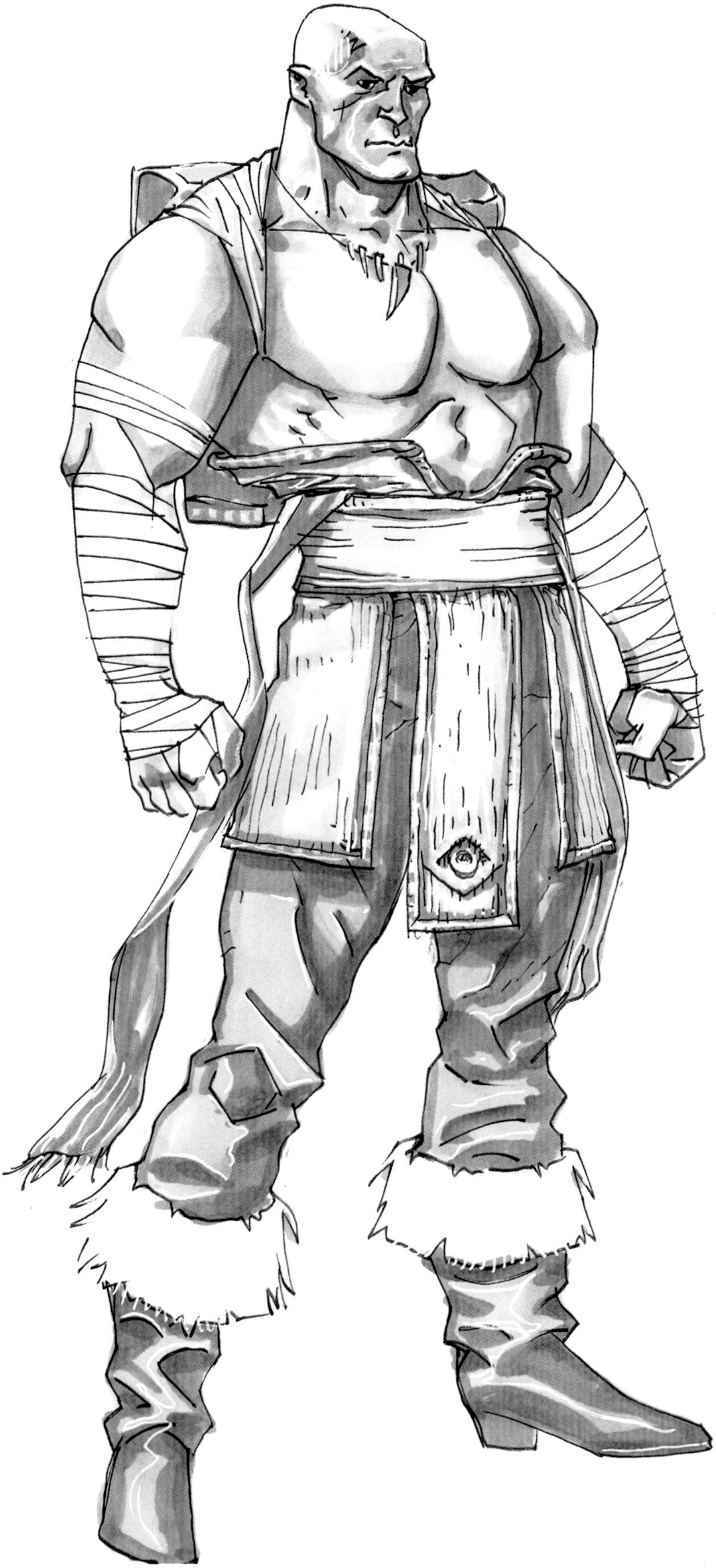

NO'MADD: SET FOR BATTLE

IN CHAPTER TWO - NO'MADD HAS JOURNEYED TO THE COAST, BUILT A HUT, SHAVED HIS FACE AND HEAD, REMOVED HIS CLOAK, AND MADE A NECKLACE WITH ANIMAL TEETH.

HE SHEDS THE LAYERS OF HIS PAST TO START OVER WITH NEW INSIGHT, DETERMINED TO SOMEHOW CROSS THE SEA AND FIND HIS ENEMIES ON THE LAND OF PLATU.

OR HERO IS HAUNTED BY THE BETRAYAL OF HIS WIFE, AND BY HIS BELIEF THAT HE IS NOT A CHAMPION WORTHY OF TION.

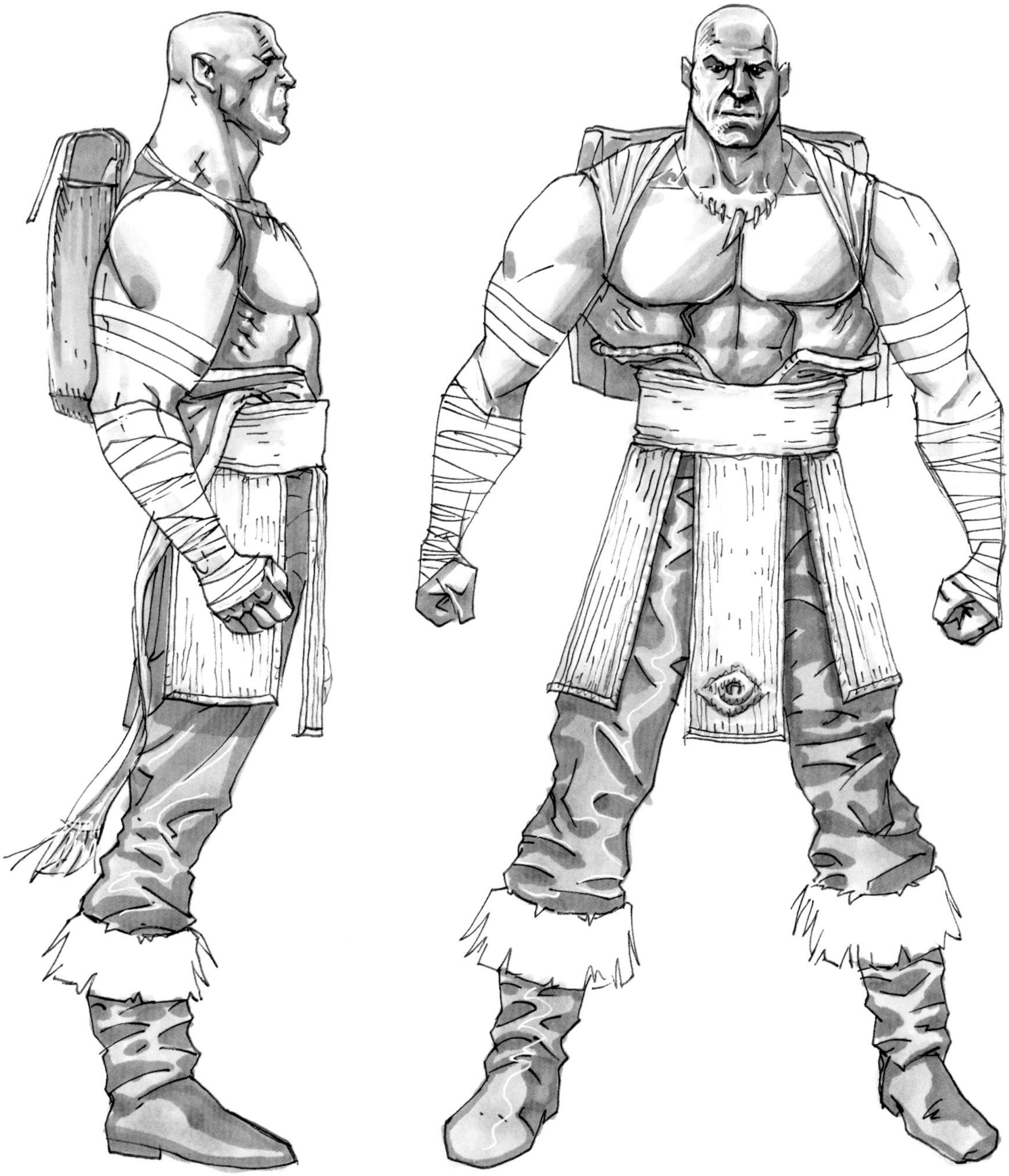

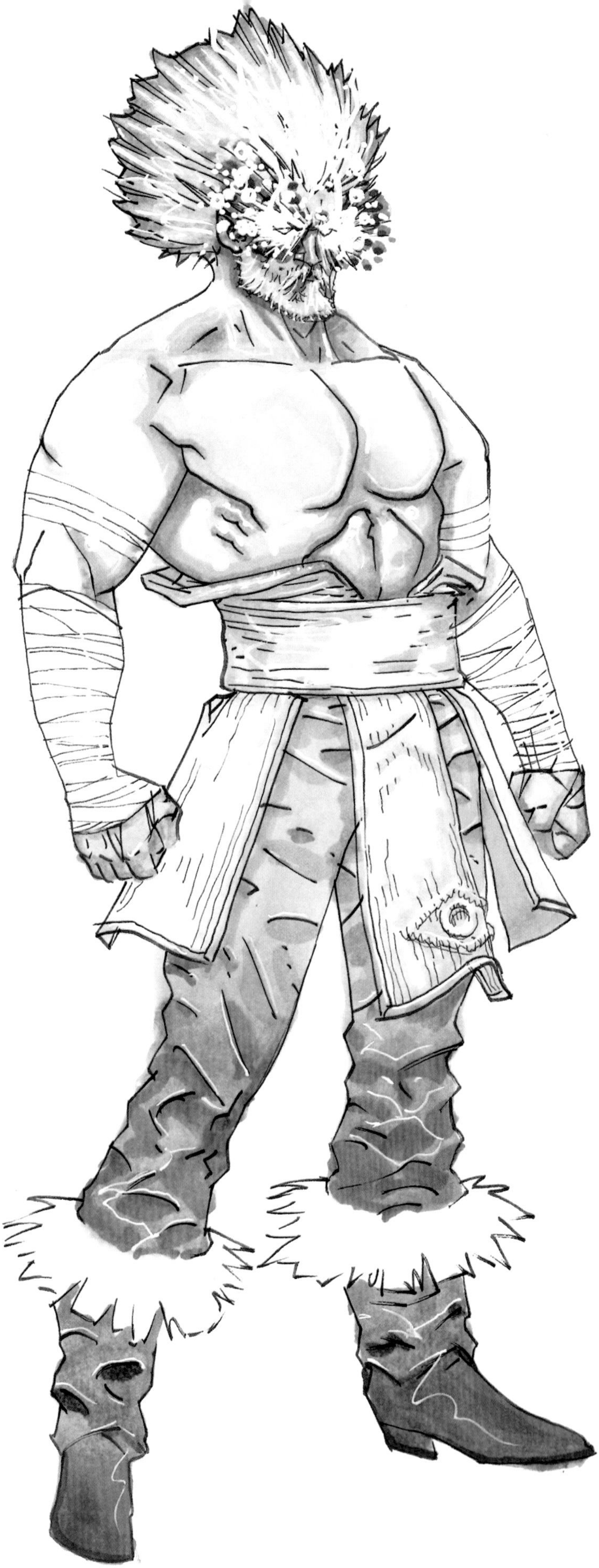

NO'MADD: THE CHAMPION OF ITH

IN CHAPTER THREE - OUR HERO PROVES HIS WORTH TO THE GODDESS TION
AND IS GRANTED HER DIVINE AMULET - A WEAPON KNOWN AS
"THE GLEAM OF DISTANCE."

THE AMULET MERGES WITH HIS BODY, AND NOW NO'MADD
IS A DEMI-GOD, THE PROTECTOR OF PLANET ITH.
HIS POWERS ARE SEEMINGLY ENDLESS.

BUT HIS WEAKNESS IS TIME -
HE NEEDS REST TO RECHARGE HIS MIGHT.

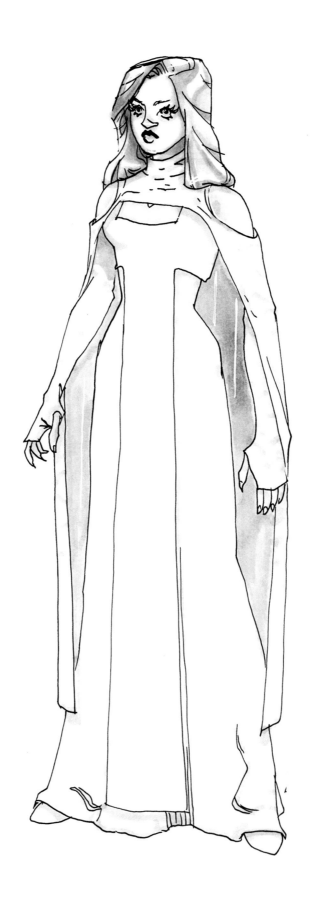

KA'SELL: THE WALKING MOON

WHEN THE GODDESS OF THE MOON - TION - CHOOSES TO TEST NO'MADD,
SHE COMES TO HIM DISGUISED AS A MORTAL WARRIOR -
AND CALLS HERSELF "KA'SELL."

KA'SELL IS OLDER, WISER, AND A BETTER FIGHTER THAN NO'MADD.
SHE LOVES HIM AND GIVES HIM A SON
WHOM SHE HELPS TO RAISE.

NO'MADD DOES NOT KNOW THAT SHE IS THE GODDESS TION -
SO WHEN KA'SELL BETRAYS HIM IN CHAPTER ONE,
HE ENDURES UNBEARABLE LOSS.

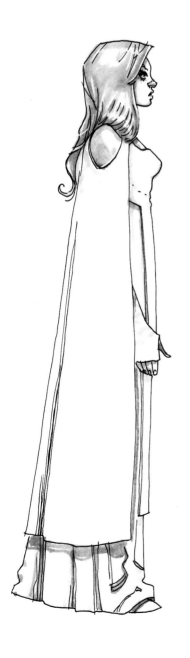
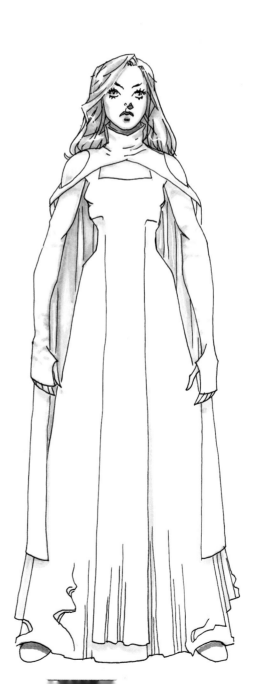

TARON: THE HEIR OF DISTANCE

THE SON OF NO'MADD HAS A DESTINY THAT REMAINS UNCLEAR, HIS MOTHER (KA'SELL) IS REALLY THE GODDESS TION - SO SECRET POWERS STIR WITHIN HIM.

THE SEQUEL IS FROM TARON'S POINT OF VIEW - AFTER GROWING UP WITHOUT HIS FATHER, THEY REUNITE.

HE IS THEN TOLD THAT HE MUST BREAK FORTH INTO THE WORLD ON HIS OWN.

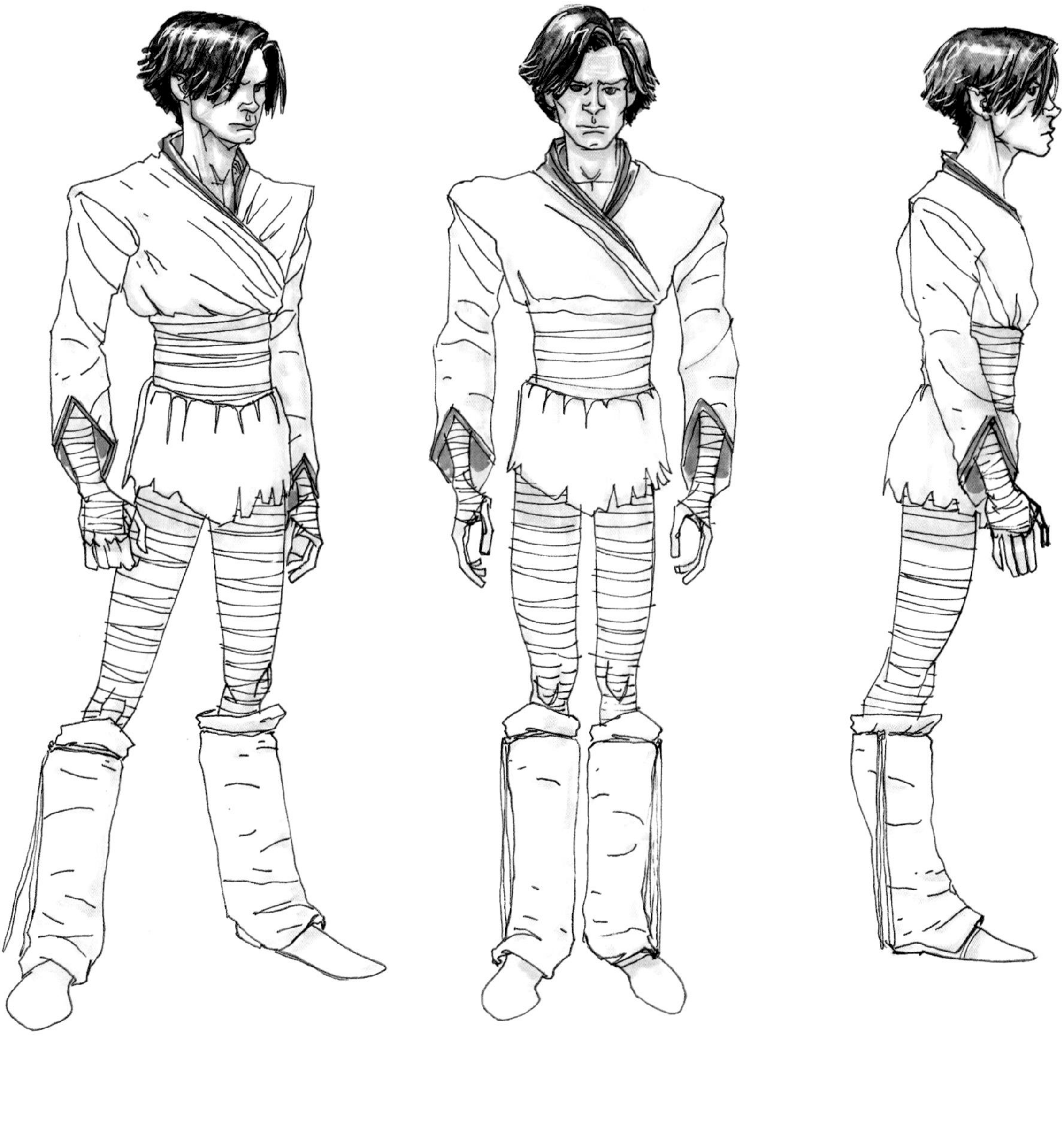

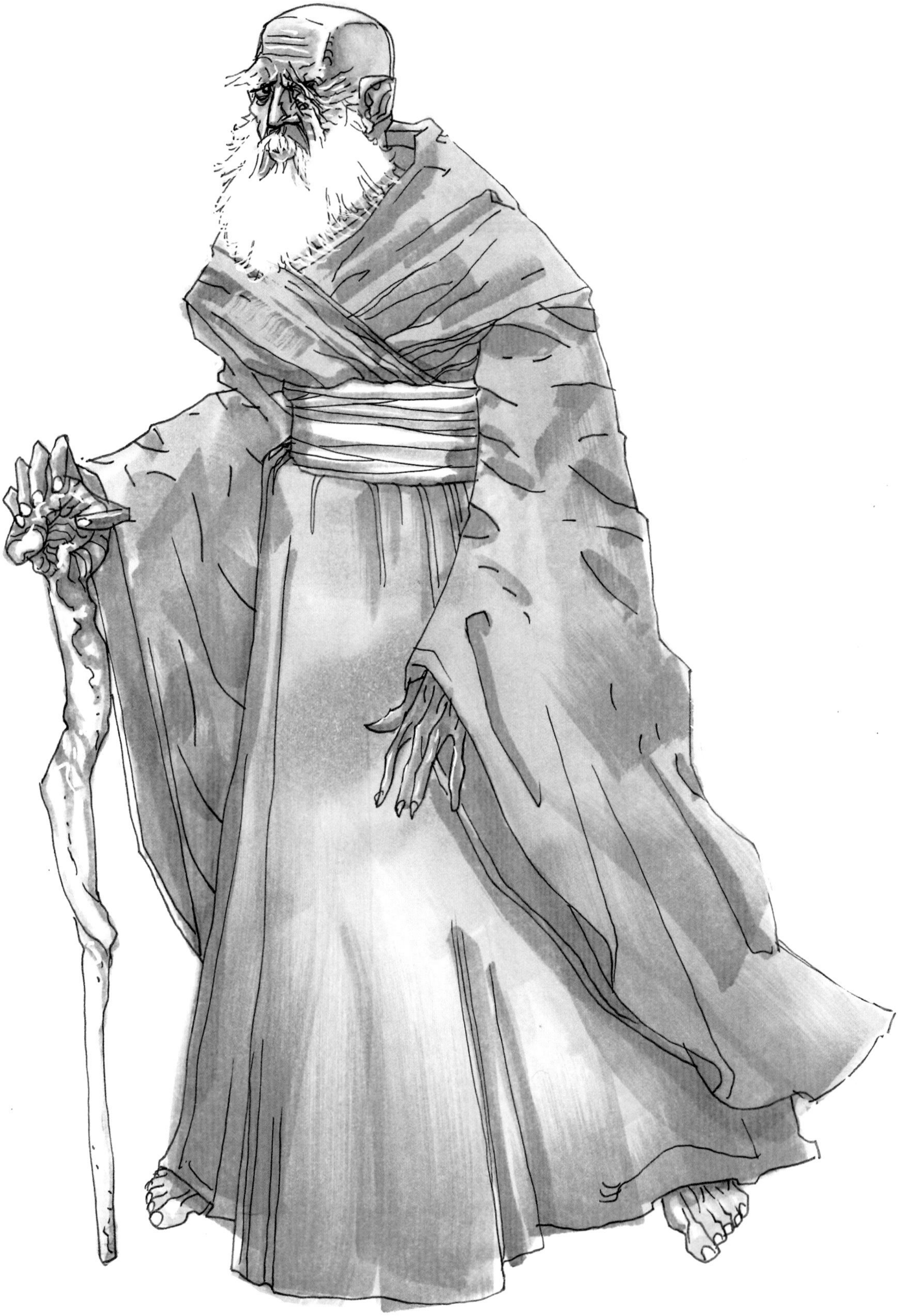

WHISPERS: HERMIT OF THE STONES

WHISPERS IS A HERMIT WHO LIVES IN A CAVE FAR FROM
NO'MADD'S VILLAGE; THE FULL EXTENT
OF HIS POWERS IS UNKNOWN.

WHISPERS IS A KA'II SEER – WHO GAVE AN EYE TO TION
FOR THE GIFT OF FUTURE SIGHT.

YET THE FUTURE IS NOT WRITTEN – SO HE CAN ONLY
"WHISPER" INTO THE EAR OF FATE.

HE IS THE "MERLIN" OF PLANET ITH,
AN UNCANNY FIGURE WHO ONLY LEAVES HIS CAVE
IN TIMES OF CRISIS.

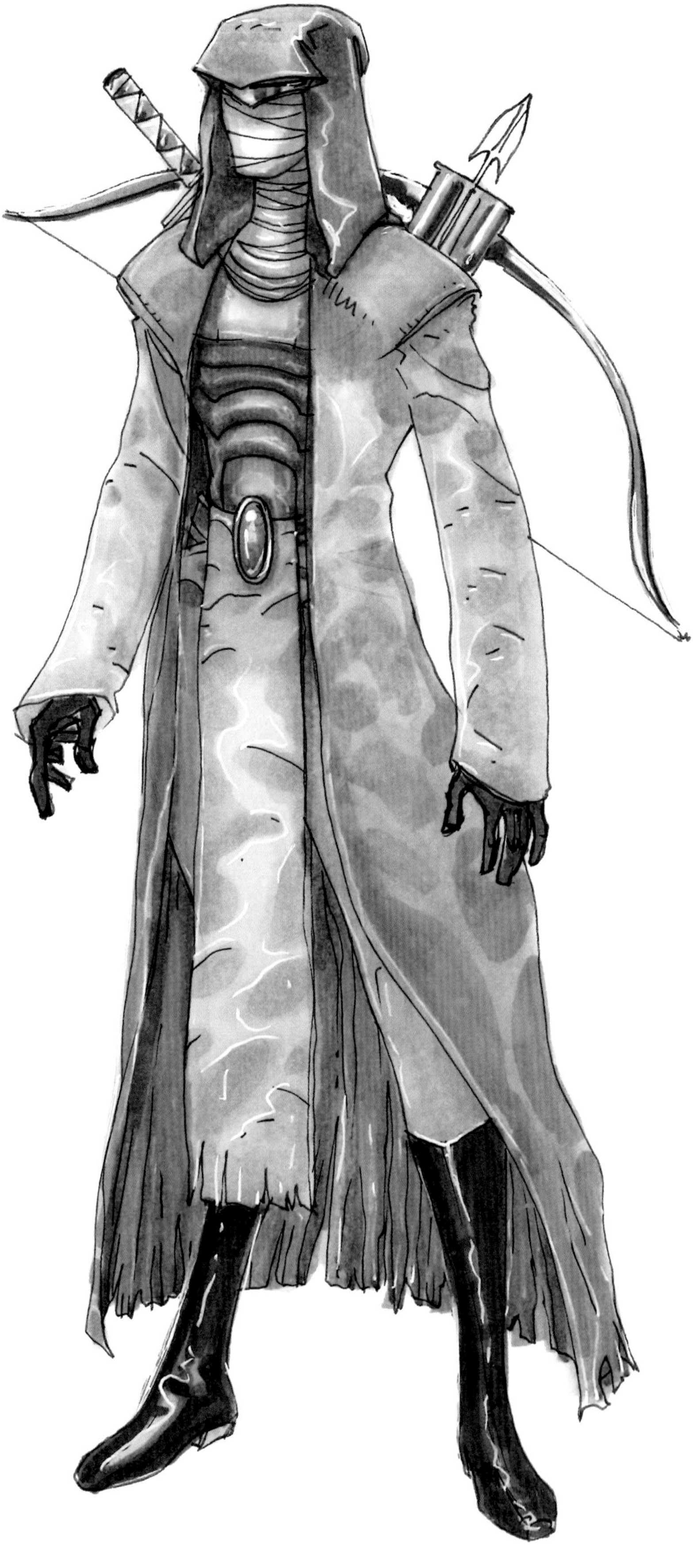

WARLORD: GHOST OF THE STEEP

LONG AGO THE KA'II WARLORDS WENT TO WAR BECAUSE THEY
THOUGHT A SHOW OF MIGHT WOULD EARN TION'S
DIVINE AMULET...BUT THEY WERE WRONG.

CENTURIES LATER ~ TION FALLS IN LOVES WITH NO'MADD
AND SHE SETS A SERIES OF EVENTS INTO
MOTION THAT WILL TEST HIS WORTH AS
THE CHAMPION OF ITH.

THE WARLORD GHOST IS REALLY TION ~ DISGUISED AS KA'SELL ~
DISGUISED AS A WARLORD. FOR TO TEST NO'MADD,
SHE MUST FIRST MAKE HIM CONFRONT
THE FUTURE, PRESENT, AND PAST.

BRUMM - THE HIDDEN SPIRIT

WHISPERS TELLS NO'MADD "THE TALE OF BRUMM,"
A DOOMED HERO WHO WAS CURSED BY A HAG
TO SHRINK OUT OF EXISTENCE.

BRUMM FOUGHT TO BREAK THE CURSE - BUT FAILED.
DESPITE HIS DEATH - THE TALE OF BRUMM TEACHES
THAT CHAMPIONS ENDURE IN SPITE OF LOSS.

FOR THE KA'II BELIEVE THAT BRUMM'S SPIRIT HIDES INSIDE
THE SOULS OF CHAMPIONS.

(BRUMM IS BASED ON RICHARD MATHESON'S
"THE INCREDIBLE SHRINKING MAN.")

BAKK'ROLL - THE SACRED FANG

BAKK'ROLLS ARE THE SACRED BEASTS OF PLANET ITH -
TO SEE ONE IS A SIGN THAT THE GODS
ARE WATCHING OVER YOU.

THE BAKK'ROLL IS A WILD ANIMAL WITH NO
COMPASSION TOWARDS OUR HERO.

WHEN NO'MADD'S FATHER IS KILLED ON A HUNT
AN ENRAGED YOUNG NO'MADD FORGES HIS AX
AND EMBARKS TO FIND THE KILLER!

NO'MADD THEN DISCOVERS THAT THE BAKK'ROLL
IS A MOTHER WHO ACTED ONLY TO
DEFEND HER CUBS

NO'MADD UNDERSTANDS THE BAKK'ROLL, FOR WHEN HE WAS A CHILD
HE LOST HIS MOTHER. HE CHOOSES TO SPARE
THE BAKK'ROLL, AND TO FOREVER PROTECT
HER BREED.

THIS HEARTFELT DEED IS HIS FIRST ACT AS A CHAMPION -
AND IT CATCHES THE EYE OF TION.
SHE WILL SOON COME TO HIM
AS KA'SELL.

FOREVERMORE - NO'MADD AND BAKK'ROLL ARE
LINKED IN DESTINY.

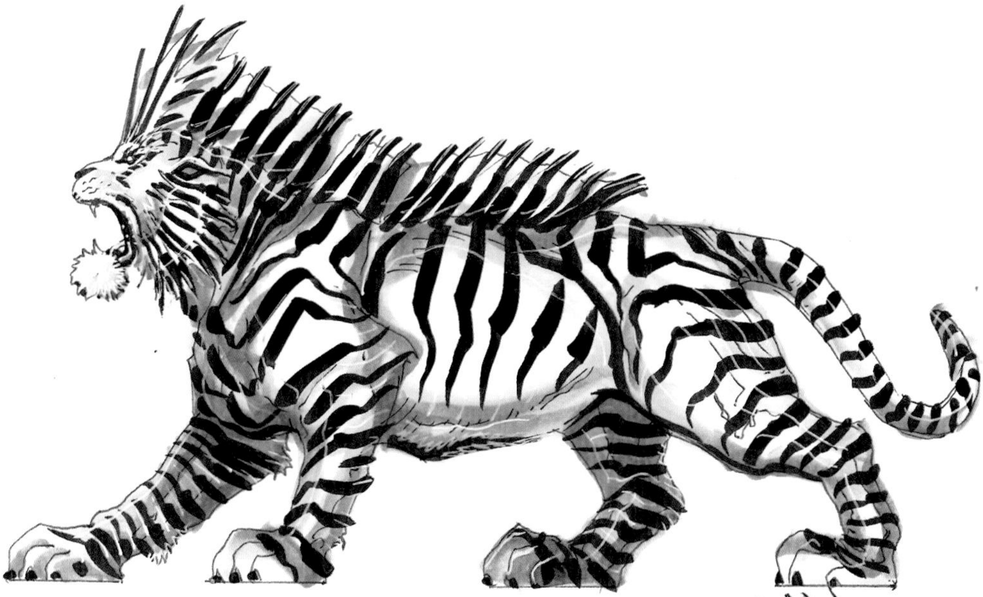

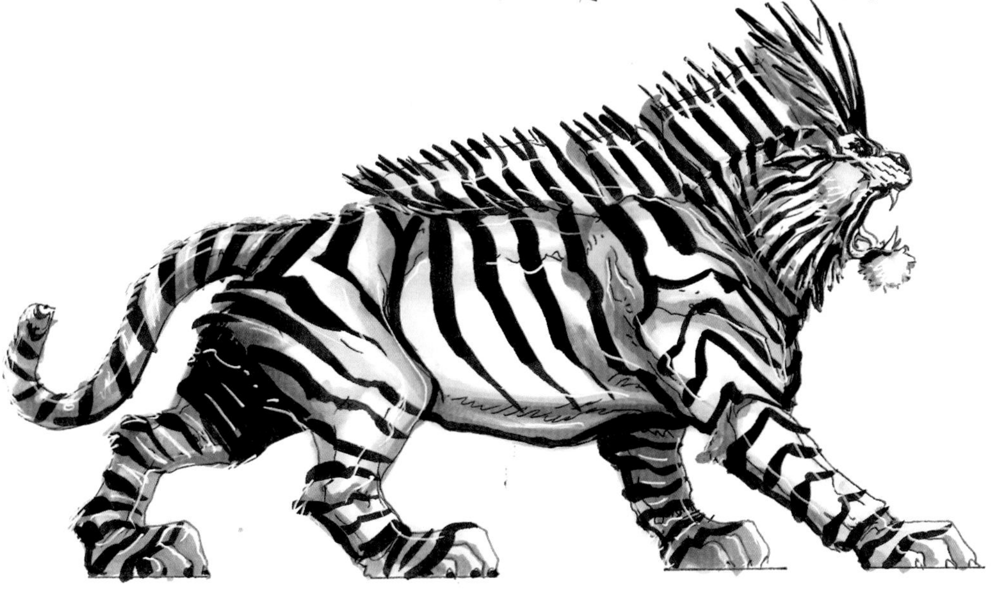

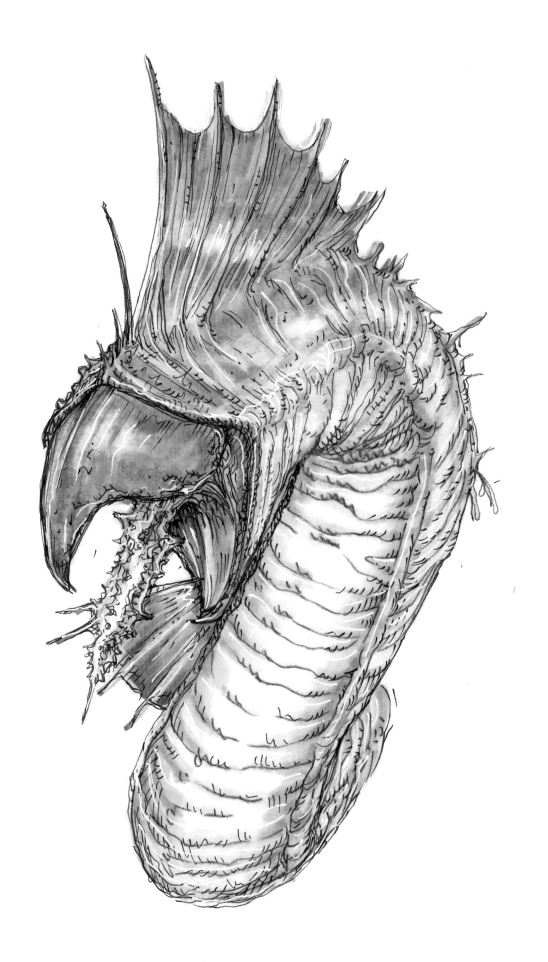

VESP – BANE OF THE TIDES

THE VESP IS A PATIENT PREDATOR
OF THE SEA AND OF THE LAND.

THEY CAN HOLD THEIR BREATH UNDERWATER
FOR HOURS, AND THEY OFTEN LURK
BENEATH THE SAND.

THEY CAN DETECT WHEN MOVEMENT IS NEARBY,
AND IF THE PREY IS BIG ENOUGH,
THEY WILL STRIKE.

IN CHAPTER TWO, WHEN NO'MADD BATTLES A VESP,
OUR HERO IS LUCKY THAT THE CREATURE
IS YOUNG.

A FULLY GROWN VESP WOULD HAVE DEVOURED
NO'MADD.

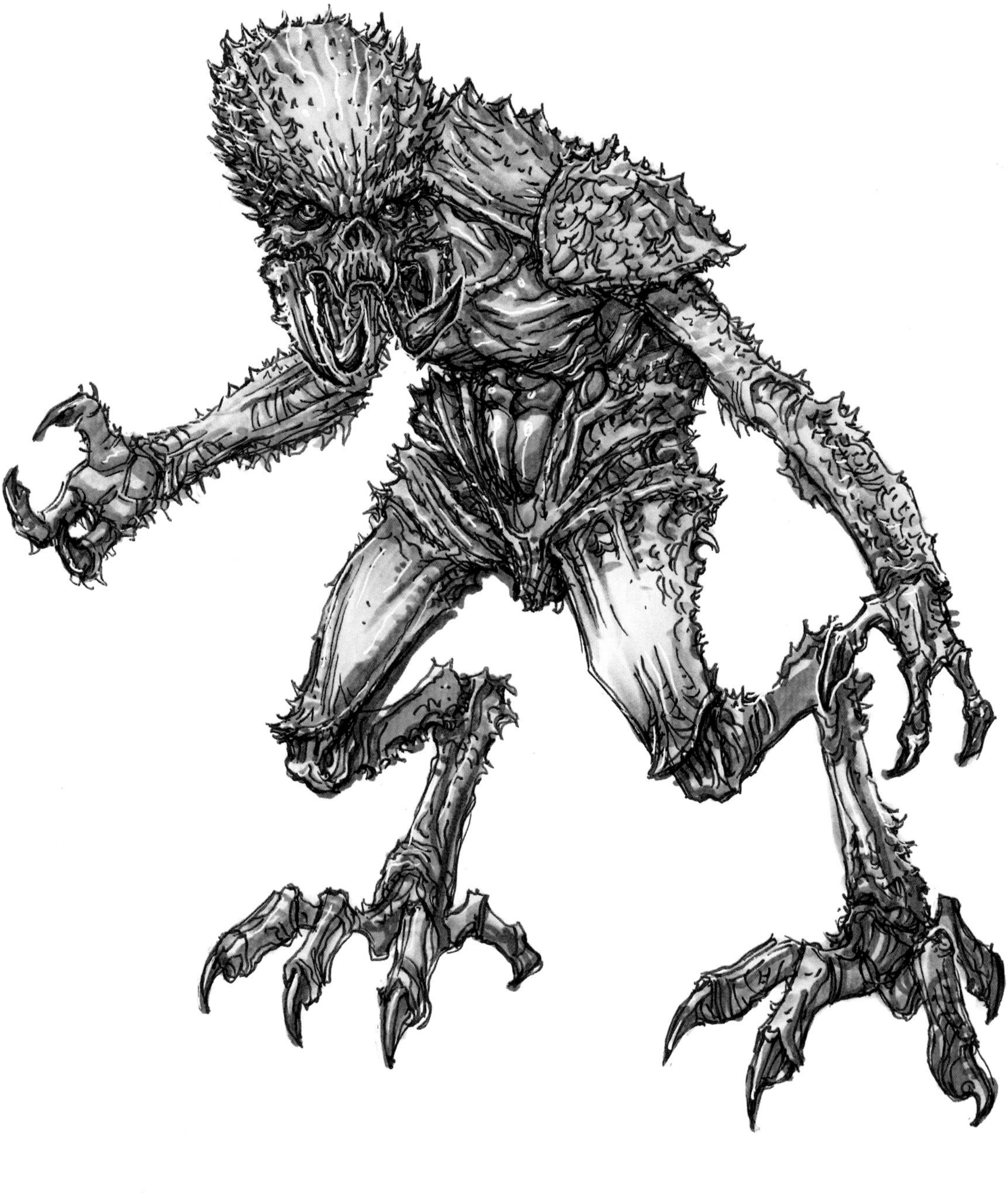

GNATZ: SWARM OF THE PIT

THESE BEASTS ARE RAVENOUS NIGHT HUNTERS
THAT LURK IN A DESERT REALM
KNOWN AS "THE PIT."

LITTLE IS KNOWN OF THE GNATZ, OTHER THEN
THAT THEIR MINDS ARE SMALL AND
THEY ONLY ATTACK IN DEFENSE
OR FOR FOOD.

IN CHAPTER ONE, WHEN NO'MADD FINDS THAT THE
GNATZ HAVE BESET THE WARLORD PALACE,
HE DOES NOT KNOW THAT THEY ARE
UNDER SIEGE BY A RIVAL HIVE.

OUR HERO FINDS THE HEAD OF AN ENEMY GNAT
STUCK ON A PIKE, AND SOON SPOTS
GNAT SOLDIERS AS THEY GO ABOUT
THEIR DUTY.

TION TRICKS THE GNATZ INTO BATTLE WITH NO'MADD
IN ORDER TO WEAKEN HIM BEFORE SHE
CONFRONTS HIM.

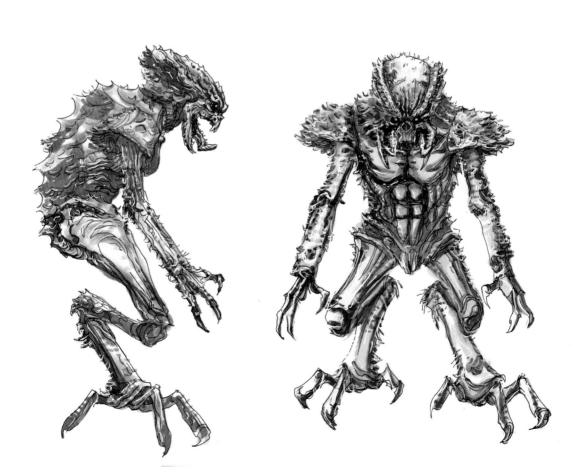

SWOTH: THE GENTLE STEED

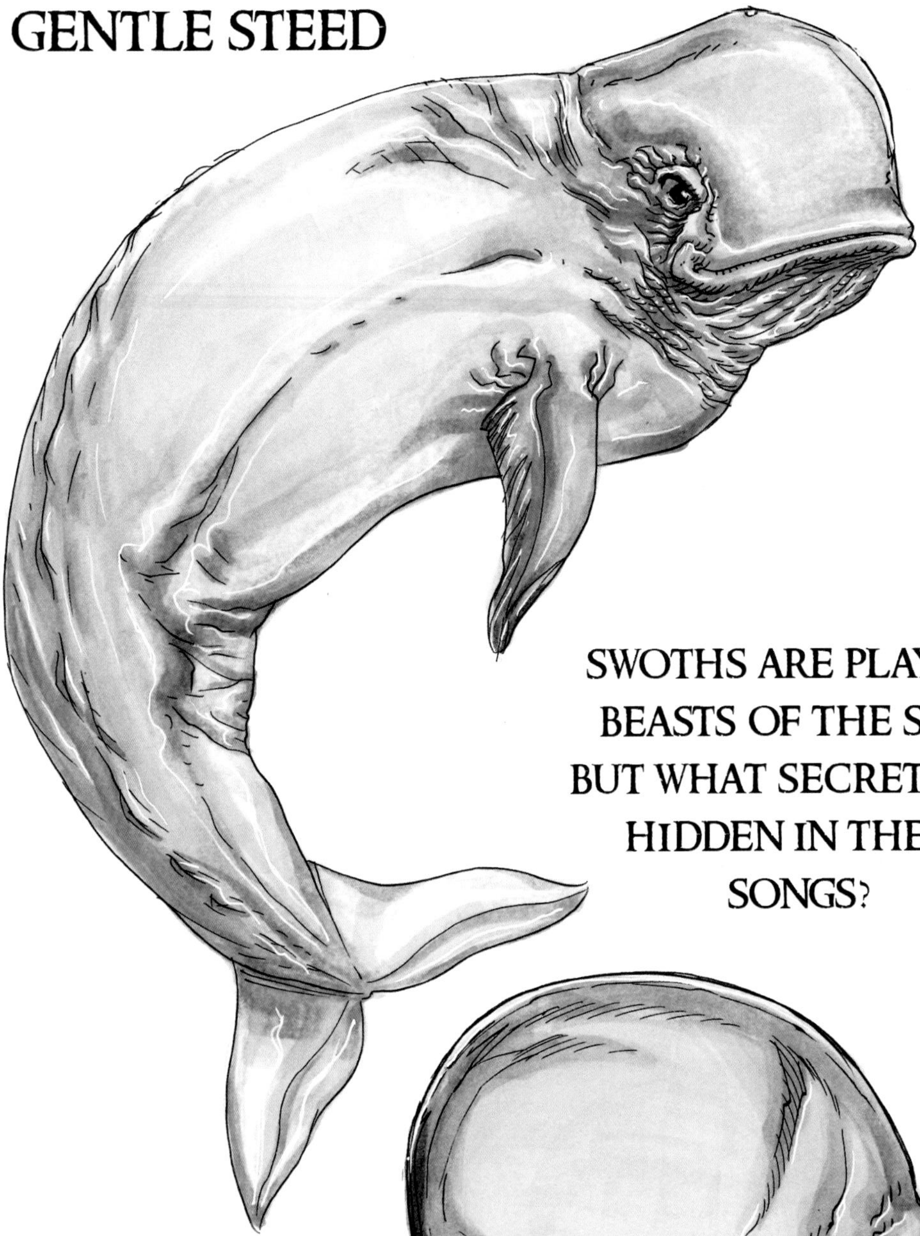

SWOTHS ARE PLAYFUL BEASTS OF THE SEA - BUT WHAT SECRETS ARE HIDDEN IN THEIR SONGS?

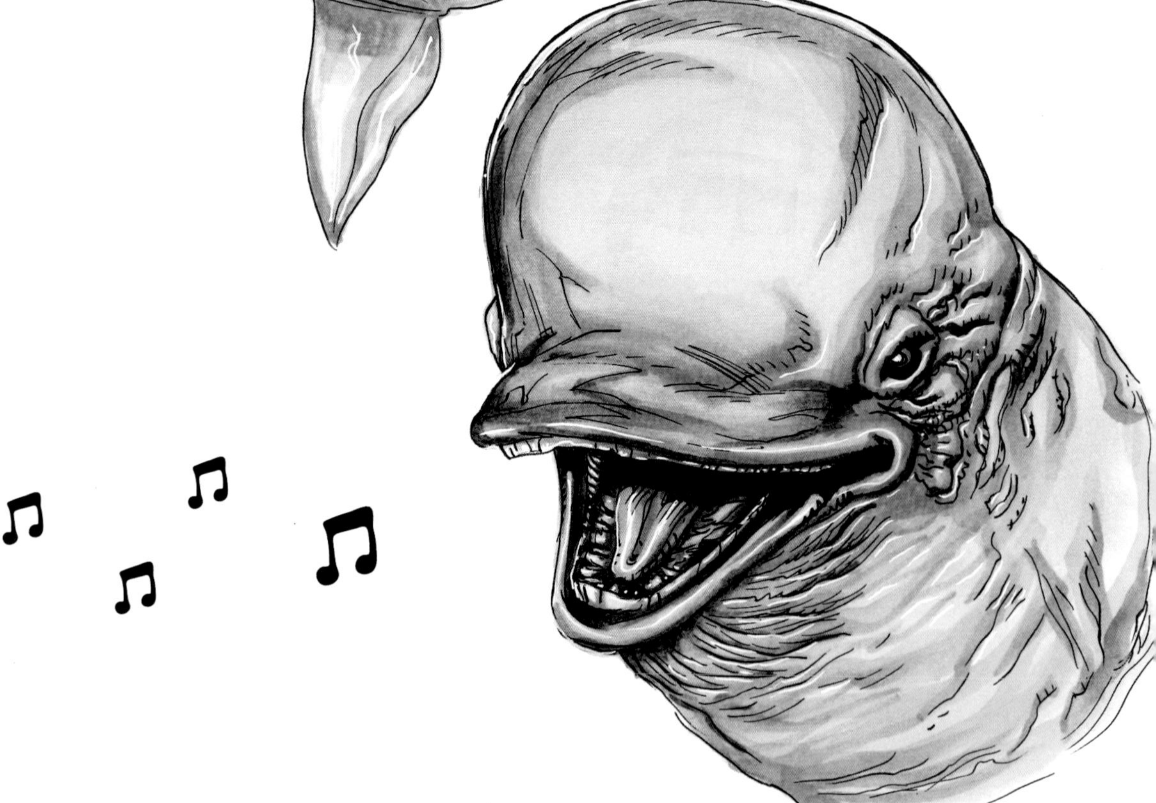

META-WEN THE AH'KEE KING

(CHARACTER APPEARS IN BOOK TWO)

META-WEN IS A CONQURED KING, WHO ONLY TOOK BACK HIS THRONE AFTER NO'MADD SAVED HIS CITY.

TODAY - HE IS HAUNTED BY THE SOULS OF THE AH'KEE WHO PERISHED IN THE V-OR INVASION.

IT IS SAID HE IS SICK - AND HAS BEEN SEDUCED BY THE SPELLS OF AN ANCIENT SORCERESS.

CAN NO'MADD REPAIR HIS BROKEN EMPIRE?

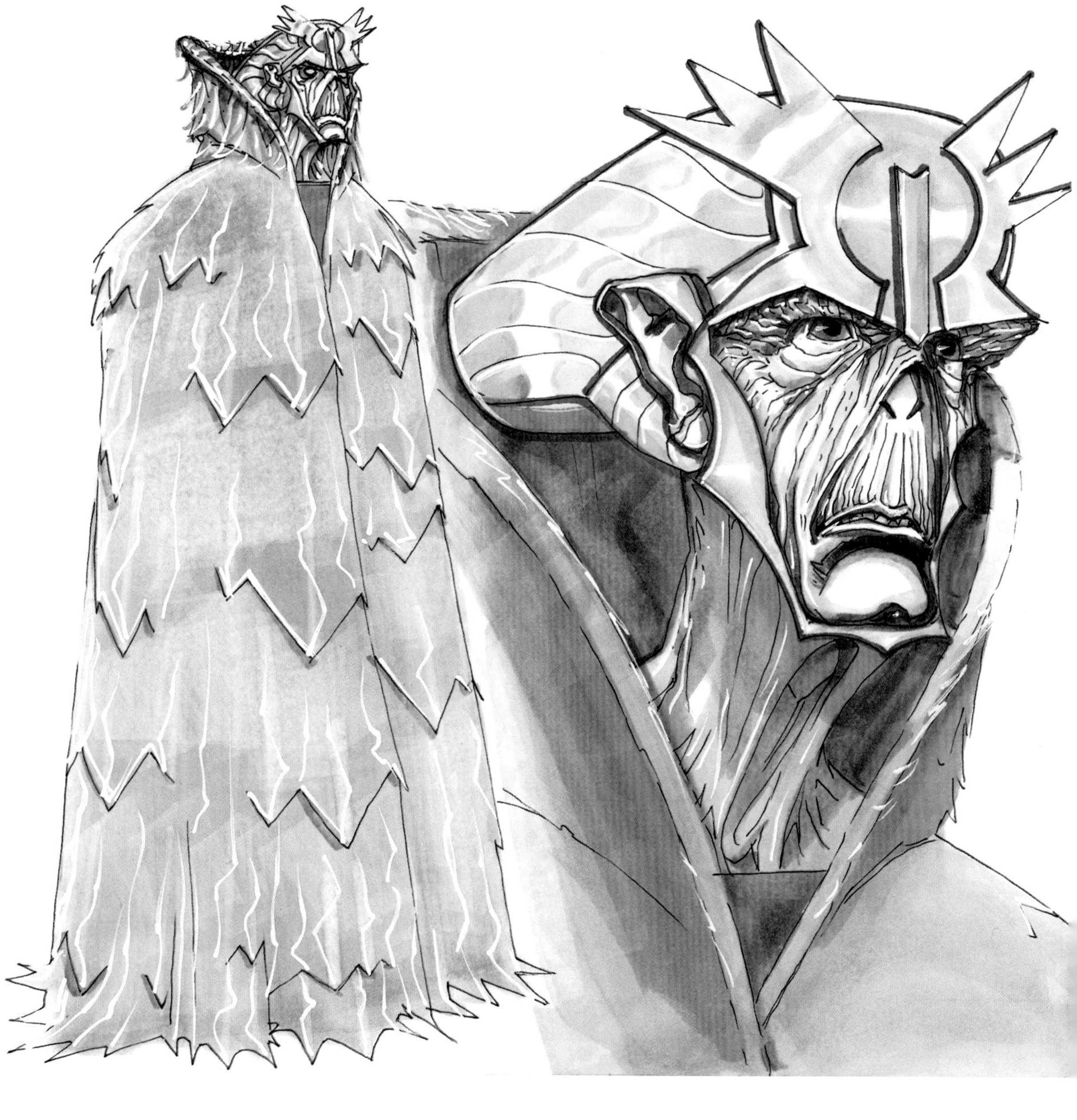

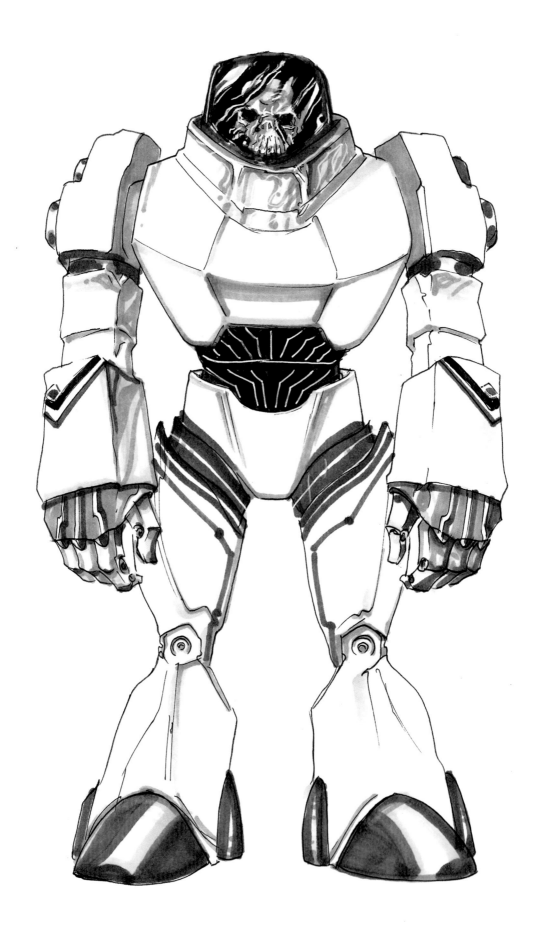

OVERLORD - MASTER OF THE MINE

THE OVERLORD IS A SLAVER ROBOT,
PROGRAMMED TO CONTROL
OR DESTROY.

THIS ROBOT CONTROLS THE PRISON MINE
WHERE AH'KEE SLAVES MINE FOR
THE ORBS OF PLATU.

WHEN NO'MADD ENCOUNTERS THE OVERLORD,
HE SHATTERS HIS AX ON ITS BODY,
AND HE SEEMS DOOMED!

FOR NO'MADD'S TRIBAL WEAPON CANNOT
DEFEND HIM AGAINST ADVANCED
ALIEN TECHNOLOGY.

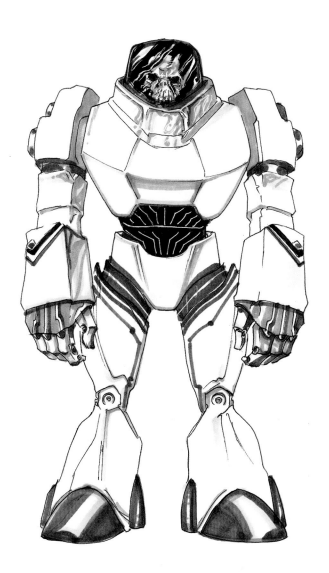
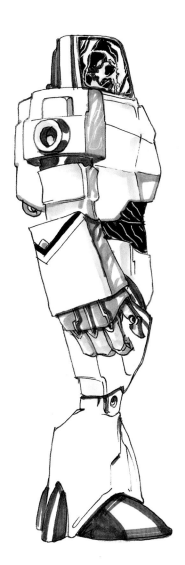

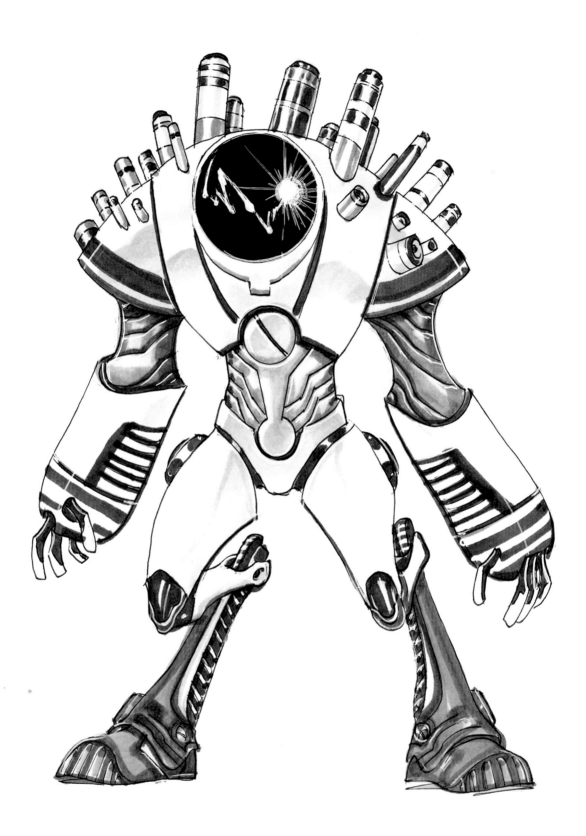

V-OR - THE INTRUDERS

AFTER THEIR HOMEWORLD WAS DESTROYED,
THESE CLEVER CREATURES BUILT
A FEARSOME ARMADA.

FOR EONS THEY HAVE LAID SIEGE
ACROSS THE STARS IN
SEARCH OF FUEL.

THE V-OR MAINTAIN PRISON MINES,
ON MANY PLANETS, USING WORMHOLES
TO SEEK NEW WORLDS
TO ATTACK.

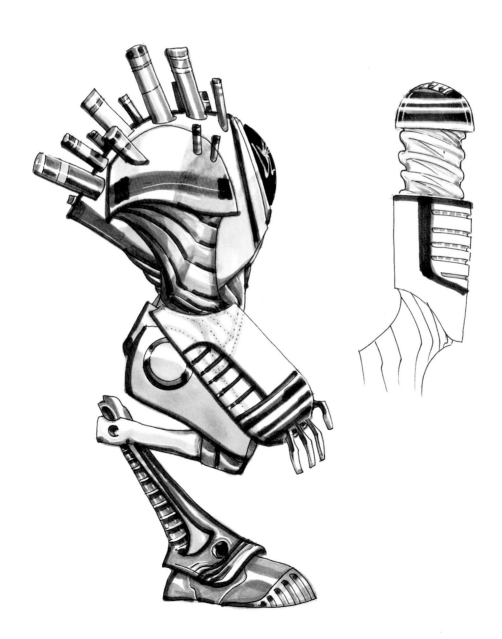

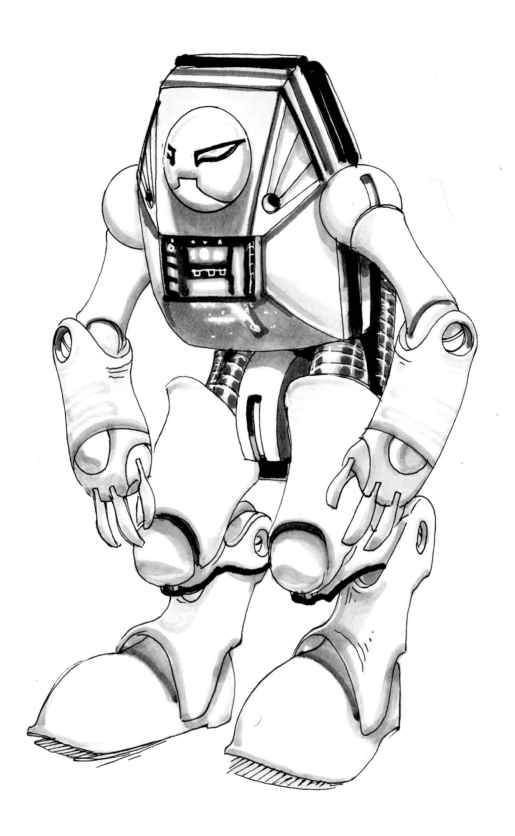

V-OR ~ CARGO BOTS

CARGO BOTS ARE DEADLY DROIDS WITH BUILT
IN WEAPONRY.

THE V-OR SEND CARGO BOTS ON MISSIONS
TO RETRIEVE FUEL.

ONE OF THESE DROIDS ATTACKS OUR HERO
WITH AN ENERGY WHIP, AND
IS DESTROYED.

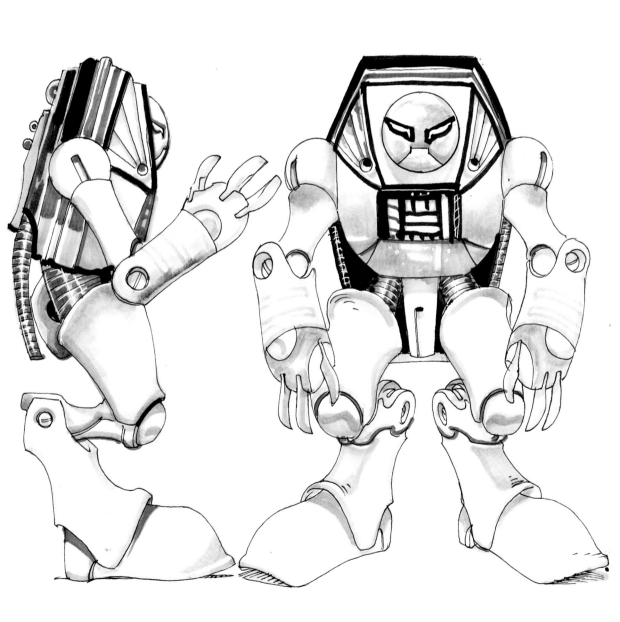

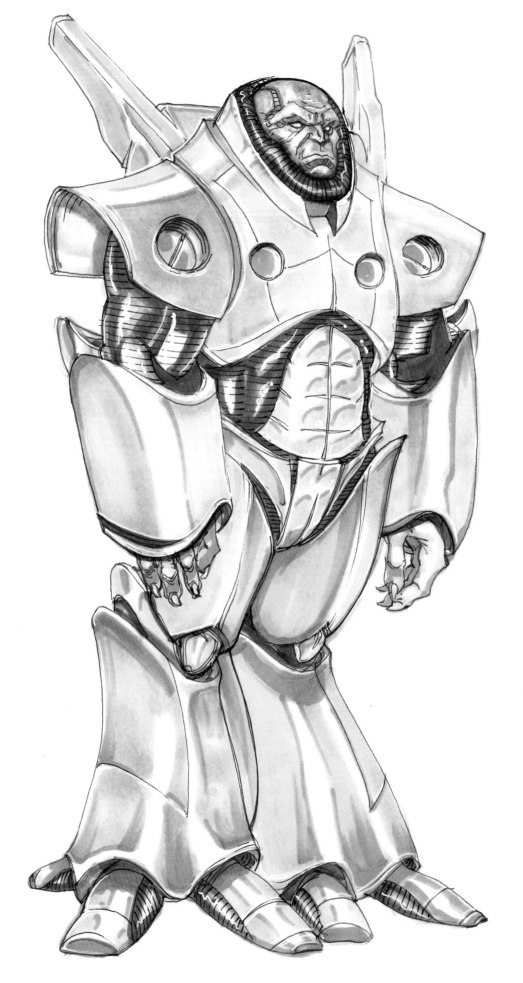

V-OR ~ CYBORG GRUNTS

WHEN THE V-OR RULERS SEND CARGO SHIPS
TO RETRIEVE STOLEN FUEL ~ THEY ALSO
SEND CYBORG GRUNTS.

THESE MEAN SPIRITED SOLDIERS ARE
INTEGRATED TO THEIR ARMOR,
AND LIVE ONLY FOR BATTLE.

WHEN NO'MADD ENTERS THE V-OR CARGO SHIP,
HE CONFRONTS TWO CYBORG GRUNTS
AND DEFEATS THEM.

IF NO'MADD HAD NOT HAD TION'S AMULET,
OUR HERO WOULD HAVE
BEEN CRUSHED.

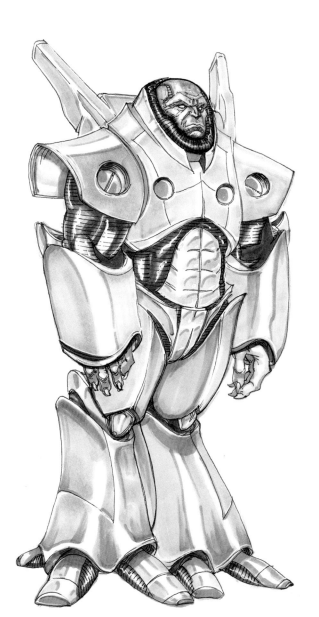
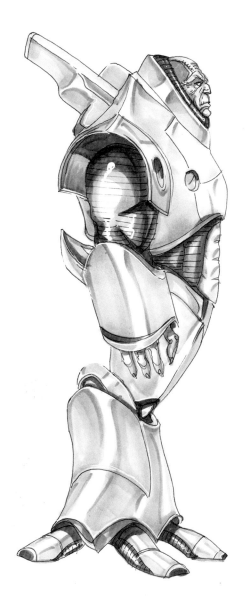